D1327850

BRITAIN'S WARTIME
EVACUEES

VOICES
FROM THE PAST

BRITAIN'S WARTIME EVACUEES

The People, Places and Stories of the Evacuations Told Through
the Accounts of Those Who Were There

Gillian Mawson

Frontline Books

BRITAIN'S WARTIME EVACUEES
The People, Places and Stories of the Evacuations Told Through the
Accounts of Those Who Were There

This edition published in 2016 by Frontline Books,
an imprint of Pen & Sword Books Ltd,
47 Church Street, Barnsley, S. Yorkshire, S70 2AS

ISBN: 978-1-84832-441-1

CIP data records for this title are available from the British Library

For more information on our books, please visit
www.frontline-books.com
email info@frontline-books.com
or write to us at the above address.

Printed and bound by CPI Group (UK) Ltd, Croydon, CR0 4YY
Typeset in 10.5/12.5 point Palatino

Contents

Introduction

In the early hours of 1 September 1939, the carefully devised British Government plans for evacuation swung into operation and millions of children, teachers and mothers began to be moved to safety. War was declared two days later.

More waves of evacuation started in May 1940, when fears of an invasion of Britain became very real. Air raids from German airships and bombers had left 1,500 British people dead during the First World War – events which led the government to the assumption that, should another war occur, the loss of life from aerial bombardment would be extremely heavy. Evacuation plans needed to be made well in advance of any future war.

In April 1937, an event during the Spanish Civil War boosted Britain's evacuation plans as German bombers conducted an air raid on the town of Guernica. In just one day, 1,654 adults and children were killed and 889 injured. Yet, even with carefully planned logistics surrounding the movement and housing of millions of British people, the psychological and lasting effects of evacuation on family life could never be planned for. Only by speaking to those who were actually involved and examining wartime reports can we discover the truth behind the evacuation experience. As a member of the British Evacuees Association, I feel it is vital that the memories of Second World War evacuees are recorded now – before they are lost forever.

Since 2008 I have interviewed hundreds of evacuees from England, Northern Ireland, Scotland and Wales. Families have also given me access to the testimony of those who have passed away. I have organised evacuee reunions, provided research to radio and television documentaries on the subject of evacuation and run a community group for evacuees in Stockport. My first book, *Guernsey Evacuees: The Forgotten Evacuees of the Second World War*, told the story of the 17,000 individuals who fled Guernsey to the UK in June 1940, just days before their island was occupied by Germany for five years. My second book, *Evacuees: Children's Lives on the WW2 Home Front*, shared 100 evacuation stories and family photographs. I have also interviewed those who, in 1940, found refuge in this country from Crown Dependencies such as Guernsey, Jersey, Alderney, and Sark, as well as the British Overseas Territory of Gibraltar, the majority of whom were certainly not sent to the safety of the countryside.

In this book I include stories from the mothers and teachers who travelled with the schoolchildren and took on a huge responsibility. We tend to hear their stories far less often than the stories of child evacuees. In some cases, schools were kept together as a unit, so the teachers became their pupils' 'guardians' for as much as five years, in a move unprecedented in educational history. These chapters include the difficult decisions made by the children's parents and the administration behind the evacuation of schools. Evacuees describe their journeys to the reception areas and how they were actually treated upon arrival. Although most children journeyed by train, we also hear about the thousands who were evacuated by ship. Child evacuees describe their emotions while facing the selection process carried out by local people, whilst evacuated mothers with infants share traumatic memories of being separated from their own children.

Evacuees share their first impressions of their new homes, wartime foster parents and new cultures. Some stories shatter the myth that most city children left the slums for pristine homes in the countryside. Many were shocked when they were placed in country cottages with no running water, gas or electricity. Some householders simply refused to take in evacuees and were taken to court, whilst others tried to get rid of their evacuees within days of their arrival. A chapter is devoted to the kindness shown to evacuees from people in Britain and from overseas. However, another contains the tragic stories of evacuees who, having been sent to supposedly 'safe' areas, were badly treated. They endured physical and mental cruelty and sexual abuse at the hands of their foster parents. It also contains details of the countless evacuees who died.

It would not be possible to paint a full picture of the evacuation experience without including testimony from the evacuees' parents and their foster parents. Wartime letters written between evacuees and their parents and between the foster parents and the evacuees' parents are also included here. They contain a wonderful mixture of everyday life, family affection and news of the war. They also give a glimpse into the relationships formed between children and their foster parents. The evacuees describe their emotions when they left their foster parents to return home. Many were delighted to be reunited with their own families whilst others had rather mixed feelings. For some, it was 'Evacuation' all over again as they struggled to readjust to life with their own families. Mothers also had to be reconciled with their husbands after years apart. For various reasons, some evacuees never returned home. In the final chapter, evacuees look back, to share the aftermath of evacuation and the way this experience shaped their lives.

The personal testimony of hundreds of evacuees, together with the wartime reports and newspaper reports paint a true picture of wartime evacuation. The stomach-churning farewells, the fear and excitement, the adventures, the kindness and the cruelty. The breadth of experiences touched upon is extraordinary, along with what binds them: the evacuees' incredible resilience and the willingness of the majority of people, from all walks of life, to 'do their bit'. Whether they lived in a ramshackle country cottage with three kids to a bed and no running water, or a stately home; if they were teachers accompanying pupils from the Channel Islands or Gibraltar, only to be exiled from their own families for years; or volunteers for the Women's Voluntary Service and Salvation Army, it all goes to show that evacuation was a remarkable feat of organisation, dedication and sacrifice.

Nowadays, the thought of sending your children off into the arms of strangers for months that turned into years is unimaginable. But for many it was a life-changing, even life-saving, experience. This book gives a unique insight into the evacuation from the mouths of those who lived through it, before they are lost to us forever. I have not attempted to put my own interpretation on the British evacuation experience in this book. I wish to allow those voices from the past to come back to life to tell their stories for future generations.

Gillian Mawson,
Derbyshire, 2016

Chapter 1

'The Bomber Will Always Get Through'

Plans for Evacuation

Government planning for the evacuation of millions of people, in the event of war, can be traced back to the First World War. German airships dropped bombs on England and Scotland in fifty-three separate raids, leaving over 500 people dead and over a thousand injured.By 1918, long distance German bomber aircraft and technology had improved, and resulted in the death of almost 1,500 British people. This led to the assumption that, should another war occur, the loss of life from aerial bombardment would be heavy.

In 1924 the Air Raid Precautions (ARP) Committee was set up to examine the problem of future air raids. On the list for discussion was the evacuation of civilians which would need to be planned before another war began.[1] Planning continued with the assumption that London would be the major target for enemy bombers, but by 1934 the Home Office focus of evacuation had changed, as 'the size, speed, range and numbers of bombers meant that London was no longer regarded as the target. Towns, cities and industrial complexes throughout Britain were now in the firing line and any evacuation scheme had to take this into account.'[2]

The events of the Spanish Civil War provided further stimulus to the UK's evacuation plans. On 26 April 1937, German and Italian aircraft attacked the Basque town of Guernica in what is considered one of the first raids on a defenceless civilian population by modern air forces. In just one day, 1,654 people were killed and 889 were injured. Ester Nickson witnessed this attack:

1

My mother and I were in a queue for food, horse flesh probably, and suddenly the air raid sirens went. We ran across the road and I looked up and the sky was blue and full of planes with black crosses. We went and sheltered and we could hear 'boom boom' and at night, the sky was orange with flame. They had chosen market day and carried out precision bombing, machine gunned everyone and the only building left standing was a municipal building and an oak tree which the Basque now consider sacred. They were the Condor Legion, Hitler's crack squadron. A few weeks later, I was sent, with hundreds of other Spanish refugees, to England. I never returned home to Spain.[3]

News reel footage of this devastating attack was soon being shown in British cinemas. Lorraine Chadwick watched one report with horror:

I was at the cinema with my friend, to see a nice musical and suddenly the newsreel showed us hundreds of dead Spanish people, not only adults but children too, and destroyed buildings. I turned to my friend who whispered, 'Do you think that could ever happen here?'

I could not think of a cheerful reply to give her, I was so shocked at what I had seen. For the first time in my life I was actually worried about what Germany might do to us in England.[4]

In 1938, every British household received a leaflet from the Home Office entitled, 'The Protection of Your Home Against Air Raids'. On the first page was a message from the Home Secretary: 'If this country were ever at war the target of the enemy's bombers would be the staunchness of the people at home. We all hope and work to prevent war but, while there is a risk of it, we cannot afford to neglect the duty of preparing ourselves and the country for such an emergency.'

In May 1938 an Evacuation Committee was established to consider the evacuation of school children, expectant mothers, the sick and the elderly. One conclusion was that if children were not leaving with their family, they should be evacuated with their schools. The Committee also concluded that evacuees would need to be billeted in private houses, and the recently formed Women's Voluntary Service (WVS) was chosen to carry out house-to-house surveys to ascertain how many places were available for evacuees.

In January 1939, householders received a letter asking them to co-operate with those conducting the survey. A letter sent to residents of Southwold stated:

> The Council have been requested by the Government to co-operate in plans which are being made for the protection of civilian life in the event of war. Recent experience in other countries has shown that under the conditions of modern warfare the greatest loss of life is caused by bombardment from the air. This danger is most acute in crowded cities. It is to lessen this danger in case our own country were involved in war that arrangements are being made now to enable children to leave the crowded cities and be received in homes elsewhere … The Government has asked each local authority in the country to find out what housing accommodation would be available in case of emergency... this note is being sent to you now in order that you may be aware, in advance of this enquiry and why it is being made.[5]

Householders were also visited by the WVS, the volunteers asking how many habitable rooms they had and how many people lived there permanently. The reception they received was not always a warm one. One newspaper, for example, noted that some householders had refused to provide accommodation to evacuees, stating that 'there were occasions during the house-to-house canvas when householders slammed the door in the faces of the canvassers. That, to say the very least, was adding insult to injury.'[6]

On 15 March 1939, hopes for peace in Europe receded further when German forces marched into Czechoslovakia.

In May 1939 those parents who wished their children to be evacuated were told to register at their school. Mothers were permitted to accompany any children under the age of five. The government then asked all local authorities to report on how many people wished to be evacuated in the event of war. Despite government appeals, parents' meetings and targeted propaganda, the registration numbers were low. The government was surprised at this reaction from the public and consequently in July 1939 it asked local authorities to canvas every house once more. The result of these efforts was that the number of child registrations rose somewhat. A government leaflet, 'Evacuation – Why and How', was duly delivered to every household, outlining the evacuation scheme.

Over the summer of 1939, evacuation drills were carried out in schools so that children would know what to do if the day came when they had to be evacuated. George Osborn recalls the practice drills which took place at his Portsmouth school:

> We had rehearsed the whole thing at school; marching along the road in orderly fashion, singing 'Ten Green Bottles' and other songs,

3

to board lines of buses which transported us to Clarence Pier at Southsea. There we dismounted and walked to the ferry terminal for the Isle of Wight. The council had decided that our school, Meon Road infants and seniors, would be evacuated there, together with other children from Portsmouth. No boats were waiting to receive us on the rehearsal day, so we did the whole thing in reverse and returned to school on a bus. Lessons on why we mustn't cry and how to wave goodbye – clean hanky please – were seriously taught to us. 'Think of it as going on holiday' must have been one of the first pieces of propaganda of the war, but as my sister Brenda and I had never been away on holiday this was hard to imagine.[7]

Jean Noble found the constant evacuation drills tedious:

Every day as we set off for school Mum gave strict instructions never to allow anyone to use our toothbrush or comb. She also impressed on me the need to keep my Identity Card safe and to memorise my number – and every day as I left for school she asked me to repeat it – DSAL 198/6.

From one day to the next we did not know if we would be returning home that afternoon and it must have been very distressing for my mother – seeing us off to school in the morning, not knowing if we would be coming home that afternoon.

Every day, mid-morning and mid-afternoon, the whole school trooped out into the playground where our teachers organised us into class lines and began checking and questioning us. Did we have our bag? Was our label attached? Then our bags or knapsacks were checked against a list to ensure everything was in order. All this took time because some children had items missing and a note had to be written to the parents. It also meant standing around waiting, seemingly for hours, to return to the classroom. Additionally there were air-raid drills when classes were interrupted and everyone trooped out quickly into the playground to be counted. It was very boring.

Now, instead of hanging up our coats and bags in the school cloakroom, we were told to keep them beside us in class and the checks in the playground increased to ensure that the contents of our bags had not changed during the lunch break. Did we have a luggage label pinned to our jackets or coats giving our name and address? Did we have another label with the school's identification number? On no account were we to remove these for, we were told, no-one would know who we were or where we came from if we lost

4

it. Becoming lost seemed to me to be a very real possibility and my mother reminded my brother (who was at the same school) and me daily that we must stay together.

At any moment we expected to be ordered to assemble and prepare to march off to the railway station or to board a bus and lessons were practically at a standstill. From one day to the next we did not know, when we left for school each morning, when or if we would see our parents again. I cannot recall any lessons taking place during this time. At the end of the afternoon, with no orders for departure having arrived, we plodded home with our bags over our shoulders only to go through exactly the same procedure the following day. We seemed to spend the whole school day lined up in the playground waiting for the news that our school had received its evacuation orders.[8]

An evacuation drill at one Birmingham school clearly did not go according to plan, with the result that the children's parents received the following letter:

At Evacuation Rehearsal many of the children had not brought all the clothing that they had been told to bring. As you know the children will be lodged in twos and threes or more, in private houses and I am sure we all wish them to be as little trouble to these people as possible, and that our children will be able to keep themselves as neat and tidy as they would be at home. They can only do this if they take with them all the necessary things given in the list. They must have changes of clothing to wear while their others are being washed. No one can say how soon you would be able to send on any extra things in such disturbed times, so do get ready all the things you know they may want and which they will be able to carry. Until this crisis is over, have their things ready, it will help all of us if we should have to go – a little pocket money would be useful.[9]

Government plans for evacuation were soon in place. *The Times* produced a special article which described 'a vast civil defence organisation, standing ready, equipped and trained. The evacuation scheme is also fully planned and prepared.' In August 1939, a Flintshire newspaper advised readers of the number of evacuees that would arrive, should war occur:

This week tenants of houses have received a notification from the Clerk indicating the number of evacuees allocated to them in the case of an emergency. The Ministry of Health has arranged for 20,700 evacuees to come into Flintshire ... a group of 100 blind people from Birkenhead will be accommodated in one building and it is hoped to make arrangements for other groups such as cripples and expectant mothers in suitable buildings in other parts of the county.

In late August 1939, a sense of impending disaster spread rapidly throughout Britain, if not much of Europe. On 23 August, the Molotov–Ribbentrop Pact was signed between the Soviet Union and Germany.

The following day, a Ministry of Health broadcast notified teachers in evacuation areas that they should return to their districts immediately and report to the schools by 26 August.[10] It was, of course the summer holiday. The school logbook for Meon School, Portsmouth, notes: 'Aug 26th – A state of emergency – Staff have been instructed to return to school to complete arrangements for evacuation.'[11]

The government gave local authorities the power to make householders take in evacuees. Large numbers of shrouds and papier mâché coffins were ordered and the Ministry of Health hired tents to provide cover for 10,000 extra air raid casualties' beds.[12] Britain was readying itself for war.

Chapter 2

'A Huge Decision to Make'

The Parents' Dilemma

Millions of British parents obviously now had a huge decision to make. Should they register their children for possible evacuation with their schools? Some evacuees remember the agonies their parents went through. James Roffey recalls:

> Increasingly I heard the word 'evacuation' being said at school, by my parents and on the wireless, but I didn't fully understand exactly what it meant. Then one day at school we were given letters to take home. Each letter was in a brown envelope with the words 'From His Majesty's Government. Urgent' printed on the front. 'Take this letter home and give it immediately to your parents! Don't lose it or get it dirty. It is very important!' said the teachers – all looking very serious and worried. I did as I was told and so did my sister Jean and our brothers John and Ernest.
>
> Our mother put them all unopened beside the clock on the high mantelpiece for when our father arrived home from work. As he opened them he became very angry, 'It's all starting again!' he shouted. 'They told us we were fighting the war to end all wars!' He had been a soldier in the First World War and had been gassed and injured. 'They will have to go,' he added. I didn't know what he meant, but our mother rushed out to the kitchen and we could hear saucepans and plates being banged about, which was a sure sign that she was very upset and probably crying.[1]

The letter taken home by James was probably similar to the one that was given to pupils at one Grammar School in West Bromwich:

Dear Sir/Madam, In the event of an emergency it has been decided to evacuate all pupils attending Higher Education Schools in the Borough of West Bromwich. I hope that one parent from each family that has (or will have in September) boys or girls at this School, will kindly attend a meeting at the School on MONDAY EVENING at 7.30 p.m. I am enclosing a circular letter from the Director of Education, and I shall be much obliged if you will fill in and return the Form of Registration attached to it at your earliest convenience, or bring it with you on Monday evening.[2]

John Hawkins vividly remembers the day that his mother first mentioned the possibility of evacuation:

Mom had bought a haversack for one of us and said that she would let the other have a case for when they practised 'sending us away'. The moment she said it, she obviously regretted having done so. The immediate flicker of alarm that crossed both of our faces at that moment reduced her to embarrassed silence.

She slipped a comforting arm around our shoulders and said quietly, 'I don't know whether to let you go or not or to send you to your Auntie Flo in Canada, like she wrote and asked me to.' I had visions of every Western film I had seen and pleaded 'Oh yes Mom send us to Canada, they have Mounties, and cowboys and Indians there!' Grim-faced, she shook her head, 'Well, I don't know. Just think, if you went all the way over there across the sea, I wouldn't be able to visit you, not ever. I think if you've got to go anywhere you'd best go to the country. It's lovely, honest, and I promise to come and visit you every week if I can.'

One morning, laden with haversacks, gas masks, suitcases and top coats, we were all once more paraded in the school playground and counted. But instead of being returned to our classrooms, Rose and I were each given a letter and sent straight home. The letter was apparently to inform her of our quite probable evacuation and asked that she attend the school that same evening, both to sign her final consent and to receive all the necessary details. The last sentence was heavily underlined and said quite simply, 'Evacuation is to take place immediately'.

We looked on in wide-eyed astonishment at Mom's sudden flood of anguished tears as she read it.[3]

In August 1939, Mr A.D. Wilshere was one of many across the country tasked with helping prepare for the evacuation of children.

He subsequently made the following entries in his diary:

Friday, August 25
Evacuation duty in Ilford has fallen to Mr Dinmore, Mr Bryce and me. We attended the meeting this afternoon to receive preliminary instructions. My party, which will consist of children under five with their mothers, together with expectant mothers, will be known as a non-school party. It will number at least 650 and will go from Southpark School.

Thursday, August 31
We learnt that the government has ordered the evacuation to take place tomorrow Saturday and Sunday. We attended a meeting this afternoon to receive our final instructions. I am going on Sunday – I know not where to. My party totals 800.[4]

Jean Burton's mother was reluctant to send her daughters away:

We lived in Dunfermline in 1939 and Mum became an Assistant Riveter at Rosyth dockyard, working on the ships and submarines. Rosyth and the Forth Bridge were considered prime German targets, so the government ordered that the local children should be evacuated.
    At first, Mum refused to send my sister Margaret and I away. However, when bombings occurred around Rosyth, Mum decided to send us to relatives in Wolverhampton, believing it would be less of a target.[5]

Anthony Pakenhem was in church when his parents suddenly decided to send him away:

My parents had made plans for me to get out of London as soon as possible – assuming that London's fate would be similar to that of Warsaw. After lunch my case was packed, and about 2pm my parents and I travelled up to King's Cross to catch a train to Letchworth in Hertfordshire which was about forty miles from Central London.
    When we arrived at Letchworth, everywhere was deserted, but we managed to get a taxi to my new 'home', namely St. Francis College, quite a large boarding school.
    In a bit of a daze, I was shown around – which in every way was a complete mystery to me. After an hour or so, I had to say my

goodbyes to my parents and just could not hold back the tears any further. I was completely on my own with not a friend in the world. Eventually I was shown my bed and locker, where the staff were trying to put blackouts up at all the windows. All was quiet and I cried myself to sleep.[6]

Like so many, Jean Noble's mother, having come to terms with the prospect of evacuation, did not want to send her children away to live with strangers:

For some time we had been practising for the evacuation of our London school. From one day to the next we did not know if we would be returning home that afternoon and it must have been very distressing for my mother. She would see us off to school in the morning, not knowing if we would be coming home that afternoon.

One day, I arrived home for lunch to find we had a visitor. It was my grandmother's brother, Frank, who lived with his daughter and her husband in Reading. To prevent us being evacuated with the school and billeted with strangers they were offering to take us in. Two days later mum took us to the railway station. My grandmother hugged and kissed us tearfully and stood at the corner of the road, waving to us until we disappeared from sight.[7]

Having taken on board all the evidence presented to her, John Payne's mother decided that her son would remain in Notting Hill in September 1939. However, she later changed her mind:

I was seven at the time with a five-year-old brother and a three-year-old sister. Mother was seven months pregnant and I think this is why she didn't want us to move away from London.

We soon noticed that evacuees were returning to London but the quietness was not to last. Bombs began to fall at night and you didn't know where they were going to land. I give thanks that I wasn't a parent in those dark days, not knowing what to do. What a nightmare for her and thousands upon thousands like her, having to make life or death decisions like that.

One night there was a horrendous air raid, so close that dust and stuff was falling on us. Our mother had second thoughts about the basement being the safest place for us so took us all into the shelter on the street. On that very night the house that we were living in caught the blast and some of it tumbled down. We were now homeless and had to stay with our Aunt. One morning our mother gathered us all together and we were evacuated, not knowing on earth where we were going to.[8]

From May 1940, further waves of evacuation were announced when Germany invaded Belgium, Holland and France. In Parliament it was said that, 'In the weeks that lie ahead, none of us knows whether he may not be evacuated from some place which at the moment appears to be quite safe'.[9]

The newspapers discussed the risk of an invasion of Britain, with one paper reporting that, 'the whole German press this morning announced that a campaign of annihilation against England was about to be unleashed. In all cafes and places of amusement, crowds sing repeatedly the German war song – we are sailing for England!'[10]

On 27 May 1940, parents in Folkestone received this notice:

> The Government have decided that parents of school children living in this town are to have an opportunity of sending their children away to a safer district. The evacuation of school children will begin on Sunday next the 2nd June. Whether it will be possible for all the children to go on the one day will depend upon how many there are to go. If there are too many for them all to go on Sunday, the rest will go on Monday, and if necessary, on Tuesday, and following days. In order that trains may be ready to take the children whose parents wish them to go, the Council must know at once how many parents intend to send their children away. If you wish your child to go, please fill in the form sent with this notice, and get your child to bring it to school as soon as you possibly can, and in any case not later than 9 a.m. on Wednesday, the 29th May.
>
> The children will go to places in the Midlands and Wales that the Government consider are safer than this town. You are free to decide for yourself whether your child should be sent away to a safer area or not. It is hoped that parents will not decide to keep their children in this town without thinking very seriously whether such a decision is in the best interests of the children themselves.[11]

Living in Folkestone at that time, Peter Campbell was one of the youngsters who may have been affected by this notice. He recalled the following:

> Our Headmistress said we would be going to a town in South Wales called Merthyr Tydfil but I had no idea where Wales was or how far away. I thought it would be very nice to go away on holiday and it sounded like fun. What I did not realise at that moment was that my

Mum and Dad and my little brothers, too young for school, would not be coming with us and we would have to stay there until the war was over. I couldn't wait to get home and tell my Mum and Dad but they already knew and were very sad, they did not want us to go to a strange place on our own. However, they knew our teachers were coming with us and the whole school would be together.[12]

The fate of pupils at Earl Hall School in Southend was decided on Sunday, 20 May 1940, when the BBC announced that East Anglian coastal towns were to be evacuated by 2 June, for fear of invasion. During a bewildering week, parents had to decide whether to have their children evacuated or not. The destination would be Chinley in Derbyshire, which was later amended to the nearby village of Whaley Bridge.[13]

Derrick McGarry lived in Oldham, Lancashire, in the dark days of the summer of 1940. On one occasion he overheard his parents discussing his potential evacuation:

My parents considered sending me to live with an uncle and aunt in the United States. I heard them discussing it while I was in bed. But a few weeks later a ship with several hundred evacuees on board, bound for North America, was torpedoed in the North Atlantic and my parents changed their minds about shipping me out.[14]

Philip Doran remembers his mother's preparations for his evacuation by ship from Liverpool:

In the weeks that followed, we had it drilled into us, what evacuation really meant; it was to be no holiday. Each child was given a list of clothes that they would be expected to take away with them, I regret to say, the list bore no resemblance to what was in my clothes cupboard at home. Needless to say, my ever-loving Mam miraculously managed to get hold of most things. At the time it didn't occur to me that she probably had to go without in order to provide everything on the list.[15]

The problem of mothers being unable to provide the required list of 'evacuation clothing' was discussed in the House of Commons:

In any future evacuation it is not sufficient to say that each should have a change of underclothing, a pair of house shoes, an overcoat and so on. They should be provided for those who cannot provide them. The parents of a family of four are told to provide four new pairs of boots. It simply cannot be done. They have not the income.[16]

The Channel Islands of Jersey, Guernsey, Alderney and Sark lie within thirty miles of France. In June 1940, as German forces approached the French coast, concern arose in the islands. Would Hitler decide to invade?

On Guernsey, Ebenezer Le Page had no doubt about the outcome of the German Blitkzkrieg:

> Well, when we saw the clouds of smoke in the sky from the Germans blowing up things across the water in France, and boatloads of French came over with horrible stories of what the Germans was doing to them, I reckon we all knew our turn was coming.[17]

Now it was the turn of Channel Island parents to decide whether to send their children away – with the destination almost certainly being the mainland. Ursula Malet de Carteret described the anxiety she suffered in Jersey:

> On 16th June I saw many troops marching along the main road towards the bay. The Germans were occupying Cherbourg and gun fire could be heard. I telephoned my husband, Guy, who was working in Malvern at the time. I told him how things were, telling him not to come to Jersey unless I phoned again.
>
> On Monday 17th more gun fire could be heard, everyone was wondering whether Jersey was going to be defended, and what was the right thing to do. On the 19th Jersey was declared an open town and would not be defended if German forces arrived. A register was immediately set up in the Town Hall in St Helier for the names of those who wished to leave the island for England.
>
> I telephoned Dr John Evans for advice, his answer was swift, you have three small children and should leave. I went into town to join the queue at the Town Hall. I can't remember how long I waited to obtain our permit, but it was some hours. I had Jill, my golden Cocker Spaniel with me and went straight to the Animal shelter. She was one of the first animals put to sleep in a humane way![18]

On 18 June, Guernsey's headteachers attended an emergency meeting where it was announced that the evacuation of schoolchildren was a real possibility. On 19 June the *Guernsey Star* announced that the evacuation would commence the following day. Ron Blicq's headmaster made this announcement:

Within a few days Guernsey almost certainly will be occupied by German troops. Consequently, starting tomorrow, the government plans to bring a fleet of boats to the island to evacuate everyone who wishes to leave before the enemy arrives. I must make it clear that no one has to go. Your parents will tell you whether you are to stay or leave. And they will tell you their own plans. The college has to be ready to leave at any time after 9 o'clock tomorrow.[19]

Rachel Rabey heard her mother and aunt whispering throughout the night. 'Then at breakfast I was told that the school was going on holiday and I could go too.'[20]

Therese Riochet found her mother in the kitchen with evacuation instructions in her hand and two labels. She told Therese that she was going to be evacuated with the school:

I asked her why and she said, 'You heard those guns last night didn't you? Well they were at Cherbourg on the coast of France. The Germans are there and people say they are coming to Guernsey.' Mother had made her decision that I was to go.[21]

Hazel Duquemin recalls her parents' anguish:

I remember how desperate my immediate family, grandparents, aunts and uncles felt when the States of Guernsey announced that everyone who wanted to would be evacuated to England until the danger passed. My father decided that our family would go and he never wavered from that decision, but a lot of islanders were undecided including my maternal grandparents (who spoke no English) and eight of my mother's siblings who stayed on the island. The evacuation eventually got underway, personally for me, after two false starts. Twice my father took me to school as instructed and both times I was brought home as there was no ship available to accommodate our school. The third time was successful.[22]

Rex Carre also recalls his parents' discussions over whether to send him to England:

I was sitting in the Wayfarer bus on the way home when someone gave all the passengers leaflets saying that the island was to be evacuated as the German armies had already reached Normandy. (We were soon to hear the guns.) There were details in the leaflet about the schools being evacuated and naturally my family fairly panicked when they read all this. We were eventually told to meet at school where our parents were faced with the choice of my going to England under the care of most of the school staff, who, bless them, must have agreed to this incredible responsibility, or the alternative of staying under an inevitable German occupation which could come at any moment.

My parents dithered – could they come after me? Could they leave their parents, especially my frail French-speaking grandfather who had made a disastrous second marriage? This was especially difficult as my mother's sister and brother and their families had already left, so my mother felt very responsible. As for me, in the great excitement of the moment, I wanted to go with my friends. So it was settled I would go.[23]

In July 1940, it was the turn of parents in the British Overseas Territory of Gibraltar to decide whether or not to send their children to an unknown destination.

In May 1940, 13,000 civilians had been evacuated to North Africa, mainly French Morocco, on orders from London. However, when France fell to Germany, the Royal Navy and RAF attacked elements of the French navy in order to stop part of its fleets falling into German hands. As a result, the Gibraltar evacuees were often treated badly by the people of French Morocco. Lourdes Galliano recalls:

Life had become a nightmare for us. My mother had tried to spend what money she had but none of the shops would sell us anything. To them we were 'Anglais'; the most despicable beings on earth.[24]

The evacuees were told they had just twenty-four hours to get out of Africa and were forced onto ships and returned to Gibraltar. Lourdes Galliano's family therefore made the decision to leave Gibraltar. Though they did not know it at this stage, their destination would be Swansea, then London:

Gibraltar suffered various air raids from Italian aircraft and from the Vichy French force based in Morocco. Spain was not willing to take us, so we were advised to pack our belongings and to be ready for our move to an unknown destination.

In the early hours of Thursday 18 July two enemy aircraft dropped fifteen heavy bombs on the southern half of the Rock, bringing the first casualties of the war. On Tuesday 30 July, twenty-four ships sailed out of Gibraltar Bay for England and our whole family travelled together. My father, a volunteer in the Special Constabulary, had been designated the charge of looking after the five hundred evacuees on our ship.[25]

As the war progressed, further waves of evacuation occurred as British towns and cities were targeted by German bombers. Gerry Mullan's family decided to leave their home in Northern Ireland:

> In 1941 we lived about eight miles outside Belfast, up in the Belfast hills. Because of our proximity to Cave Hill, quite a lot of bombs fell near us, together with shells from the anti-aircraft guns. Many did not explode so were scattered around where we lived, which was very dangerous. We had a close call during one air raid when my father was sitting on the windowsill inside the house with my brother, Peter, on his knee. A shell exploded about one hundred yards behind the house. It blew my father and Peter across the room and as a result of that shock, Peter didn't speak properly until he was almost five years old. It was a very frightening time, so my father sent my mother, my brothers and I to Fintona, County Tyrone, where we had lived three or four years earlier. He remained in Belfast.[26]

Dan Muir remembers his mother's decision to leave Clydebank with her children:

> My sisters Betty, aged nine, and Helen, aged five, and our mother and I were evacuated on Friday 14th March 1941, after a night of German bombing. We had spent the night of the 13th in a cinema where we had gone to see a Shirley Temple film. We came out at 6 am to devastation and the news that two of our uncles had been killed. Our house was not habitable, so we had to leave town. Our father had not been at the cinema with us and we did not know his whereabouts.
>
> We travelled upriver to Glasgow in the back of a lorry then we got a bus which took us on to Helensburgh and eventually ended up in a big house in Millig Street. The family who took us in were called Snodgrass and our mother became their housekeeper. Our father eventually found us after a two day search, but soon after he was called for service in the RAF. We lived in Helensburgh for two years and I have two years of mainly happy memories. The only sad ones were watching our mother who kept looking around, hoping to see our two uncles, whose bodies were never found.[27]

16

During the war, there was one more major decision to be made by parents of those children who had been ecavuated. Should they leave their children in the 'safe' areas for the duration of the war, or should they bring them home before then? In some cases, a lack of enemy bombing resulted in the gradual drift home of evacuees. John Partridge, for example, remembers that, 'after five months living in Cheshire, Mum decided to bring me and my sister back home to Manchester so we could be with Dad'[28]

For his part, Ben Howard recalled that by March 1940 over half of the boys from Catford Central School had returned home.[29] This drift home led to some criticism. One newspaper in Northumberland reported:

> In a bus going to Morpeth the other day was sitting a woman who was talking to friends, on their way to see their evacuated children. The woman was going to fetch a little boy home, saying, 'One place is as safe as another, he's not happy there, he says he is always getting into trouble. His father says he might as well be home.' Presumably this fond mother came from a vulnerable area. She preferred her son to live with her in danger of being killed than that he should live with someone else in danger of getting into trouble.[30]

The *Manchester Evening News* expressed similar concerns in a report published in its edition of 20 August 1941:

> Manchester's evacuated school children are returning to their homes at the rate of 40 a day. The summer raid lull has converted the trickle into a stream. Nearly 2,500 have drifted back from the country during June and July. There were 11,387 scholars from Manchester schools in safe areas at the end of May. Two months later, the figure had dropped to 9,125. So now 72,358 children are going to Manchester schools again. Education Committee officials told the *Evening News* today, 'We have done everything possible to persuade the parents to leave their children in the evacuation areas.'

However, a report issued by the Manchester Child Guidance Clinic argued that, for many families, the impact of evacuation was just as loathsome as the impact of aerial bombing:

> There are cases in which the parents wished to take the child home. The commonest reason was just that the parents wanted the children home, despite the risk of air raids on Manchester. Some of these cases are worth quoting. One child was evacuated in September and

brought home in November. The mother reports, 'I was afraid something might happen to her. I thought she wasn't happy.' A boy aged 17 whose father committed suicide; the boy was brought home because the mother was lonely. Another boy, aged 12, is a difficult, very anxious boy whose mother was in a state of chronic ill-health. He was taken home suddenly by his father because the foster parents complained that he was difficult to manage. Another boy, aged 11, ran away from his billet taking another boy with him and they started to walk back home, a distance of some 50 miles. They eventually stopped at a police station and were returned home. The general conclusion to be drawn would seem to be that the immediate effect of evacuation, which is separation from parents and a known and accepted environment, is worse than the fear of air raiding.[31]

In some cases, those evacuees who returned home before peace was declared were going to face many issues and risks. May Hill was living in Lincolnshire at the time and mentioned the return home of London evacuees in her diary:

> 13 September 1944: Evacuees are streaming back to London in spite of contrary advice. Gerry may still have something up his sleeve and apart from that, practically half the houses in London are down or damaged, so accommodation will be a problem for some time, tho' I can quite understand the people wanting to be home if it is reasonably safe.[32]

On 20 September 1944, *The Times* reported the following tragic story:

> Children who had only just returned from evacuation were among those killed by flying bombs which were sent over the southern counties, including the London area yesterday. Two months ago when flying bomb attacks showed no sign of slackening a little girl named Margaret aged five, and her two sisters were evacuated from their home in southern England to Birmingham. Then a few days ago the menace seemed to be ending and the parents, who now had also a baby boy, decided to bring the children home. On Friday there was a family reunion. Now only Margaret is alive. The others were all killed while they slept. When the house was demolished early yesterday, rescue workers dug for two hours. They could hear Margaret crying for help and found her with the mother's arm around her.

Such were the dangers faced by those who had decided to return home before the end of the fighting in Europe.

Chapter 3

'Evacuation Begins'

The Journey

In the early hours of 1 September 1939, the Government's plans for evacuation swung into operation and the majority of the schools, teachers and mothers were moved before war was declared on 3 September. Such was the scale of the operation that Mr James Ede, the MP for South Shields, announced in Parliament, on 14 September 1939, that 'we have during the past few days seen the most remarkable movement of the civil population ever recorded in history'.

Jessie Hetherington (née Robertson) was a Gateshead teacher who described the evacuation of her senior school, as being part of that 'remarkable movement':

> As I prepared to leave home that morning, news came through that Germany had invaded Poland, and that Britain and France were mobilising. So, with a heavy heart and many forebodings I left home for school. During the afternoon teachers, children and tearful parents gathered in the playground where information was given as to our various destinations in the many pit villages of County Durham.
>
> My destination was to a village near to Bishop Auckland with my pupils – about 40 thirteen and fourteen year olds. As the practice was to keep families together, there were younger brothers and sisters in my care. After tearful farewells between parents and children we boarded coaches to go to catch the train.[1]

Maureen Brass described the evacuation of children from St Dominic's Infant School, in London, to Kettering:

19

The week before the evacuation, we gave parents lists of what the children should bring with them, made labels showing their names, the name of the school and the school number. Ours was school number 0302. On the morning of September 1st 1939, all the children assembled in school around 7.00am. The staff had arrived at 6.00am. At 8.00am we set out from the school, waved off by tearful mothers, grandmothers and others. The groups, Seniors, Juniors and Infants, with staff and helpers walked in fours to Kentish Town West Station. We all boarded a train that was waiting for us and set out into the unknown.[2]

Having helped prepare for the evacuation of Southpark School in Ilford, A.D. Wilshere went on to recount the moment of departure:

The playground was swarming with people. I made my way across it and found my helpers in the classroom. I read the instructions and distributed armbands as far as they would go. When I opened the door and found, not only the playground full but most of the ground floor as well, I confess I felt a momentary wave of helplessness. However I rallied a few staunch masculine helpers and kept the people where they were – confused bunches of women and children, husbands, friends.

We moved them upstairs into the respective classrooms, getting some order out of hopeless chaos and checking their names against my lists. We were now working against time but the checking was finished and the Town Hall was on the phone wanting to know my numbers. There were 430, but only to be expected as half of them had turned up in yesterday's evacuations. Coaches had arrived and husbands were hastening to Seven Kings station with the evacuees' luggage. At the station I handed over all the tickets and one list of names and then all into the waiting train.[3]

Many child evacuees remember leaving without an opportunity to say goodbye to their parents. Harry Flack's mother took him to school that day, as usual, then returned home. 'In less than fifteen minutes we left for the railway station. It was so quick that that my poor mother was unable to return in time to wave goodbye to the train that she knew I would be travelling on. She never forgot it!'[4]

James Martin and his brothers set off for Bridgwater, Somerset: 'One day we were evacuated and a neighbour ran to tell our Mum that we had been taken to the train station. Mum ran to the train to wave goodbye, she had no idea where we were going.'[5]

When children did not return home from school at their usual time, parents gathered at the school gates to read the short, stark notices which announced the destination of the pupils and staff. When some of the children from Doreen Frisby's school were put onto the wrong train, it caused confusion: 'We girls had been put onto the wrong train at Waterloo Station to Templecombe in Dorset whilst our boys were sent to Petersfield. It was a couple of days before our parents knew where we had gone and a notice could be posted at our school.'[6]

Syd Hodges wrote to his wife, Hetty, regarding the evacuation of their daughter:

> I walked by the school this morning and there was a poster outside saying that the school party had arrived at Keswick safely and that parents could write to their children thus:- Elizabeth Hodges, Central Newcastle High School, c/o Post Office, Keswick.[7]

Whilst some never had the opportunity to say their goodbyes, others were more fortunate. Nine-year-old John Hawkins described leaving Birmingham with his sister Rosie:

> I arrived at school where a teacher was marking names off a clipboard. I joined Mum and Rosie then a teacher touched Mum's arm and said softly 'You can leave them now, Mother, they'll be safe with me.' Mum's lips begin to tremble - she crouched down and kissed us tenderly on the cheek. The teacher shepherded us both into the waiting lines and handed us our evacuation labels. I slipped the bootlace over Rosie's head, then my own, then tried to catch a glimpse of Mum amongst the crowd who waved at us through the railings. On we children marched, past the houses, shops and factories that we all knew so well, from which poured housewives, factory workers, shop assistants, men and women, young and old, to loudly cheer us on our way.
>
> When we reached Tyseley station, Rosie and I hoped that we might catch a fleeting glimpse of Mum, but were swiftly ushered into a compartment. Howls of alarm arose from brothers and sisters who, with all the pushing and shoving, found themselves separated. Suddenly, everyone turned in amazement to see a frantic mother dash from the crowd and blindly force her way through the barrier onto the platform, to scoop her tiny, frightened daughter into her arms. She then ran, sobbing bitterly, from the station. Finally, when the platform was emptied and all the carriage doors had slammed noisily and firmly shut, a shrill whistle blew and the train slowly

moved forward. Suddenly the watching crowd at the station erupted into a waving, shouting mass, whilst from every carriage window, little arms waved back frantically in reply, and kept on waving, until Tyseley station and their weeping parents, had completely disappeared from sight.[8]

On Guernsey, Ron Gould said farewell to his father: 'He gave me what he had in his pocket, which was a ten shilling note [50 pence} and a nice, nearly new, penknife. The ten shillings lasted for two weeks and sadly I lost the knife on the River Bollin later in the year.'[9]

Lily Dwyer was six years old when she was evacuated from Liverpool to Gresford, North Wales: 'I remember being at the railway station with my mother and lots of parents and young children. Quite a lot of the children were pleading with their parents not to send them away. I didn't cry. I just accepted what was happening to me. However, my mother did cry and she kept on hugging me.'[10]

Marion Wraight was evacuated from Margate on the Kent coast with her brother:

> Mum came to school to say goodbye to us and she had a parcel of clothes for Bill and me, but somehow I lost it. I didn't mind being evacuated. My Mum, Rosa, had left my Dad in 1938 and took my sisters Lillian and Jean with her. Dad was really violent towards Mum, and I was frightened of Dad because he used to hit me with a belt when I was just 3 years old. He was a drinker, possibly alcoholic, I wasn't too happy a lot of the time. I loved my brother, Bill, he was 2 years older than me, and he looked out for me when we were evacuated.[11]

Doreen Acton (née Mason) left Southend with Westcliff High School:

> I remember waving good-bye to my mother at our house and was surprised to see her eyes fill with tears. There did not appear to be any immediate danger either to my parents or to us. We had no idea where we were going and as the long train journey progressed, rumours began to circulate. Finally we were told it was to be Chapel-en-le-frith in Derbyshire. We had been told to bring sleeping attire and a change of clothes and toiletries. It was rather like going off to Guide camp.[12]

Jean Noble will never forget the chaotic and even traumatic scenes she witnessed at Waterloo railway station:

Just before Mum took the two of us to Waterloo, my grandmother hugged and kissed us tearfully and stood at the corner of Rectory and Brook Roads, waving after us until we disappeared from sight. Having experienced being taken fighting and screaming from home on a stretcher when I had been ill, I realised there was nothing I could do to prevent what was happening so I just accepted it. Waterloo was busy - the forecourt was packed with people, buses, coaches, taxis and cars mobilised to bring school children and their escorts to the station. The noise in the concourse was tremendous with hundreds of bewildered children, panicking parents, agitated teachers, concerned station attendants, WVS members, and assertive charity workers, some carrying a banner with a school number on it, milling about while trying to gather their groups together.

The crush was frightening with children trying to keep connected to their own little group while being pushed and jostled towards various railway platforms. Many appeared bewildered or close to tears as they were pressed forward towards the gates to the platforms as those in charge tried to prevent their group breaking up while trying to keep some sort of order. I learned later that parents were not supposed to accompany their children to the station unless they were helping with the evacuation arrangements because there was no room for them, but many parents were trying to link up with their children at the station before they boarded the train. I held tightly on to Mum's coat as she juggled with two large suitcases and two children aged 7 and 10.

Because we were not being evacuated with a school she was allowed to accompany us onto the platform where she reminded me that my brother Bern, who was three years older, was in charge. On reflection - for a ten year old he took his responsibility seriously and was stoical and not showing any sign of distress. Mum found us a carriage with seats by the window and then waited on the platform, calling out last minute instructions to behave ourselves and who to look out for when we arrived. I sat letting all this flow around me and then, as the guard blew his whistle and the train started to pull away, I saw my mother's face crumple in abject misery and her floodgate of tears opened, which set me off and I grizzled for the rest of the journey.[13]

Alfred Goble also has vivid memories of evacuation day:

We went down to Hollington School down in Battle Road. My dad and elder sisters couldn't go, but my younger sister, myself and mum went. We waited for the buses and it seemed eternal! All we kept saying to Mum was 'Let's go home!' Anyway, at last the coaches came to take us to the station. We got on the train and it took ages and ages. They had to keep stopping because of air raid attacks along the way and some of them were a long time waiting, making us fed up and miserable.[14]

Some evacuees remember very little about the journey to their new home, whilst others can recall almost every detail. Peter Campbell travelled by train to Wales, a journey which seemed endless:

It was a terrible journey - the sun was too hot through the windows of the train and there were air raids. We did not reach Merthyr Tydfil until 5.30pm. There were no buses to meet us so we were told we would have to walk to a mission hall, which was at the top of this steep hill. We set off to walk in twos hand in hand. People were lining the street right to the top, waving flags and cheering. I think they were trying to make us welcome, some were crying especially the women. I suppose they felt sorry for us.

Half way up the hill the string on my parcel came off and I dropped everything all over the street. Some kind ladies ran forward and picked them all up, wrapped them up again and carried it up to the mission hall. When we arrived we were given lemonade and cakes to eat while the teachers and staff decided what would happen next. We were all very tired and wanted to sleep. After a while they came to us, that is me and my brother and sisters, and told us we would not all be able to stay together, that me being the youngest would stay with my eldest sister Pat which was good but my other sister Ivy would be on her own, as would Gordon and Terry. Soon a couple came to us to take us to their home, a Mr and Mrs Evans.[15]

Peter Hopper's mother died when he was six months old so it was his father who made the decision to send him away with a group of Grimsby evacuees: 'When my father prepared for war service with the RAF, the choice for me was to be placed in a children's home, or be evacuated. So I joined the train taking three hundred other children heading for Skegness.'[16]

Audrey and Gwen Woodhatch were evacuated to Devon in early June 1940 and Audrey recalls:

We had our photographs taken in the garden at Kangley Bridge Road and then, with our gas masks on our shoulders, we waved goodbye at the local school and boarded a coach. The journey from London on a steam train for 5 hours or more was obviously very boring for a little 5 year old so I remember passing the time with my knitting.[17]

Alan Boast lived in a children's home in Lowestoft and remembers the journey to Derbyshire during his evacuation in great detail:

On this Sunday, us Home boys were told to be ready for Church early! This was unusual, as I didn't think it was the Sunday for Holy Communion – something was going on! We had some breakfast, which proved the point because you didn't eat before communion. However, gas masks at the ready off we set. To our surprise we didn't turn into St. Margaret's Church but carried straight on past the big tree in the road, over Rotterdam Road Bridge and through the town. Straight to the station we went, which was near the bridge.

The sight that met my eyes when we arrived at the station was something I will never forget. There were children everywhere, hundreds of them – and I was one! We were told we were being evacuated for our safety, and would be going school by school, not as Home boys. We were told that along the road, at the side of the station, our teachers would be waiting for us, as they were coming with us. So us Home boys were split up into our school classes. We then had to wait until our school was called. We were taken to the front of the station where ladies were waiting for us.

They had lots of labels and wrote our name, school and age on each one and tied or pinned it to our clothes. This must not be taken off, we were told. On to the platform where our train was being reversed in. If needed – go to the toilet, as it would be some time before we could go again! We were then lined up, and more ladies arrived, with a trolley-full of boxes. They gave us two sticks of barley sugar each. These were long sweets. We were told to wait until we were on our way before sucking them, as they were to combat 'travel sickness' – whatever that was! Where on earth they produced barley sugar sticks from I shall never know – but somebody had thought about it - talk about being organised! Into the carriages we were shown, teachers and all, and off we went! Major Humphrey (the Mayor) spoke to every child that left that day. He told us that the honour of Lowestoft rested on our shoulders, and we had to be well-behaved. A lot of the boys had never been on a train before, but of course, having lived at Yarmouth with my Uncle Fred (a train-driver) I knew all about it.

The journey took a long while and we stopped twice for toilets. On the platform were ladies of the WVS with urns of lemonade, cakes and biscuits etc. The organisation was spot-on – this had all been arranged in such a short time! While everybody was milling about on the platform, I took a stroll down to the front of the train, to see the engine. I wanted to see what kind it was, didn't I – well that's me! I recall speaking to the driver and fireman. When I returned to the carriage, I was told off, and also told not to wander about as it was dangerous. All aboard and off we go again and at last we reached our final destination. There it was, a little village station – the name plate on the platform said Clowne. I said, 'Clowne? Hang about – they are funny people who run around in a circus!' As things turned out, it was to be my home for the next year and nine months.[18]

During his journey, Francis Rutter was separated from his brothers and sisters:

The train ride from London was cramped and we didn't even have access to a toilet. Some children had to wee on the floor, including my poor sister as it was such a long journey. However, the hardest part was saying goodbye to my brothers and sisters when they all got off the train at Oxford. Being so young I didn't understand why we couldn't all be together. I had to stay on the train until we reached Redruth, Cornwall.[19]

Many other evacuees remember the lack of toilet facilities on those overcrowded trains. When a group of mothers was put on a train to Wrexham which had no facilities, the matter was subsequently raised in the House of Commons: 'They were taken a journey of 120 miles in a non-corridor train. Who was responsible for that?'[20]

During these long journeys, a great deal of kindness was shown to the evacuees by volunteers, many of whom were members of the Women's Voluntary Service. John Mallett recalls: 'We were not allowed off the carriages, so the ladies held up to us unbuttered fresh bread and hunks of cheddar cheese, which up to that day I had not particularly liked. To this day, I look at cheddar cheese with great respect and liking!'[21]

When Irene Wood left Salford for Hambleton, Lancashire, she was given a bag which contained food items. 'Among these were a thick block of chocolate, a packet of biscuits and a packet of cream crackers,' she recalled. 'The mischievous older lads began shouting "When this is gone, that's your lot. You're going to starve to death" which reduced some of the girls to tears.'[22]

Thousands of evacuees travelled to their new homes by ship. One of these youngsters, George Osborn, was evacuated from Portsmouth to the Isle of Wight:

> The great engines, powered by steam from the coal-fired boiler, slowly turned the two large paddles, thrashing and churning a watery roadway of bubbles in their wake. What a thrill, and how very different from the little paddle boats we had seen on the boating lake at Southsea in the summer months. When we arrived at Ryde Pier, my sister Brenda and I were no more than six miles from our home in Portsmouth, as the seagull flies, but we may as well have been a hundred miles away.
>
> At the reception end, things weren't quite so well organised. They had not been told how many children were coming, what time they would arrive, their ages, how many mothers were coming (with children under five years of age), and many other things. In fact it was so chaotic that an immediate thinning out was achieved at the reception end, by several mothers and their toddlers or babies simply catching a return train and ferry back home to Portsmouth! We then boarded a train at Ryde pierhead. Children, helpers, teachers and a few mothers with their under-fives were then dropped off at each railway station between Ryde and Newport.[23]

After a five-mile walk to Dagenham docks, Derek Trayler's school boarded paddle steamers bound for Yarmouth:

> I remember being got up for school while it was still dark and our parents coming right into our class and talking to our teacher and the other parents. Then we were going along Kenneth Road, Dagenham, which runs parallel with the High street. We came out into Station Road at the foot of the bridge that leads up to Chadwell Heath railway station. Two roads converge at this point with Wangey Road and Station Road merging to go over the station bridge. There was a crocodile of children going back as far as you could see and going up the bridge until they disappeared down the other side.
>
> We joined the procession and started to move up the bridge to the station at the top. This is about 100 yards and normally takes a few minutes but we were moving very slowly.
>
> It was still dark at the bottom but dawn was breaking by the time we got halfway. It was completely light by the time we got to the top and could see the other side. What we saw was the most amazing sight and one I hope we never see again. From the station and all the way

down Valance Avenue was a complete line of young children going on into the distance. Out of each side turning there were more crocodiles of children emerging. Each one was adding to the line which by now was spreading half way across Dagenham. It was as if some modern Pied Piper was luring away all the children from the borough.

Eventually we arrived at Dagenham docks after walking five miles. Facing us were three paddle steamers tied up at the wharf. These normally took Londoners on excursions to Southend and Margate but had been chartered to take evacuees out of London to avoid the Blitz. We crossed the gangplank with the usual cries of, 'Don't look down' but of course we did!! On deck we were told to go on round to the other side where we crossed an even longer gangplank to the next ship. Finally we got to the far side and hung on the rail without moving, all the way down the Thames, up the East Coast until we turned in to Yarmouth.[24]

Ronald Brash left Pollokshields, Glasgow, with Kelvinside Academy, for the Isle of Arran:

At the entrance to Hampden Park football ground were to be seen groups of boys, teachers and parents. Rector Mr S W Clark was going around talking to the boys, some of whom, perhaps, he was speaking to for the last time. Arrangements were made for cars to carry all the luggage to Crosshill Station whither we now set out. After final farewells to parents and friends, we trooped down into the station and boarded the train. Soon we were speeding away from Glasgow, on the rarely-used Caledonian line to Ardrossan.

There the difficulty of transporting luggage from the train to the boat arose, but somehow or other we managed it. The excursion steamer Duchess of Hamilton was being used as an 'evacuee ship' as there were so many children from other schools being brought to Arran as well as ourselves. The calm sea was a deep blue and a heat haze enveloped the lofty peaks of distant Arran which was to be our home for – no one could tell how long. We stood on the upper deck eating sandwiches, cold pies and other victuals we had brought with us to sustain ourselves on the journey, whilst a cool breeze fanned our faces.[25]

Ralph Risk was also evacuated with Kelvinside Academy:

I was six years old and do not remember the train journey from Hampden Park to Ardrossan, nor the ferry trip. This is surprising as my father was President of Queen's Park Football Club! However, I remember being very upset that evening, and was comforted by Mrs Young, the junior school teacher. The following day was fateful for Britain but also for me. It was my 7th birthday and at 11am it was announced on the radio that Britain was at war with Germany. I had received a present of a Dinky truck complete with a wind-up barrage balloon, and was very upset when the older boys used the balloon as a football and damaged it beyond repair.[26]

Over 25,000 school children, infants and mothers were evacuated from the Channel Islands of Jersey, Guernsey, Alderney and Sark in June 1940. Although some left by air, the majority crossed the English Channel in overcrowded mail and cargo boats. Ted Hockey, the harbour signaller, heard officials persuading people not to leave Guernsey:

> They said that trade would carry on as usual, there would be no worry or trouble and if it came to the worst, they would see that everybody got safely away. They had cars going round with posters saying 'Don't be yellow.' As a result of this, I saw one ship which could have carried 4,000 people and I doubt she carried more than 50.[27]

Also on Guernsey, student teacher Merle Roberts recalled 'people trying to decide what to do. The noise was terrific, with broadcasts telling people "not to be yellow" or not to leave the island.'[28]

During this confusion, some parents changed their minds about sending their children to England, and Guernsey's Education Council noted:

> Throughout the evacuation, the ship's crews were greatly handicapped by parents changing their minds. Actually 755 teachers and helpers had registered at the Vale and Torteval schools but there were many withdrawals at the last moments. We were able to get 76 Alderney children aboard the *Sheringham*, in addition to the local schools.[29]

The crew of the SS *Antwerp* assisted with the evacuation of Guernsey and Second Officer, Cliff Witchell, noted in his journal:

> Thursday 20 June - Left at 12:30. Air raid on. Planes overhead but no action. Fires started in Southampton. Arrived at Guernsey at 8:35 and left at 9:45 with 1200 women and children. Arrived Weymouth

and anchored at 3:00. Hove up at 6:15. Alongside 6:45. Left at 8:15 and anchored. Bed at 10:30pm. Saturday 22 June – Some day! Arrived Guernsey 6:30am. Paddy, self and Warrant Officer busy for 2-3 hours taking evacuees by car to (SS) Sheringham. Sailed at 1:00 with 1978 passengers. Arrived Weymouth and anchored 6:15. Alongside 9:45, but only 1000 allowed off. Passengers sleeping all over decks and my cabin full up.[30]

John Petit was shocked by conditions on board his evacuation ship:

The vessel taking us to England was the *Batavia IV* and the whole school, with its teachers, filed in an orderly fashion on board. We descended into the acrid-smelling between decks and lower holds of the ship. The holds emitted a strong smell of excrement and urine and we learned later that the vessel had been used to evacuate British troops from St. Valery in Normandy.[31]

Violet Hatton's husband, Elijah, was among the troops who had been evacuated from Normandy. Violet fled Guernsey with her mother, sisters and six-month-old son, Brian. When she reached Weymouth, she was offended by the reaction of some of the volunteers: 'There were French interpreters who thought we spoke a foreign language and that we wore grass skirts! One of them even showed us how to use an electric light! We told them we were British citizens and that we had everything like that in the Channel Islands.'[32]

Leonard and Alyce Garfath Cox fled Jersey with their four children. Leonard later recalled:

Our sons were put onto a cargo boat but the rest of us could not find room on any ship. I returned to the boys' boat, asking 'Will you please just take my wife and daughters? I'm too old.' The man on the gangway agreed, then as he saw our tearful farewells, said 'Oh come on, old man, get on!' We settled down on the hatch-cover of a hold as the sun was setting on a calm sea, and after an uneventful night, we berthed at Weymouth. We were asked if we had relatives or friends who could accommodate us in the UK, but like us, the majority had nowhere to go and very little money.[33]

Graeme Cox adds to the family story:

We boarded a train and soon realised that we were heading north. The following morning we pulled into a station where I managed to read a painted-out sign 'Rochdale.' I had never heard of the place, but someone mentioned that it was where Gracie Fields came from. This trivial bit of information was strangely comforting. I had seen Gracie Fields in films and felt that if they were like her in Rochdale we would be all right. We were taken to a large empty house where women and girls were placed in some rooms and men and boys in others and my father was put in charge of the group. Our reception by the local people was basic but wonderful because they were so welcoming.[34]

During this hectic cross-channel activity and despite the very real and growing threat of a German invasion, on 22 June 1940 a holiday advertisement appeared in *The Times*: 'Channel Islands, Jersey. St Brelade's Bay Hotel. The safest place on earth. Dream in peace to the whisper of the warm south winds, where summer is ever a reality.'

Marjorie Lewis will never forget the kindness of a London policeman:

We travelled on the *Duke of York* to Weymouth then, through the army, we got tickets to go to where Bert was stationed in Yorkshire. We stopped off in London to have a break for a day and night, but could find no lodgings; I broke down and sat down on the street and cried that no one wanted us. A policeman came and rescued us and took us to his lodging room, however, the two ladies that rented his room to him didn't want to know and refused us his room. I ran down the stairs into the street crying, 'They don't want us either.' The policeman brought us back and explained to the two old ladies, they could not have been kinder to us all. On Monday, Bert went to the army people and he got tickets for Rosemary and I to travel back to Weymouth to join the other evacuees.[35]

Miss Grace Fry arrived in Weymouth just as an air raid warning was taking place:

My pupils and I were pushed out of the building onto a bus, then to my horror, the driver locked the door and disappeared. The children had been sick on the boat and were dropping off the bus seats in the dark because they were tired. After an hour, I had given up and thought, 'Well, this is the end, if a bomb falls on us, I hope it happens quickly!' Then the driver unlocked the door and said 'Out!' I had to feel with my foot under the seats in the dark to check whether I had all the children or not! We were then sent to the railway station.

Young soldiers began to push the children onto a train, then suddenly this big Major came out of the darkness, and said 'Madam,

31

will you go on with your children?!' and I said 'But where?' Well, the
train started to move, and a young Lieutenant came running down
the platform, grabbed my hand and said 'Can you run?' and we set
off at a terrific lick! A steward appeared in a white coat, at the open
train door, and this young soldier pushed me into his arms, and then
off we went. We were sent to Pollokshields, Glasgow, where one of
the volunteers asked me if my group were Belgian![36]

Mr Frederick Veale acted as a Liaison Officer, assisting thousands of
evacuees:

Whilst the evacuation was proceeding, very little was known of the
final destination of the refugees in England. I was selected as one of
three Liaison Officers who would deal with matters between the
English and Guernsey authorities. We left Guernsey on 22 June and
were received with courtesy in Weymouth, but found that most of
the refugees had moved on with others volunteering to join H.M
Forces. We were advised that care had been taken to place food and
water on all the trains.

I later discovered that many had travelled long distances without
refreshments, and that some were actually locked in trains without
sanitary conveniences. They had arrived at their destinations in a
distressed condition. In some areas the officials were working
closely to the Ministry's instructions for dealing with 'foreign war
refugees' and restrictions which were designed to deal with groups
of aliens – causing some friction between the officials and the
islanders, who are of course, British subjects.[37]

Philip Godfray was Headmaster of Alderney School and he described
the Channel crossing:

The total length of the journey from Alderney to England was sixty
hours, with the delays. For the whole of this period the amazing
spirit and faith of the children enabled them to respond to our
guidance without a single whimper or word of complaint. At
5.30pm the ship parted from the historic quay. The National Anthem
was struck up as the gap quickly widened between the silent crowds
on shore and on board. It was, as any other music would have been,
ridiculously inappropriate, but both sides, linked across the space
by so many ties of parenthood and 'islandship' felt the need for a
parting act together, and so that unique and mercifully short music
filled the gap.

I was standing just below the boat's bridge when the Blue Warning was brought down to me – an Air Raid at sea. I sent the boys down into the hold, while the others crowded under the shelter of the superstructure. Ten minutes crept by, half an hour. The gunner looked about him with a slightly disappointed expression. His rugged face seemed to say 'Just let me have a shot at the blasted Nazis.' More time passed. We began to nibble the sandwiches made in Guernsey. This frugal meal broke the spell. Ninety minutes. Suddenly the transmitted buzzed and spluttered into welcome staccato. It was over. And then, to the delighted eyes of our boys and girls, came the Cliffs, the long lanes of ships, the Docks, the trains, each to be explained, each part of the blessed wonder – of England.[38]

In July 1940, Lourdes Cavilla was evacuated from Gibraltar with her mother and younger siblings:

Before we sailed for the UK, I remember my father sewing with a huge needle a large white stencilled material with our name on it, which contained our personal effects. He made a great job of it. We did not possess or couldn't afford suitcases. It felt like a long time on board the ship, I think it was seventeen days to the United Kingdom, zigzagging due to U boats. We were treated very kindly by the sailors but it was very uncomfortable in the hold of the ship. I have hated boats ever since, especially the smell![39]

The Gibraltar evacuees endured terrible journeys due to overcrowding. Lourdes Galliano also recalls that there were food shortages on her ship:

Due to poor storage conditions and the intense heat, everything was covered in green mould. A human chain was formed on the deck and out of the hold came the meat, bread, fruit and vegetables that were to have fed us for the rest of our journey. They were thrown overboard to give the fish a good meal! The next day we were given boiled rice, which we could not eat because it was full of weevils, but the day after that when the rice came round, we decided it was better than nothing. After that, rice became our daily ration (the weevils were pushed to one side) till the end of our journey which was still 12 long days away.

As the days passed, our rice ration became smaller and we began to develop boils and mouth sores. Some days later there was excitement as we saw land. As we neared the harbour, small craft came alongside and asked, 'How are you? is there anything you want?' We were leaning out over the deck and someone shouted 'We are hungry! We want bread!'

After a while two speedboats appeared which were loaded with baskets full of loaves of bread. We sat down on the deck and people handed each person a whole loaf, then a basket of tomatoes appeared and we had one each. Finally a basket of eggs. We berthed, but that evening the ship had to raise anchor and move out into the Bristol Channel as a big air raid took place. We watched, terrified, as bombs fell and exploded on the town. They eventually died away and we were allowed to berth once more.[40]

Chapter 4

'We Will Find You a Nice One'

The Evacuees' New Homes

Prior to the arrival of evacuees in the designated 'safe areas', reception centres were established in public buildings in towns and villages all over Britain. Thousands of volunteers and council employees brought in the necessary chairs, camp beds, food and blankets, some of which were donated by local people – but unfortunately, the washing and toilet facilities in these buildings sometimes proved inadequate for such a large number of people.

The following accounts paint a picture of the different ways in which evacuees were received by communities. They also highlight the difficulties encountered, the highly emotional atmosphere and the cultural differences between evacuees and those who received them.

A.D. Wilshere arrived at Glemsford village school in Suffolk with 430 children:

> The local committee began sorting out the evacuees. I was anxious to get one poor woman with three-month-old twins and another child settled, since she was near to collapse. She was pathetically grateful and relieved and I was glad to find later in the day that she was excellently situated. There were two Irish sisters with six children between them who were blunt to the point of rudeness. They were oblivious of the trouble and inconvenience that they were causing other people and I could not but admire the patience and tact of the slow speaking Suffolk villagers in dealing with them.
>
> When I mentioned the matter of the helpers who were with us, there was surprise and difficulty. The reception officers had received no definite instructions – indeed they had not known whether they

were to have children only, or women and children. Although they were prepared to accommodate people like me for one night, they could not understand the purpose of the helpers. They would arrange for me to stay for one night but I had best take all these ladies back with me tomorrow.[1]

Mary Richardson arrived in Kent with children from Cork Street School, Camberwell:

Each teacher was assigned 10 children and after a long train journey, we arrived at Sevenoaks where we were neatly put into cattle pens to be counted. We then caught another train and arrived at Brasted station, which is quite a distance from the village, so when we arrived at the church hall we were a sorry sight – tired, thirsty and afraid. Mothers came and chose us and I was seized upon by the lady at the village shop and bakehouse. We had promised to try to keep families together but with four Peabody girls and four Sparrowhawk boys, this proved impossible.

By morning we were met with distraught mothers. Some of the younger children had head lice, some had wet their beds and their clothing was dirty, ragged and unsuitable. However, the Kent ladies were brilliant, extra clothing was found, menus were changed to accommodate townies who never ate greens, cuddly toys were given to comfort the weepy ones and we teachers set about de-lousing. Because of transport difficulties, few London mothers came to Brasted but the children grew strong and rosy cheeked due to the love and care they received.[2]

Mary's comment on children who had arrived in the reception areas with inadequate clothing was a recurring issue. The House of Commons discovered that men and women working in the Lancashire cotton mills had bought clothes and shoes for child evacuees who had arrived poorly clothed: 'I could take Hon. Members to little shops in Great Harwood which have been sold out of children's clothing for the first time ... because the kind hearted weavers of that village were rigging out the children.'[3]

When Guernsey teacher Ruby Nicolle arrived in Cheshire with her pupils, they were taken to the local town hall:

From Weymouth we were sent by train to Stockport and several Guernsey schools were sent to the town hall. Hundreds of camp beds and blankets were laid out for the children and the teachers slept on the balcony. There were only the cloakroom facilities one gets in a public hall, four wash basins with only cold water and a limited number of toilets. We adults were allowed to use the Town Council facilities in a separate room – lavish toilets and hot and cold water in the wash basins. The first night a nun from the convent school was quite downhearted. 'I see no future before me' she moaned, which I thought was a fine attitude for the girls in her charge! One of our teachers was in tears too. I had been brought up in the rough and tumble of a large family and it didn't bother me, though I had left my future husband behind. We had been due to marry in August 1940.

A few weeks later we were moved to a church hall in Bowden where people approached the children they fancied and arranged to take them into their homes. The great mistake was that the teachers were not consulted and there were many misfits. Bowden was the district where many Manchester business owners had their huge houses. In Bowden Vale were the humble folk who did the washing and cleaning for the high ups! Some of the Guernsey children came from working class homes and found themselves in the grand houses, like fish out of water. Other better class children were in council houses. The Bowden people said they were quite relieved to have country children as their previous evacuees had been from the poor parts of Liverpool, and they had preferred beer and chips to jam butties.[4]

John Glasgow was just a young boy when his mother, Edna, pulled shut the front door of their home on Alderney. Having left with all the other evacuees on Sunday, 23 June 1940, Edna would never see her house again. In fact, she would never return to the Island. Seventy years later, John still has some recollection of his departure:

Six ships came and church bells rang to tell people it was time to go. They were allowed one bag per person – pets were left behind to fend for themselves or be shot. We spent June 24 travelling and my mother was already ill.[5]

John recalls the tragic events which occurred three days later:

On arrival in Glasgow, boy scouts were on hand to assist the carrying of bags, cases etc. Small children were carried by members of the Strathclyde Police Force and a photograph taken that day shows me and another child, unknown, being carried by policemen.

We were put on coaches and taken up a hill, some had recognised the Scottish accent and asked whether it was Edinburgh, but no, Glasgow. Destination, Stobhill where on arrival all luggage was placed on the grass and us evacuees taken into a very large building that was a former workhouse. Inside were very long tables with food comprising tea and bread and margarine. By this time many were so tired and distraught, in tears and unable to eat.

On the coaches again, to church halls this time, and in my case to the church hall of The Holy Cross, Knightswood. Here the first proper medical screening took place. My mother was diagnosed as having advanced pulmonary tuberculosis and on 26 June was sent to the Ruchill Hospital in Glasgow which specialised in infectious diseases. I was sent to the Castlemilk Children's Home ... we were never to see each other again. She died on 4 October 1940 and was buried in Glasgow, on 8 October, in Sighthill Cemetery in the common burial ground, a pauper's grave. She was 29 years old.

My father, who had already enlisted in the Army, had been notified of my mother's death, collected me from the children's home and took me on a train journey which ended about a mile and a half out of Winchester. He knocked on a door randomly and asked if I could be taken in temporarily. The lady couldn't help as she had two small children of her own but she suggested trying over the road. A lady there had no children but was fond of them. My father asked if they would look after me for a couple of days whilst he tried to find somewhere more permanent for me. They said yes.[6]

Mrs Marie Duquemin and her 2-year-old daughter, Mavis, were sent to Stockport Sunday School in Cheshire with two hundred Channel Island evacuees. At that time, it was the largest Sunday school in the world, containing a hundred rooms with beautiful stained glass windows.[7] Mavis recalls:

The people there were kindness itself, but the only washing facilities were the sinks in the toilets. We lived there for three weeks, sleeping on old mattresses and when we left, we found that we had lice and fleas. My poor mother was so embarrassed. Then we were taken into the home of a lady who had a child the same age as me. She asked for a lady with a little girl who had dark hair and we 'fitted the bill'. She was very kind, my mother was extremely embarrassed about the fleas and lice that we had caught from the reception centre, and she helped to sort us out. We stayed with her for 3 happy months in all.[8]

However, Mrs Duquemin did not know the whereabouts of her older daughter, Hazel, who had left Guernsey with her school. Hazel explains how the family were eventually reunited:

> I ended up in Rochdale, then, along with two of my schoolmates, I fell ill with German measles and we were put into isolation. Unknown to me, my mother and Mavis had left Guernsey two days after my departure and my father left a few days later. He joined the army and was stationed in North Wales. After making enquiries as to my whereabouts my mother established that I was in Rochdale and travelled from Stockport to see me. This was quite an undertaking for a country woman with a young child who had no experience of trains and double decker buses.
>
> Furthermore, at the house where I was supposedly living, she was directed to the hospital and having arrived there, could only communicate with me through a glass door as I was in isolation. Not a very joyful experience for either of us! Whilst I and my friends were in hospital, our school was moved to Alderley Edge. So when we were discharged from hospital we were sent there. We were taken into the homes of local families but I was not happy there and naturally missed my mother very much, which made her determined that I should join her and Mavis in Stockport. This took quite a long time to arrange but eventually I was released by my Guernsey school.[9]

Mrs Duquemin was fortunate to have been placed with a couple who were willing to take a mother and child into their home. Many British families were happy to provide a home for a child, but few came forward to take in evacuated mothers with their children. The *Rochdale Observer* reported, 12 October 1940, that, 'The accommodating of mothers and children presented great difficulties and in the final stages, compulsory powers had to be exercised.'

Travelling with his mother and sister, Alfred Goble arrived in Somerset:

> They gave us a bun and a cup of tea and put us into this hall for the night. The next day we had to go to Wells and the same again there – no one wanted the 3 of us. I remember standing by the Cathedral and Town Hall and being kept waiting and do-gooders came and said 'It won't be long now, we'll find somebody.' A few people were taken then the rest of us were taken off in coaches and ended up in Priddy in the Mendip Hills. We finished up at the vicarage there and

waited again. Nobody wanted us and we were taken back along this track and, as luck would have it, a farm cottage said they would take us in. They'd already got two evacuees from London who were afraid of the animals, as they'd never seen them up close like that![10]

Sarah Murray and her mother were evacuated to the opposite end of the country, to Dunning, a small village in Perth and Kinross in Scotland:

I was quite sad when we had to be evacuated, there was all that hustle and bustle and here you were with tags tied around you and gas masks. I cried because I was frightened as well as it being a great wrench in life to me. I was quite unhappy even though my mother was with me. It was such a long day getting here and we were stood about waiting. My feeling was that everybody else was getting away to billets and homes and we were left standing about.[11]

Sheila Brown had a similar experience at a reception centre in Stockport: 'If anyone came to choose me, my Mum came forward and said she was with me, but they didn't want an adult with three boys and a girl as well.'[12]

Jean Le Prevost was another who experienced such issues during the evacuation process, having struggled to find lodgings for herself and her daughters:

At the reception centre, women would try to take one of my girls to live with them, and I would say that we wanted to stay together. Some women actually said to me 'Sorry love, but I don't have room for you and two kiddies.' One whispered, 'My husband wouldn't tolerate two women in our house, he thinks that one is enough as it is!' In the end I had to let my kiddies go to two separate families until I found an empty flat for us all.[13]

The separation of mothers from their children, both during the evacuation journey and in the reception centres, made it difficult for families to be reunited. Wartime communications were poor. There was a lack of telephones in ordinary homes and the postal service was slow and unreliable. It could take months for a mother to find her children which inevitably caused distress to everyone concerned. Miss Grace Fry recalls:

During our first three months in Scotland, the mothers eventually turned up to get their children. Then suddenly the Public Assistance department phoned me and said that a father had turned up on a day's leave to collect his two children. I had Jean but I didn't have Walter. He had been billeted up the road so I went round to the house. I was sorry for Walter and the people he was with because he was playing in the garden and he was beautifully kept. I told them that the father had turned up so they had to part with him. Walter didn't really want to come.[14]

John Tippett was evacuated with his Guernsey school to Shawlands Cross Church, Glasgow where he was looked after by the caretakers, Mr and Mrs Robinson. John's mother, meanwhile, sailed to England separately, and arrived in Stockport. After several weeks she discovered John's whereabouts and he was escorted by train to Stockport. He walked into the Town Hall and was horrified by the scene:

The noise and the smell, all the camp beds lined up, people's belongings all over the floor! According to my Mum, I didn't take my coat and gas mask off. She said to me, 'Take your coat off' and I kept saying to her, 'No I am going home.' She was fascinated by my Scots-Guernsey accent! I actually thought that I was just visiting Mum for the day, and that I was going back to Mrs Robinson in Glasgow![15]

One mother spent weeks searching for her daughter to discover that she had been placed with a family in Scotland. She was reunited with her daughter in Lancashire but quickly sent a letter of complaint to the Billeting Officer:

I opened her suitcase and found she had so little clothing, she had only a few items and no sleeping garments whatsoever. The socks she had on needed darning and her summer frock was filthy! I was disgusted! But what annoyed me most, half of her clothing coupons had been used and there was not a single thing to show for them![16]

Joan Simon described her anger and frustration when she was told that she should not look after her own children but should offer them to local families for the duration of the war:

The billeting officer put pressure on me. He wanted me to place my children permanently with a local family! He told me that we women could not possibly cope without our husbands. I felt sure that I could somehow manage to look after my own children! They were all that I had left and my husband was fighting in the forces.'[17]

If mothers with children were offered their own flat or house it was often in a very poor condition. This matter was also raised in parliament when Mr McGovern stated:

> I have here in my pocket a postcard which one woman sent to her husband in which she said she was satisfied because she had got into a condemned house. Things have come to the state in which a woman, evacuated from her own home, is satisfied when she can be accommodated in a condemned house.[18]

Mrs Savident was offered appalling accommodation in Manchester and her son recalls:

> We moved into a house in Ashton-Under-Lyne which was in an appalling condition - we were constantly covered in flea bites. We were then moved to 55 Wellbeck Street, which wasn't much better. In fact the upstairs of the house was too dangerous for us to even go into. I remember my mother sitting downstairs, knitting, with mice playing around her feet.[19]

Ida Donaldson was evacuated with two small children and a baby: 'I was given a house which was a bit of a shack. The house next door was bombed in an air raid and we were told that our house was not safe.'

Margaret Jones, from Liverpool, was given a flat which was also in a very bad state of repair:

> There was so much damp on the walls that when I put my hand on them it came away wet. I could not imagine staying there with a baby and not falling ill. There was no furniture except a chair and a rickety single bed. The roof leaked and I had no coal to light a fire with. That first night I cried my heart out, feeling so far away from my husband and home.[20]

A similar case was brought to the attention of the Minister of Health: 'Is the Minister aware that a Government allowance of 5 shillings for each adult and 3 shillings for each child is being paid to the owner of a house in Shotley for two evacuee mothers and their children although the roof was leaking and the house uninhabitable?'[21]

Anne Mauger encountered similar conditions in the house that was given to her parents. 'There was water running down the walls and the house was full of cockroaches,' she said. 'During air raids my parents had to stand in the cellar, knee deep in cold water, passing me back and forth between them.'[22]

Marjorie Townsend, her mother, sister and brother, were evacuated to Baslow, near Chatsworth:

> We were given accommodation with the wealthy Crossley family. They had a chauffeur, a butler and maids but we evacuees had to live over a barn full of mice. I don't know how my mum put up with it; we had one room and slept on iron bedsteads. Another woman with two children lived in the other room. There was no running water and no stove. A maid brought food to us on trays and a jug of hot water for washing. We couldn't go into their house, and we used the maids' toilet.[23]

Later in the war, a reporter from *Picture Post* magazine visited housing in Wales occupied by one group of evacuated London mothers:

> Here, women with children live in communal houses taken over by the Government and divided mostly into two-roomed units. I visited one house high up on a hill in Corporation Avenue, Llanelly. It was an ample 11 room house that once must have seen much good and gracious living. There was little that was gracious about it now.
>
> That it was still the scene of much living was obvious from the moment one crossed the threshold. Five mothers and 15 children were billeted here. Mrs Florence Spackman of Brixton, who stubbornly stayed on in London with her five children until the fly bombs blasted her home. Mrs Chisnel, whose husband is in Italy and who has moved with her two children five times since the beginning of the war. Mrs Spackman told me about the house and what it was like for 5 mothers and 15 children, each with a highly developed sense of family privacy, to share one house.
>
> These wives of working men and servicemen were so utterly absorbed in the problems of keeping families fed and clean that there was a complete vacuum where, under easier conditions, there might have been those things that nourish the mind and spirit of family. There were no books of any description, no periodicals, no newspapers, not even a children's crayon book.

In many instances, such conditions prompted mothers to return home. Indeed, on one occasion Northumberland County Council reported:

Some of the billets allotted to mothers with children were disgusting and although in a state of normality it would have been possible to adjust the difficulties after a few days, the women were naturally in a nervous condition and took the easiest course of going back to familiar and comforting homes.[24]

For some parents, the complete change of environment was simply too much to cope with. John Payne recalls the day his mother arrived at their billet with her four children:

We reached a house that I thought were only in story books, a thatched cottage – we thought we were in fairyland. We were introduced to the elderly couple who lived there and were taken up the winding stairs to where we were to sleep. We couldn't believe how small the windows were with the thatch hanging over them, the floors were all sloping and during the night we could hear things moving around in the roof. The toilet was a shed outside and there was a well with a bucket on a chain to collect the water. After two days my mother said that if they didn't find us somewhere else we would move back to London. To be honest, we were more frightened here in the country than in the air raids in London. It was so quiet.

There will be some people, who read this, that think we were being unreasonable, that we should have been thankful to have been lifted out of the blitz London hell hole. I wouldn't blame them but you have to think about it and weigh up the situation and what we had left behind. For us, and in particular, our mother, we had just been through a traumatic experience. We were very jumpy and nervous, so was our mother.[25]

John's mother was not alone in finding the quiet of the countryside extremely daunting after spending her whole life in a busy town or city. Mary Sinclair recalled that, 'In Kent, the children settled well but the mothers resented "being dumped miles from anywhere, no shops, no buses, not anything." They had nowhere to go during the daytime.'[26]

Frances Gillies' family took in a Glasgow mother and her children:

The first evening they were with us, they all set off after tea (mother and five children and our old pram) and we found later that, like many of their friends, they had been to Arrochar and Teighness in search of a chip shop. They returned much later footsore and weary and not at all impressed by the local amenities! Sadly most of the evacuees did not stay too long – I suspect that village life was too quiet for them and so they returned to Clydebank only to become victims of the Blitz.[27]

In the House of Commons, Mr Sorensen raised the issue of mothers who had been told to stay out of their billets during the daytime, so that they would not 'get under the feet' of the woman of the house. 'One said, "What am I do to? My hostess told me immediately I had my breakfast that she could not have me in her house as it was much too small and I must clear out. I have been sitting in the cemetery and sitting here, but I am wondering when I am going to bath my baby."'[28]

Luckily, many of the mothers sent to Bury in Lancashire were pleased with the accommodation they were offered – which took the form of new houses on a council estate. Letters of thanks were sent by parents to Miss Roberts, the town's Billeting officer. For example:

> Dear Miss Roberts, how can I possibly find words to describe adequately my thanks and appreciation for the generosity you have shown to my family. I am ever so delighted to hear that they have now such a comfortable home. Please accept my heartfelt appreciation for your kindness and believe me to remain yours, very sincerely, Sergeant Aylward.[29]

The selection of children in the reception areas varied from place to place. Evacuees describe a 'cattle market atmosphere', a situation in which girls were chosen before the boys because they could help around the house, or where older boys were chosen to help with farm work. In some cases, there appears to have been a total disregard for the feelings of young children who had just been torn from their homes and all that was familiar to them.

Peter St John Dawe, aged seven, was evacuated from a London orphanage, then left alone all night:

> I was evacuated after the orphanage was hit by a bomb. The surviving kids went to a convent, but nuns and children don't mix, so we were evacuated to different places. I was shipped to Leighton Buzzard by train in the guard's van, like a parcel, with a label round my neck.
>
> My baggage was a paper bag with a bun, half a bar of chocolate, a three-legged piggy bank containing tuppence, and a pocket knife with a bent blade. The van was windowless, so I passed the time trying to straighten the blade of my knife against a wooden crate, but the guard stopped me. So the blade stayed bent. On arrival,

nobody knew what to do with me. So I ate my bun and chocolate, and spent the night in the station waiting room. The next morning, I broke the piggy bank and bought a sandwich at the station buffet.

Eventually the Billeting Officer came, a short lady, with a short temper. She housed me temporarily with an elderly couple. That was all right except that their house adjoined an abattoir for pigs. The squealing was terrible. From upstairs, I could see what was happening.

Next morning, the short, short lady called. We went together to the Town Hall. It was market day, with pens full of sheep, cows, and pigs. One was crammed with pigs, and some men were poking them. The pigs squealed; the men laughed. I decided to straighten the blade of my knife under the latch. So I got to work. But I didn't expect the gate to spring open. The pigs didn't wait a second; they rushed out like demon-filled Gadarene swine. They hurtled through the market, knocking people over, and upsetting stalls. After that, I wasn't wanted in Leighton Buzzard.[30]

George Osborn and his sister Brenda arrived in the Isle of Wight with their infant school:

Our reception centre was Wootton village school where we infants were herded together for the final humiliation – to be paraded round like cattle in an auction. The 'buyers' were would-be foster parents, many of whom seemed reluctant to take on these strange speaking, unkempt, evacuees from over the water. On top of all this we were hungry, thirsty and bursting for the toilet.

Those boys who couldn't wait did it now in corners of the school playground. Strong looking lads had no problem being chosen as they are always useful in a farming community. Likewise, older girls were soon found a home because they would be helpful around the house. But small boys – well, there simply wasn't much demand for them.

My sister was snapped up by a Mrs. Gallop; a name easily remembered by me because I always have this picture in my mind of a 'horsey' woman swooping down with a whinny and a clatter of hooves, snatching my sister from me and galloping off into the sunset. 'Won't you take the boy as well Mrs. Gallop? He'd be much happier with his sister?' 'Sorry, I can't do it' she replied.

The sad bunch of left-overs, including me, were finally trudged around the village from door to door. Small suit cases and bags became much heavier than they were before and cardboard boxed gas masks hung like lead around the neck and shoulders. Adult helpers helped where they could and smiled cheerfully through strained and worried faces; they must have been tired too.

The walk took us from the school and along New Road to join the main road which ran through the village. Brenda walked a short way with me, until she reached the gate of her new home which was in New Road. She pretended not to cry, but her face was wet as she waved goodbye, saying it wouldn't be long before we would be together again. But big boys don't cry do they? They just ache inside. We turned right, into the main road and walked up the long hill, knocking on doors and waiting. Some of us were taken in – the desperate Billeting Officers appealing, persuading and at times almost threatening the reluctant villagers to take 'just one.'

If I was not the last, I was certainly one of the last to be taken in. The house was close to St. Mark's Church in Station Road, where a large lady called Mrs Wilson, arms folded across her ample bosom scowled down at me. After trying every argument, which by now the Billeting Officer had all the answers to, she agreed to take me in, on the strict understanding that it was temporary, very temporary. 'Thank you very much Mrs. Wilson and good day; you won't regret it,' lied the official as he raised his hat in farewell.[31]

Terence Frisby was evacuated from Welling, Kent, to Dobwalls in Cornwall. He was accompanied by his brother Jack:

About sixty of us were herded into the centre of the main schoolroom and the villagers crowded in after us and stood round the walls. What a scene, this auction of children with no money involved. The villagers slowly circled us and picked the most likely looking. They used phrases strange to us in thick accents we could barely understand. 'Hallo my beauty,' 'There 'y're me handsome.' 'What be your name then?' 'This one yere will do.'

Inhuman as it all could be judged now, I can think of no quicker, better way of dispersing us. At least our new guardians were given some sort of choice in who was going to share their homes, even if the children were not. Not that anyone in authority in those days would have thought of consulting children about their welfare. Some people took three or four children to keep families together but others were split up.

A female voice said to me, 'What about you my pretty? Do you want to come wi' I?' 'I'm with my brother,' I said. 'Two of you?' 'Yes, he's with me. We're staying together,' said Jack. 'Two boys is a bit

47

much for we,' and the owner of the voice moved on. A hand grabbed my hair, an action I always hated. There was quite a lot of it and it was fair. 'I'll have this one yere, little blondie,' said a female voice. 'Ow, that's my hair.' 'I know boy. Could do with a cut, too.'

Although the hand that had ruffled my hair had been less then gentle, she herself did not look intimidating. Her accent was different again, much easier to follow than much of what we were listening to. 'You've got to have my brother too.' 'Got to?' she replied. 'Mum said we've got to stay together.' She regarded us, before saying, 'That's right then, if your mam said.'[32]

Three-year-old Peter Hopper arrived in Skegness with a large group of Grimsby evacuees:

We arrived at the Tower Gardens, a public park, for selection. Mrs Elsa Barratt, who became a lifelong friend to me, was the Evacuation (Billeting) Officer and took me under her wing right from the start.

My first evacuee home lasted just a week. I might not have been the type of child that the family hoped for, as I blotted my copy book when I swore because a toy bus would not run well on the eiderdown across my bed. Or so I was told. There were other factors, too, but I will not go into that.

I was moved swiftly on to the four members of the Willis family, just around the corner in Briar Way. I arrived at my new home carrying a small hessian bag which was known in Grimsby as a 'fish bass.' It contained just a few items of clothing and I had my Mickey Mouse gas mask. Rose Willis, my foster mother, was fiercely protective of me, especially if she thought I was being bullied. Sometimes the over-protectiveness was embarrassing in front of friends of the same age, but she always meant well and we had a good relationship throughout. However, when I was naughty or rebellious, the boot was on the other foot. I was constantly reminded that I could be 'sent back to Grimsby'.[33]

During July 1940, Lourdes Galliano's evacuation had seen the move from Gibraltar into the heart of the London, where the Luftwaffe's Blitz was soon to be unleashed:

My mother, my two sisters and I arrived in London and were taken to the Empress Hall in Earl's Court, a skating rink that had been

converted into an evacuee reception centre. The rows of tiered seats
in the hall had been closed and folding camp beds had been jammed
into the gaps – there were 750 of us!

We were very tired but as we lay on our camp beds we could see
that the domed ceiling was entirely made of glass. Not very
reassuring had we known what was to come! The next morning
there was no sign of our luggage but ladies from the Women's
Volunteer Service had set up long tables full of second hand clothes
and underwear. We also received a medical and a hot bath.

The conditions were impossible as there were always queues for
the toilets and the washbasins and they both deteriorated
progressively. I remember one morning, carrying my soap and towel
to a basin, and just before setting them down, noticing that the bar
of soap, already there, seemed to move by itself. I looked closely and
sure enough it was so covered in lice that it actually moved!

One night the lights had just been turned down when we heard
the loud wail of the air raid warning. Everyone jumped out of bed,
but we didn't know where to turn with this menacing glass dome
above us. We were directed to a shelter outside and a couple of hours
later we crawled gratefully back to our folding camp beds, only to
find most of them covered in glass from the panes that had fallen in
during the bombing.[34]

Harry Flack describes the selection process at his evacuee reception
centre in Devon:

We arrived by train at Petrockstowe and, following a long day, a
crocodile of tired children marched into the Church Hall. Then
began 'The Selection Process.' This involved all the children being
lined up and chosen by the people who were going to take them into
their homes. Do I really need to say that the girls went first? These
were followed by the larger boys who, dare I say could be useful.
Then followed the 'squirts' that included me!

However, I was chosen by a wonderful couple, Mr and Mrs Fred
Cooper. They were most welcoming people who took me into their
home and hearts.[35]

Irene Wood arrived at Hambleton village hall. Her welcome was most
inviting: 'Waiting for us were sandwiches, grapes, apples and
lemonade. It was the first time some of us poor Salford kids had eaten
a grape, and the food was gone in less than ten minutes.'[36]

Norton Myhill, meanwhile, also recalls the billeting process, this time in Lydlinch, a village about three miles west of Sturminster Newton in the Blackmore Vale in North Dorset:

> We assembled at the church hall which later became our school. After welcoming speeches, we had our even more welcome lunch as we were hungry and tired. After lunch we – my mother (who was only with me until I found a billet), myself, and another boy set off with a volunteer lady in a car to a village called King's Stag. We were going down the front path of our assigned new home when someone screamed out, 'I asked for girls!' so we got back in the car. It was now quite late so our volunteer tried the manager's house of a cheese factory in the same village. After some discussion the manager and his wife agreed to take us on a temporary basis until we could find somewhere else.[37]

It is surprising how many evacuees believe that they were among the last to be selected by host families. When Doreen Moss was evacuated from Leigh-on-Sea to Kniveton, near Ashbourne in Derbyshire, she was horrified by the events unfolding around her:

> Twelve children, mostly brothers and sisters, were gathered in the school hall where prospective foster parents assembled. I had a label round my neck saying 'brother to follow, has chicken pox.' This meant I was left till last and went home with Muriel and her mother.
>
> Unfortunately, next morning Muriel was found to have German measles. I was immediately taken to a children's home in Hartington some distance away. Imagine the shock, horror of a child, the first time away from home! On the third day our headmaster found me and somehow, my mother and brother appeared. She was asked to stay in the village to keep an eye on the evacuees and this she did.[38]

Philip Doran was evacuated twice from Liverpool. On the second occasion, he found himself in a village hall in Caernarfon:

> There were hundreds of children, joined by young mums and babies. Despite the age difference between us, they looked just as insecure as we did. Not only were we in a strange town, but they also spoke a strange language – Welsh! The five of us huddled together, secretly hoping that we'd all be taken to the same destination; we were joined by two friends from our area, Teddy

Ralph and his little sister. People came in and inspected the children, one by one they made their choice and left; slowly the room began to empty until we were the only ones left. By now it was dark and even the women from the WVS were beginning to show signs of concern; what on earth could they do with these seven 'scallies' if nobody else turned up? They suggested that we gather up our things and follow them to the local hospital where we would have to spend the night; a decision would be taken in the morning as to what could be done with us long term.

We were about to leave when the door opened and a lady walked in. There was a long conversation in Welsh, none of which we could understand. Eventually, a WVS woman came over and explained that Mrs Roberts only wanted two children; our hearts sank. Which two? It would make sense to take Teddy Ralph and his sister, leaving the four cousins and me to spend the night in the hospital, unwanted. With that the WVS woman continued, although Mrs Roberts only wanted two, she was prepared to take the rest of us, so we could all go! I cried then and I cry now as I relive that memory; the memory of a woman who had a big heart and showed us compassion, compassion that was so far missing in this miserable episode of our lives. She would not easily be forgotten.[39]

Having been evacuated from a Lowestoft children's home, Alan Boast found himself in a Co-Operative Stores hall in Glossop, Derbyshire:

There were lots of chairs so we all sat round, wondering, whatever next? In came these people from the village to select which boy, or boys, they would take in and look after. 'I'll have him, I'll take those two' etc. I put on my best beaming smile but nobody picked me! Soon the hall was cleared and there were only two of us left, myself and a boy called Peter Harvey. He wasn't a Home boy but I knew him from school. In came two ladies and after a lot of talking one said 'I'll take them as I have room for two.'

We were the last ones picked out. So off we went with these two ladies into what turned out to be a different world entirely – believe me! One of the ladies introduced herself as Mrs Townsend and said we would be living with her. We followed them out, under the railway bridge and into Clowne. I, as usual was chattering to Peter about where we were going.

Mrs Townsend looked round and said in a broad Derbyshire accent, 'If thou don't shut thee rattle, I'll belt thee tabs!' I was taken aback – I will never forget it!

'What did she just say?' I asked Peter. He shrugged his shoulders, saying 'I couldn't understand it.' It was our first experience of the local dialect, which took some understanding. I have often wondered since, what they thought of our Suffolk twang! For those of you who don't know it meant, 'Stop talking or you'll get a thick ear!'[40]

Joseph Parry and his brother were the last to be chosen when they arrived in Southport, from Bootle:

We were loaded onto a bus to travel to Norwood Road School. The Norwood children had been given half a day off to allow us to go into the school to be billeted. I was sitting with our Phil who had his arm in plaster of Paris, after falling off a wall back in Park Street.

When people came in to choose their evacuees, I think they saw Phil's arm and thought, 'Sod that, we'll have to take him to hospital all the time!' and passed us over so we were the last to be picked. Luckily for us, a kindly Mrs Rimmer took us home to live with her husband Mr Rimmer and their son John.[41]

Ben Halligan was evacuated to Shropshire with his brother and two sisters:

We were placed in cattle pens in the local market and people came and took their pick. We were not picked and were then taken to a small village about four miles away named Tetchill. We must have looked a pathetic bunch as we stood in the school playground. My sisters were taken away, whilst my brother and I were taken by a farmer.

Two days later we were placed with a Mr and Mrs Roberts. I did not know it then but that was the luckiest day of my life. They were over the age limit for taking evacuees but when Mrs Roberts heard where we had been billeted, she insisted on taking us in. Six months later that farmer was arrested for strangling his wife. Mrs Roberts must have seen something in his character. There was an aura about her, when she looked into your eyes she looked into your very soul.[42]

Barry Fletcher describes his experience in a village hall in Feckenham:

At 8 years old I sat there, on a long wooden seat, facing anxious children on the bench opposite, some crying, but most wide eyed, tired and wishing they were back at home. I became aware of strangers arriving in the hall, pointing at children, usually the girls, and within a few minutes child and adults disappeared out of the door.

This process continued until only a handful of children remained. I spoke to the older boy sitting next to me. Harry was nearly 10 years old, two classes above me at Station Road School. A teacher reassured Harry and I that someone would soon arrive and we would be chosen and a home found for us. A further long wait before an elderly couple entered the hall. I sensed immediately that this was a reluctant act of kindness of their part, dutifully carried out to provide a temporary home for two very tired, lonely, hungry boys.[43]

Derek Trayler recalls the ordeal of finding a new home in Yarmouth:

The quayside was packed with people who must have come miles to see the convoy of ships loaded with Dagenham children. By then I must have been told that we going to stay with people we didn't know which didn't stop us trying to pick out our likely hosts from the sea of faces staring back at us. We needn't have bothered as we were not destined to stay in the town permanently. That night we stayed in a school hall where we were issued with straw mattresses and blankets and soon fell asleep. In the morning we were told 'War has been declared' which didn't mean anything as it was completely beyond our experience at the time.

I remember going into the school toilets which were never intended for such a large number of very grubby children to use at the same time. The sinks were black and there was a filthy roller towel hanging down as if ashamed of its condition. My brother decided that we would end up even dirtier if we tried to wash there and I had no objections. Like most 7 year olds, I hated washing. My next recollection was the evacuees standing at one end of the village hall with the villagers at the other end. Somebody was calling out from a list and children went forward to meet their new foster parents and left the hall. The numbers dwindled until only my brother and I remained - and one couple with a young girl of my age who decided to take us home.[44]

Kenneth Grant was horrified by the route march endured by evacuees in Morpeth:

We had something to eat then they marched us all round Morpeth. Looking back maybe it was a weakness in the system. We were well organised leaving our homes but the reception areas seemed weak. We were only nine years old and they actually marched us around various streets, knocking on doors, 'Are you taking children?'

Now I'm not sure whether these good people had put their names forward but it seemed rather odd that they didn't take us straight to the houses that were allocated. Then it started getting dusk. Now that's the only time ... I didn't cry but I got a little anxious. Will we get billeted before nightfall? I would be in the last dozen – we walked along High Stanners then we turned left into a council estate. We walked up Holeyn Street knocking on doors and they knocked on number 12 and the lady came to the door, 'Are you having evacuees?' 'Yes.' So I was allocated to number 12.[45]

A Northumberland newspaper highlighted faults in Morpeth's billeting system:

The original plan was that children from specified areas should be evacuated in prearranged numbers to certain centres, where billeting accommodation was known to be sufficient. After them should come the expectant mothers, invalids and mothers with children of preschool age. In practice, the plan did not work successfully. In the first place, many children registered for evacuation did not present themselves at the entraining centres. This meant that during the first days of evacuation, many areas scheduled to receive evacuees did not do so.

A second batch of evacuees was then sent out, with little warning to the reception authorities, in some cases to areas which had declared that they had no more billets. The billeting officers did their best to fill up the billets left vacant by the small numbers in the first batch.

Unfortunately, between the first and second evacuations there had been some unofficial exchange of billets by dissatisfied people. In addition a number of the billets originally listed some time previously were no longer available either through private occupation of the premises, death or illness of the householder or similar reasons. The result was that evacuees were detrained, sent off to billeting centres and had to be returned because of a lack of accommodation.

The effect of this on the morale of the evacuees can be imagined. In Morpeth the number of evacuees so far exceeded the billeting accommodation that some of the late arrivals had to be sent off to neutral areas, whilst forty children were billeted in the ballroom of the local hotel – with unsatisfactory toilet arrangements.[46]

Chapter 5

'It Was Like Another World'

First Impressions

The arrival of large numbers of evacuees in towns and villages unsurprisingly created quite an impact. In some cases the population of a village could double overnight. In Lancashire, on 15 September 1939, the *Bury Times* remarked upon 'the large number of child evacuees walking around our streets with their smiling faces, greeting everyone with a cheery Hello'.

Many evacuees retain strong first impressions of their new homes and of the people who cared for them. The environment was often unfamiliar and they encountered differences in housing, dress, food, language, dialect and religion. Many remember the immediate kindness of their foster families.

Audrey Patterson, for her part, found herself in a house in Bideford, where,

> My sister Gwen and I were very lucky to be placed with Mr & Mrs Shute, a lovely couple who were very kind to us and where we were both very happy. I remember she used to make junket, a white sloppy substance sprinkled with nutmeg which I hated, perhaps that's why I remember it well. My most vivid memory is of their canaries which were always singing in their cages in the little garden room leading from the sitting room and of an old eccentric cousin, who lived a few doors away, had bright red hair, red lipstick, yellow fingers and who always seemed to have a cigarette dangling from her mouth.[1]

With his mother dead, 3-year-old John Glasgow's father, who was serving in the Army, had knocked randomly on a door, asking if the family could care for his son. Luckily, Frederick and Winifred Grant, said 'Yes' and John remained with them for the duration of the war:

> When my father had left me there before returning to the Army, he said 'this is your new mummy now.' As I already had my father, my foster father was known as Uncle Fred and foster mother as Mum or later Ma. They also had a live-in lodger, a Scot from Dumfries, Robert Monks. He became like an adopted uncle to me, known as Uncle Bert. These were my surrogate family now. I was three and a half years old and had been embraced into wonderful loving care, all by chance.
>
> Could it happen today? Some years later when I was old enough to understand, my foster mother told me that my father had told her that some of my mother's last words to him were 'Look after John for me.' A mother thinking of her child to the last. He did look after me.[2]

Dagenham evacuee, Derek Trayler, was billeted with the Keeler family in Yarmouth:

> Mr and Mrs Keeler took us back to their house and it was only later we realised the problem. My brother had insisted that we were not to be split as he had promised our mother to look after me. Mr and Mrs Keeler had a 6 year old daughter and had to give up their own bedroom to take us in. Nowadays parents would be even more reluctant to foster two unknown boys as my brother was nearly 13 at the time. They treated us very well with the same loving care that my parents would have done for their children if the roles had been reversed.[3]

Rita Roberts, aged six, was evacuated with St Thomas's school, Birmingham, to Bromsgrove:

> I thought I was many miles away from home and at that time Bromsgrove was all countryside, trees and fields with lovely big farm houses. I was one of the lucky ones chosen by a family who seemed quite wealthy. Mr King was a departmental head at the Austin Motor Company. Their house was called Blackmore Lodge, a large black and white country house with a plentiful garden.
>
> The Kings were very good to me; they bought me new clothes and nice books to read. I was allowed to go to the farms to help with milking cows, feeding chickens, collecting the eggs, making

butter and cheese, having a ride on a horse, but the best was seeing a lamb born. Another exciting time was being taken to Aberystwyth in Wales to see the sea, which I had never done before. All I could say was 'Ooh, look at all that water.' To my surprise, Mr and Mrs King had bought me a brand new swimming costume which I immediately changed into and ran splashing along the sea front.[4]

Ron Gould, from Guernsey, was billeted with the Yearsley family in Hale, Cheshire:

I remember waking up on the first morning, we were in a lovely sunny bedroom and went down to breakfast. It was all rather strange, we were told which seats to sit on at the table and we used the same ones every day. We did not want for anything as Miss Yearsley was very kind and showed a lot of interest in us and our families. Soon after our arrival a photo was taken of us and it was clear that we were busting out of our jackets and trousers. Anyone knows that as 12 year olds, you are growing by the day. Miss Yearsley took us both into a big department store in Manchester and fitted us both up with a new grey suit each. I am sure they paid for this themselves.[5]

There is a common misconception that most evacuees were sent from poor urban housing to the countryside where the facilities were far superior. As former evacuee, James Roffey points out, 'To this day many people still assume that all evacuees came from inner city slums, were dirty, had head lice and were not "house trained"'.[6]

However, this was not always the case, as Jessie Hetherington recalls the poorer facilities that she encountered in Bishop Auckland:

We were welcomed warmly by our prospective hosts and, after distribution to our new homes, a long day ended. Mine was to a village comprised of long rows of pit houses with outside 'netties' (toilets) and very few bathrooms. Saturday was spent seeing that the children were settling in. They had all come from a new housing estate where every house had an indoor toilet and bathroom and most were housed in homes without either – as I was. The kindness of most of the hosts made up for the lack of amenities.[7]

Philip Doran was surprised by the toilet facilities in his Caernarfon billet:

The seven of us travelled with Mrs Robert to our home through the lovely countryside in a beautiful pony and trap. We travelled through places that not only had we not heard of, we couldn't even pronounce. Cwm-y-Glo, Brynrefail, it was pure heaven!

Eventually we turned off the main road and crossed over the bridge of the beautiful Lake Paddern. Just over the other side we entered a small farm; on the gate it said Penlynn Farm. We stopped outside and Mrs Roberts said, 'Come on my loves, we're here'. Once inside, we met Mrs Roberts's children, Bobbie who was fifteen and Grace who was nine. We also met Tom – Tommy Roberts, the Dad! Tom didn't look too happy, he wanted an explanation as to how his wife had left to collect just two evacuees and come back with seven!

Mrs Roberts obviously had a way of handling Tom, and eventually he calmed down. Tom's first job was to show us where the 'lavvy' was. I didn't want to go but Teddy was desperate. He came back and said quietly to the rest of us, 'Yer wanna see da lav, it's just a bit o' wood wid a hole in it, yer do it into a bucket and it stinks'. It was Tommy's job to empty the bucket – a job that he did once a week. Now with seven new inhabitants it would have to be done on a more regular basis; maybe this was what he was upset about and who could blame him. I recall that first evening with great pleasure; we had a lovely tea and Mrs Roberts asked us all sorts of different questions, 'How many are in your family? What do your dads do, and what religion are you?' She seemed to really want to get to know us.[8]

Bob Cooper also remembers the subject of toilet facilities and his experiences in Cornwall:

Billy Shipman and I were both chosen by Mr and Mrs Old, a couple who lived in a tiny hamlet called Ladynance. Mr and Mrs Old had no gas, electricity or running water, we collected water from a well, and used a bucket for a toilet. It was normal to them but very strange to me! They looked after us well and I called them Auntie and Uncle. On our first day there, Billy and I went out for a wander and as we were passing some trees we heard a noise overhead and looked up - it was the local children looking down on us as if we were from outer space.[9]

Mavis Robinson immediately noticed the lack of facilities in Wales:

In Caerleon I had found a lovely surrogate family even if the surroundings were rather different. Baths were taken in front of the fire in a tin tub. There was no bathroom and the lavatory was across the yard in a little pantiled building. It had a scrubbed wooden seat and was flushed by emptying a bucket of water down the hole.[10]

When Liverpool evacuee Richard Singleton asked his foster mother where the toilet was, 'she took me into a shed and pointed to the ground. I asked her for some paper to wipe our bums. She walked away and came back a few seconds later with a bunch of leaves.'[11]

June Somekh was evacuated from Manchester to Winster, Derbyshire. Not only were the facilities at their destination less than satisfactory, but she and her brother quickly noticed the strange behaviour of one of the women in the house:

> My brother and I had left a large house in Manchester with facilities and were taken to a much smaller one with no electricity or running water. Miss Smith was somewhat older than my grandmother, but she was very kind and I grew to love her. However, the problem was a much larger lady who used to shout, 'You licker newt, you kipper 'addock!' at us.
>
> With hindsight I think she had Tourette's Syndrome, but we were terrified and thought we were staying with two witches! We decided that one of us should stay awake at all times. Needless to say, we soon dropped off.[12]

As June goes on to recount, there was often little consideration given by the host to the religion or ethnicity of an evacuee:

> I came from an Orthodox Jewish home and my brother was billeted with the local pork butcher! I could go into more detail such as my attendance at Sunday School and my brother's singing in the pub run by his hostess's daughter. I am quite sure that my mother had never seen the inside of a pub. Had my parents known any of this I don't think we would have been allowed to last the course.[13]

Brenda Harley also shared her first impressions of the home of the Davies family in Aberdare in South Wales:

> This was a miner's household with no bathroom, an outside toilet and a tin bath in front of the kitchen fire (a culture shock). They were a kindly, welcoming family but endured much hardship.
>
> I remember the girls had a plate of broad beans on their own for dinner. The bread was made at home and cooked across the road in

the baker's shop oven. Their house had four bedrooms and three downstairs rooms. There were lodgers in the front room. The wife was a dress maker and the husband was ill in hospital, returning home to die of septicaemia (I declined the invitation to look at the body laid out, having been advised to do so by my teacher). In time I learned to read and pronounce Welsh by singing hymns in Gadlys Chapel.[14]

John Martin, aged just seven, was evacuated from Dagenham to Lancashire in 1943:

I had a very nice place to live with Mr and Mrs Bromley at 5 Lawn Street, Colne, near Burnley. It was a nice clean house with a small back yard. There wasn't a bathroom and the toilet was outside. It was next to a coal mine and from my bedroom window I could see the miners going into the lift cage which took them underground. They did not have any children of their own so I was looked after very well.

After six months Mrs Bromley became ill so I had to go to another family. This time it wasn't so good. The house was shoddy and not clean, they had no idea how to look after children. My room was the junk room in the attic, full of old stuff which they had no use for. The bed was never made and the room was never cleaned the whole time I was there.[15]

Peter Staples, aged eight, arrived in Norfolk where the facilities were less than modern:

I was allocated, with another boy, Donald Self, to live with Mr and Mrs Scarff in Brumstead, near Stalham. He was a cowman at a local farm and the couple had two sons, Patrick and Derek. They had no gas or electricity, drew water from a well and cooked on a primus stove and range, which shocked my Mum when she came to visit us from London. Despite this basic existence, they were a delightful family, and it was great fun for us boys![16]

The different dialects and languages required some adjustment. John Honeybone attended school in Portland, Dorset where, 'the local children were unfriendly. Our accents stood out and we were called "incomers".'[17]

In his account, Liverpool evacuee Richard Singleton remembers hearing the Welsh language in Bronant, near Aberystwyth:

My brother Ron and I were chosen by Elizabeth (Liz) Morgan and travelled with her in the dark to her farm. Inside was a slate floor, a room with a table in the middle and sitting on the couch was a man who looked old, wearing a greasy trilby hat. There was a lovely fire burning, stoked with peat. Aunty put a pan of milk on the fire, cut a couple of rounds of bread and two lumps of cheese, she poured the milk into cups. The last time we had eaten anything was a sandwich and a cup of tea when we had changed trains at Shrewsbury.

When we finished, Aunty told us to say 'Goodnight' to Uncle Moses, who replied 'Nos Da' (He spoke Welsh and no English.). She then took us to a room in the hallway. There was a double bed and a chair, on the chair a candle in a saucer. We put our pyjamas on and climbed into bed. Aunty told us to get out of bed then told us to kneel down and put our hands together. She said 'Now say the Lord's Prayer and ask God to keep your Mother and Father safe'.

We grew very close to Aunty Liz because she looked after us, and if she went anywhere, we would be right behind her. If one of us got hurt she would give us a hug and say 'Come here my love' (in Welsh). Our mother would never have said that, it would be 'Don't be a cry a baby'.[18]

Clifford Broughton was another of the many evacuees who were sent to new homes in Wales:

My sister and brother had already been billeted with Blodwen Thomas, a miner's widow, at her house 'Glanpedol' in Twyn, a mining village. In December the London 'Blitz' intensified, so I went to join Mavis and John. It was a sea-change in culture, moving into a rural Welsh-speaking mining community but we were safe, save for the nights when Swansea was bombed in February 1941! We could hear the explosions even though we were 20 miles distant. Auntie Blod was very generous to accept all three of us and for that we were eternally grateful because it lessened the blow of leaving our parents.

The village was at the confluence of two rivers at the head of the Amman Valley. One of the rivers was known as the 'black river' because it was literally black from colliery workings upstream. Auntie Blod's neighbours gave us a demonstration of how to kill chickens, and what with a pig slaughterhouse just down the road we were certainly indoctrinated into country life.

Although I only had a few Welsh friends – I think the evacuees tended to keep to their own – I learned a little Welsh. I remember going around households on one New Year's Day, probably 1945, singing a little traditional verse 'Blwyddwyn newydd dda' and collecting a few coins.[19]

Jean Burton was privately evacuated to relatives, whom she did not know, in Wolverhampton:

I was three years old when I arrived there from Scotland. My Aunts, Marjory, Barbara and Jean, worked shifts at the Boulton Paul aircraft factory. I spent most of the time with Barbara which led some of her neighbours to assume that I was her own child! Wolverhampton was very different to Dunfermline, and I had to get used to the different accent. There were actually more bombing raids in Wolverhampton than at home! German maps found at the end of war show that the aircraft factory was a major target. It survived because of a dummy factory built two miles to the north which was bombed three times by the Germans![20]

Ken Chamberlain found it difficult to adjust to his new environment in Eccleston in Cheshire:

There were no buses, no trams, no cinemas like we had in Liverpool and we had to walk everywhere. It was a four mile round trip to school. At the school, everyone had a totally different accent to mine so there was a certain amount of bullying by some of the other children. This went on until another Liverpool boy came to live in the village and took my side.[21]

The experience of encountering different accents and dialects is one that Eric Scott remembers from his time as an evacuee in Kettering:

We arrived at the Henry Gotch School from where a car drove me to 12 Hillcrest Avenue. Having knocked on the door a lady answered and said 'He'll do' and I thought 'Oh this will be alright' although I was surprised by her quite broad Midland accent. I met her husband Charlie on his return from work and as he was a quiet, gentle man, I had no concern for my safety because Hilda and Charlie Petit were very kind to me.[22]

When over 25,000 Channel Island evacuees arrived in Britain, local people often assumed that they were foreigners. Ruth Alexandre wrote in her diary that, 'I told the girls at the Co-op that I was from Guernsey and was surprised to hear them say, Fancy and you speak perfect English too!'[23]

Olive Quin will never forget her arrival at an evacuee reception centre in Burnley:

> The ladies from the WVS made 'signs' for us to start eating. We thought this rather odd and would have had a jolly good laugh at their miming had we not been so tired. Suddenly the penny dropped, as they say. They thought we were all French and as they could not speak French they had performed this sign language. They were very relieved when they learned we could all speak English![24]

Agnes Camp was pregnant when she left Guernsey with her four-year-old son:

> We arrived in Yorkshire where kind people had prepared a nice buffet for us and lots of cups of tea. Dennis wasn't very well and I was quite worried. We spent the night on camp beds with an army blanket to cover us. The Northern people knew very little about the Channel Islands and thought we were all going to be black people; they were also amazed that we could speak English.
>
> I phoned my husband in Guernsey and told him that we were safe, gave him our number and asked him to phone me the next day. That call never came because the Germans invaded Guernsey and all communications were cut. Then Dennis came down with pneumonia and nearly died.[25]

Rex Carre remembers hearing his wartime foster parents' Oldham dialect:

> In contrast to my Guernsey family of growers, my new family were nearly all teachers which scared me a lot at first but not for long. The Oldham dialect took a lot of getting used to, e.g. 'If thou does out for nowt, do it for the sen!'
>
> My foster father, Sam Morgan, was a junior school headmaster at Watershedding, near Oldham Rugby football ground. He was the finest real gentlemen I have known. My foster mother was his second wife. She was a jolly happy person with a great sense of humour. Things were difficult at first, getting to know these new people and trying to fit in. Auntie tried her best on the first day by taking us to Alexandra Park – including a boat trip on the lake – about the last thing I wanted after a traumatic Channel crossing![26]

Just before the Channel Islanders arrived in the UK, at least one newspaper published an article which told readers to beware of strangers and people speaking foreign languages who might be spies. 'If Strangers ask you, don't tell!, it advised.[27]

When Guernsey evacuee, Adolphus Ogier, arrived in Stockport, he changed his name to Bill because of the hatred of the name Adolf. As well as speaking English, some of the adult Guernsey evacuees spoke a 'Guernsey patois' which was based on Norman French. Margaret Duquemin's mother occasionally spoke patois to other evacuees. 'Passers-by would give her odd looks, I was scared that they would think that we were German, and although only 7 years old, I would walk behind her, ready to run for help if needed, or escape.'[28]

Derek Dunn's Guernsey family experienced similar difficulties, this time in Wales:

> The whole family, my grandparents, their four children and we four or five grandchildren lived in one house, a family to a room. It was a difficult time for the adults as they had nothing! Just a totally empty house to furnish and equip. I think they must have been very resourceful when faced with the problems. But it all seemed very difficult as there was no meeting of minds between exceedingly insular Welsh who had no idea who we all were and where we were from and I believe that we were regarded with considerable suspicion.
>
> As I believe happened elsewhere, my grandparents were reported to the police so many times as German spies because they were speaking patois to each other in public that they called and asked my grandmother in particular to stop! But my grandfather was instrumental in catching a German sympathiser/spy who was allegedly signalling to planes from a tree. Maybe the guy was a nut-case but taken away. After the war my grandfather would not talk about it as he said that the man had probably been shot.[29]

However, it was often the Channel Islanders who felt they needed a translator when they first heard the unfamiliar British dialects. During Raymond Carre's first evening in Manchester, an air raid took place and he found himself 'in a shelter, with over a hundred people, young and old, all talking a broad Lancashire dialect that we could not understand'.

When evacuees arrived in the reception areas, they encountered very different environments to those they had left behind. Children from urban areas discovered the open spaces of the countryside. Coastal children settled into urban towns and rural villages, whilst thousands of Channel Islanders were sent to noisy, industrial towns and cities. John Honeybone was evacuated with his mother and sisters from Barnet to Portland, Dorset:

> We went to stay with Mum's brother who lived on a council estate right next to Portland dockyard. The tunnels next to the dockyard were used as ammunition dumps, so if a bomb had hit them that would have been the end of Portland!
>
> My parents were constantly worrying about this. They were a very down to earth family and kind to us. Aunt Ada used to walk round with an uncut loaf of bread under her arm and ask, 'Are you hungry duck?' and if we said 'Yes' she would cut us a slice of bread and spread it with butter.
>
> I really wanted to see the big ships in the dockyard, so one day I walked to the gates, there was no one on guard duty so I walked in. Suddenly blue lights were flashing and I was arrested! It was even mentioned in the local newspaper![30]

Marion Wraight left Margate to discover farm life in Staffordshire:

> Mr and Mrs White (later Auntie Millie and Uncle Dick) came to pick us up, and took us to Sunnyside Farm. It was the first time I had seen a cow or an egg, as we lived mainly on bread and margarine in Margate and plum jam. Auntie Millie ran the farm and there were 2 farmhands – Freddie Adamson and Bill Crisp. They had pigs, cows, sheep, geese, chickens; I got some pigs for my birthday!
>
> I was very happy there, it was much better than where I had left. I milked the cows every day, 6am before school, fed the pigs, helped in the house, cooking etc. Auntie Millie was kind but didn't show love. I liked Uncle Dick as he liked horses and I was given a pony called Taffy and learned to ride. I would never have had a horse if I hadn't been evacuated.[31]

When David Forbes arrived in Dunning, Scotland, with his mother, brothers and sisters, he was amazed by the huge open spaces:

> It was exciting, coming from tenements to a country place. We stayed at first in Baadhead Cottage on the farm up behind Keltie Castle. It probably took me a year to get used to it, to the big open spaces. There were two cottages, I think they were servants' quarters

for the Castle. Another evacuee family called the MacNabs stayed there too. We'd come from a big housing scheme in Glasgow and when you went out to play there were twenty or thirty kids to play with. In Scotland, at Baadhead, you felt at first lost and lonesome, just your family.[32]

Terence Frisby recalls the moment when he and his brother Jack saw their new home in Cornwall:

We swept past a farm with a huddle of outbuildings, which grimly showed their backs to the weather and the outside world. We topped the brow of a hill, a lone oak tree growing from the hedge, all the branches blown one way. We would soon learn to know those south westerly winds that blew across Cornwall. The man, Mr Phillips, spoke. 'There we are. See? That's where we live. We're the end one. There.'

We stared across a field at a terrace of Victorian cottages – more slate and granite. They looked tiny and grim. Seven of them, as it turned out. How could seven families live in so little space? 'That's Doublebois,' he said, 'Doublebois is French. It means two woods.' The taxi stopped and we went to the house at the far end of the terrace which had a wooden wash-house beyond it and some hens in a wire-enclosed run on the right.

Neighbours looked out of doors at us. A woman said 'Thought you was only getting one.' 'They was on special offer,' said our man. 'They looked too good to leave behind,' said his wife.

We entered and stared in wonder at a black shining range with a cat curled beside it, at a canary in a cage, at a green velvet tablecloth and oil lamps – no electricity here; at two First World War shells in their cases, over six inches tall, standing on either side of the clock on the mantelpiece. But the glory came last. Outside tucked down in a cutting and breathtakingly revealed was the main London to Penzance railway line with Doublebois station practically below us.

In the short time before we went to bed, the rural silence was occasionally shattered as an express train roared by a few yards below, steam and smoke belching over the cottages. Our Dad worked on the railways, so we two railway children couldn't have invented, couldn't have dreamed of arriving at such a place. Our satisfying new address was 7 Railway Cottages.[33]

Alan Boast was sent from a children's home in coastal Lowestoft to the village of Clowne, in rural Derbyshire:

We eventually arrived at number 9 Oxcroft Crescent which was to be my home for the next 21 months. Mr Townsend was a miner and worked at Oxcroft no. 2 pit, at the back of the house, down a hill. It was a cosy little semi-detached with two bedrooms, a kitchen, bathroom downstairs and a big front room which served as a dining room and lounge etc. In this dining room was what was known as a Yorkshire Range. It was a warm cosy home, and I liked it.

Well, Sunday it was, so Mrs Townsend cooked a Sunday dinner. We sat down at the table, and she served it up. A Yorkshire pudding was put on our plates and then covered with gravy which was very nice. Peter Harvey and I looked at each other, and didn't know what to say! So I opened my big mouth again! 'Is this all we are going to get?' said I. 'Eat your Yorkshire,' said Mrs Townsend.

Nobody had told us that in the north of England you ate your Yorkshire pudding and gravy first, then had your meat and vegetables afterwards. We, of course, were used to having it all on the plate at the same time! This was just one of the many differences in the lifestyle 'up north'.[34]

In many cases, Channel Island evacuees had left behind a quiet, rural island way of life to be plunged into noisy, industrial towns and cities in England and Scotland. Muriel Parsons, for example, wrote in her diary that, 'There were rivers and canals, viaducts, trains and noisy railway stations. There were cotton mills belching black smoke into the air and coating everything with a dark grey dust.'[35]

When he arrived in Oldham, Bob Gill saw, 'Tripe in a butcher's window. The people were very friendly but the accents, clogs, shawls and mills were very unfamiliar and different.'[36] Lawson Allez, for his part, recalled that: 'People were very friendly but everywhere seemed so noisy after living on a quiet island.'[37]

When Ron Gould arrived in Eccles, Manchester, he thought he was imagining things when, 'A large cargo ship, many times larger than our Guernsey mail boats, went steaming by, forty miles from any sea! I soon found out it was the Manchester Ship Canal.'[38]

Ted Hamel was asked by locals what he thought of Bradford and he wrote later the following: 'Well, I just couldn't tell these kind folk that I thought I'd been dropped in the Black Hole of Calcutta could I? So I compromised. I said I was not thrilled at living in a city but the wonderful welcome we had received in Bradford made up for being so far from home.'[39]

Evacuees who lived in the countryside had never seen 'smog' before, the mixture of fog and coal smoke which poured into the air from the chimneys of urban houses and factories. Len Robilliard described trying to get home on his bicycle in Stockport: 'I could hardly see my hand in front of my face and walked past my street three times.'[40]

In Leeds, Joan Wilson also encountered smog for the very first time. 'It was pitch black,' she noted. 'I wondered what on earth had happened, it was only 3 o'clock in the afternoon. A bus suddenly appeared out of the darkness across the main road and nearly hit me!'[41]

Mrs Evelyn Brouard was shocked when she arrived in Manchester:

We lived at 34 Marshall Road in Levenshulme. I had my own room but we shared the rest of the house. It was dirty, all smoke and soot. So many houses, you couldn't touch anything, your washing got black when you put it out. The houses were all back to back; there was an alley at the back and then another big row of houses, all the same. Very different to Guernsey.

Air raids too, a bit close. We had an air raid shelter in the garden but we always went under the stairs, in the cellar. We had a bomb that fell two rows of houses behind us. We heard the bomb, we went to have a look and there was a car on the second floor of a house. It had been blown up there by the bomb.[42]

For some evacuees, their first encounter with their wartime carers was not a happy one. Some households simply refused to take in evacuees, whilst others grudgingly accepted them. James Roffey describes the day when he and his sister arrived at a cottage in Pulborough, West Sussex:

The young man who had brought us there knocked loudly on the door. No one appeared and the door remained tightly closed, so he knocked again, much louder this time. Suddenly the door opened and a very cross-looking woman appeared. 'Who are you and what do you want?' she shouted.

The young man, who was obviously taken aback, replied, 'I have been sent by the Billeting Officer to bring these two evacuees'. She immediately answered, 'Well you can take them away again. I won't have any bloody evacuees!' and slammed the door shut.

He knocked on the door again and the woman immediately opened it and again started shouting at him, but this time he put his foot in the doorway to stop her shutting it. Then he pushed us inside, saying, 'You've got to take them by law; if you don't I'll call the police.'[43]

Philip Doran was grudgingly taken into the home of Mrs Burgess:

> She certainly seemed to resent the fact that I would be interrupting
> her cosy lifestyle. She made it clear to me on the way home that I
> would have to do as I was told. She had a child of her own called
> Kenneth, he was about my age; like his mother, he too made it clear
> that I was not welcome. It was only a few hours before, that I'd left
> my own dear Mam, in tears, waving to me at Lime Street Station.
>
> Here I was in a strange town, with strange people, unwelcome
> and certainly unloved. To be fair, Mr Burgess was a really nice man,
> he seemed to see the difficult situation that I was in. I got a real sense
> of genuine sympathy from him, although he never showed it in front
> of his wife. Like me, Mr Burgess also seemed somewhat
> downtrodden.[44]

Jessie Hetherington, a teacher from Gateshead, remembers the
unfriendly and somewhat icy atmosphere that existed in her billet:

> The long dark evenings were the most depressing. My elderly
> hostess, Mrs Smith, and I had nothing in common and conversation
> at any depth was nil. She would retire to bed early and I was
> expected to do so as well.
>
> I tried, frequently, to 'sit her out' and on those occasions the fire
> would have gone out before the cold sent me to bed. Her late
> husband had been a preacher in some religious sect, and I remember
> the text at the end of the bed, 'The Lord Loves You.' Every evening
> I thought, 'No, he doesn't' and turned it over.
>
> Every day I found it correctly placed. Never a word was
> exchanged between us on the subject. I can only explain my actions
> on the fact that I was homesick and desperately anxious about what
> was happening at home. We knew that Tyneside, with the
> Armstrong Munitions Works, the ship yards and factories, would
> be targets for enemy bombs.[45]

John Windett and his younger brother were sent to a house in
Derbyshire. In the days that followed they were often hungry, though
this was a situation that did not last:

> We were moved from Whaley Bridge to a little village near a quarry
> and there was a small boy living there already. We weren't fed very
> well at all and I can recall being given sandwiches containing bacon
> rind while the couple had the bacon!

Soon after moving in, our mother visited us with our baby sister and informed us that our father had joined the RAF and that she was making arrangements to come to Whaley Bridge to look after us. While she was visiting us she made arrangements with a small restaurant for me to have lunch when I came out of school. Around this time my Grandmother, plus my father's youngest sister and their dog, moved up from London. Luckily, my Mother managed to rent a small cottage in Furness Vale at the side of the canal. Now we were all together again.[46]

Jean and Bern Noble were sent to the home of their grandmother's brother, Frank, in Reading. Jean remembers their arrival:

So began a bitter-sweet period of my life in Reading. Bitter because we were not happy living with our foster parents, but sweet because it introduced me to the countryside. On arrival, we were shown our bedroom and I was pleased to discover it contained a lovely dolls house filled with furniture, a Noah's Ark and a lovely doll about 2 feet high with beautiful clothes. They had belonged to the daughter of the couple we were staying with, who had died when she was quite young. These took the edge off my homesickness but a few days later I arrived back from school and they were no longer there. No explanation was given. Perhaps they reminded the parents too much of the child they had lost.

Life was very different in our new home. The whole atmosphere seemed cold, stern and Victorian, so different from the loving family warmth we were used to and I do not recall ever being cuddled while we lived there. Our foster parents were accustomed to a different diet to the one we were used to at home. One meal served was tripe and swedes neither of which we had ever seen let alone eaten. The food stuck in my mouth and I gagged, while Bern did manage a couple of mouthfuls.

Unable to eat the food we were told we had to go hungry until the next meal and were lectured at length about wasting food in war time. We often went hungry when we found ourselves unable to eat some of the meals served. Pigs trotters, brains, brawn and the infamous tripe and swedes.[47]

George Osborn never forgot his first foster family on the Isle of Wight:

I was put with a Mrs Wilson and family. She had a short temper, but not as short as Mr. Wilson's, and positively sweet compared to that of her father, a wizened old man who mumbled discontent for the whole of his waking hours. There was also a very spoilt daughter of about eighteen years of age called Mavis, who sulkily mooned around the house waiting for her betrothed – a lusty Naval Petty Officer – to come home on leave. Mavis disliked me intensely but she seemed to dislike everybody – except her Petty Officer.

There was no room for me in the house, it was as simple as that. When it came to sleeping I couldn't stay in Mr. and Mrs. W's bedroom and Mavis wasn't going to be lumbered with a small boy in hers. The dog slept on the couch downstairs so I ended up in the grandad's bedroom. Firstly in his bed with him, then relegated to the bedroom floor on some sort of mattress when he said I kicked and moved about too much in bed. His loud snoring kept me awake and things deteriorated over the next few weeks.

Mrs. Wilson wouldn't let my sister Brenda into the house, even though she walked home with me from school. Her billet was at the other end of the village. At weekends Brenda took me for walks but always had to leave me at the garden gate. It was the loneliest feeling in the whole world to me, watching as she walked away waving until she disappeared from sight.[48]

Children who were placed in homes which were superior to those that they had left behind had to find their place within the hierarchy of family and domestic servants. As will be shown in later chapters, some of these children found it difficult to re-adjust to 'normal life' when they returned to their families.

Marjorie Parker and her sister were evacuated from Lowestoft to Glossop, where they were sent to a very large house:

> They moved us into Talbot House, an enormous house which belonged to Lady Partington who owned mills in Glossop. She had five maids, a cook, two gardeners and a chauffeur. There were three Rolls Royces in the garage. We lived in the maids' side of the house and the maids – Nellie, Muriel, Bertha, Ellen and Ethel – made new clothes for us and gave us hugs. We had everything we wanted but, at times, the maids could be quite strict with us. When Lady Partington had dinner parties my sister and I used to wait on her guests, wearing little aprons.[49]

The Headmaster of Guernsey's Torteval School, Frank Le Poidevin, arrived in the village of Alderley Edge in Cheshire with his family and pupils. Frank's family was billeted with one of the wealthiest households in the village, but they did not really fit in. His son, Nick, recalls:

> We found ourselves dwellers in a no-man's land, in an invidious 'between stairs' position. We were given a bedroom on the same level as the family, but we were considered to be below them in social status. We were told to use the servants' staircase that led past the kitchen and the servant's wing, but we were considered too highly placed to be welcome there.[50]

Doreen Acton was billeted in Bowden Hall. Located in the High Peak of Derbyshire, the imposing Bowden Hall was first built by the Bowdon family after the Black Death. From the period between the wars to 1963 it was occupied by Francis Alexander Lauder. Unsurprisingly, Doreen vividly recalls her arrival:

> After a short drive in a chauffeur-driven car, my friends and I arrived at an impressive mansion outside Chapel-en-le-Frith. We were greeted by a friendly looking elderly gentleman who shook our hands. Freda and Beryl were directed to bedrooms in the mansion to unpack. Audrey and I were taken to the chauffeur's cottage, a snug little dwelling close to the house. We did not know then that the chauffeur and his wife had hospitably given up their bed to us. We went back to the main house and again met our host, Mr Lauder. It appeared his wife was away visiting their daughter.
>
> Chrissie, the Scottish maid, was a very good cook and we were served up delicious meals. I had been used to breakfast, dinner, tea and supper – we now switched over to breakfast, lunch, evening dinner and a hot drink before bed. After about a week or two, Mrs Lauder returned home.
>
> At first I got the impression that she thought we had been allowed too much liberty. We were consigned to the kitchen for meals. Very soon however she realised we were quite house trained and not a threat to peace and good order. From then on she treated us as kindly and generously as her husband.[51]

Another Doreen, in this case Doreen Holden, would describe her arrival at her new home, which also turned out to be an impressive Derbyshire building:

> We arrived in Matlock and I was taken into a Manor house with two lads from my class. It had its own grounds and a nursery. They put

us in the nursery and we played with some children's toys. We were allowed in the kitchen and garden but not in some of the rooms. Mum made breakfast for us during the week that she was there.

One day, the man who owned the Manor house shot himself as he was worried that he might go bankrupt due to the war. I was then sent to another nice house on Starkholme Road. The husband and wife chose me because my name was Doreen, the same as their little girl's![52]

Jim Marshall recalls his first impressions of a manor house in Gloucestershire:

My brother and I were chosen, along with 5 other boys, by Mrs Percival who lived at a huge manor house, Priors Lodge. It was dark when we arrived and the next morning we looked out of the window, with disbelief, to see a huge long drive which seemed to disappear for miles into the distance! We had been very fortunate to land in the lap of luxury!

Priors Lodge was enormous, with around 40 acres of grounds, a boat house, a trout lake, and tennis courts. As well as Mrs and Major Percival, there was a cook, two housemaids, a gardener and a woodsman. Mrs Percival was very involved in the local Women's Institute, whilst the Major was in charge of Bream's Home Guard unit. They had two sons who had been evacuated to Canada so it was nice for them to have boys in the house with them.[53]

Michael Stedman, aged five and his brother, Mark, were also taken to a mansion – though in their case it was on the opposite side of the Atlantic in Canada:

My Canadian-born mother took me, aged 5 and my brother Mark, aged 7 from Dundee to Vancouver then quickly onto Victoria on Vancouver Island. This was to get us away from the bombing aimed at the U-boat bases in Scotland. We were welcomed by relations in a huge mansion, Sissinghurst.

They built us a Wendy house in the front garden and a large sandpit at the side of the terrace overlooking the fine croquet lawn. They had plenty of staff, Chinese cooks, gardeners and drivers but it was not really a suitable home for young children as they were all very old.

Later Mark and I were sent to live with Mr and Mrs Sendey in a small house on the outskirts of Victoria.[54]

For six months, Dorothy Ogier lived in Glasgow with the Thornton family, who provided her with the finest of food, clothes, toys and books:

> Eventually my mother, who had arrived in Stockport from Guernsey, managed to locate me and I was put on a train to Manchester.
>
> As I waited on the railway platform I spotted my family. My heart sank as I looked at this scruffy woman with her grubby kids. I wanted to go straight back to Mrs Thornton, who was clean and respectable with nice clothes and a gentle voice. It started to sink in, we are still poor and this is real life, and life in Glasgow was like a dream, just pretend.[55]

Along with his friends, John and Ronnie, Len Roberts moved into the home of the Mayor of Bury, in Lancashire:

> Me and my two pals were chosen by a tall, elegant lady, Mrs Whitehead. We had followed her and her uniformed chauffeur to a Rolls-Royce car. Arriving at the home of John Whitehead, landowner and Mayor of Bury, the servants were lined up in the hallway and we were introduced. The extensive grounds had cascading ponds, summer-houses, a tennis court and an orchard. We found ourselves in a fortunate position, and were made a great fuss of by the staff. Eventually I was reunited with my family who were also evacuated to West Yorkshire. We had left our Guernsey home and all our possessions but we now had each other again.[56]

When Jessica Young left West Sussex with 200 disabled girls, she never dreamed they would be sent to the stunning Peckforton Castle in Cheshire:

> We drove up a dark, tree-clad drive to a full-sized eighty-roomed castle, all dark and shadowy. As we entered the castle in the dark because of the blackout, Mrs Thomas reassured us by saying, 'Now the dark is like blind man's bluff, so hold on to the one in front.'
>
> With a teacher holding a torch to show the way, we went down the spiral steps, leading down into the long corridor which went the whole length of the castle. We passed lots of rooms until we reached the big servants dining hall which had one long table nearly the length of it and lots of trestle tables with forms, each for eight children to sit at.

The walls were white washed and decorated with heads of foxes, deer and antlers. A local potter had made us all a pretty flower mug each, in several designs, they now contained soup. How good it tasted with a thick slice of bread to eat with it. After supper we climbed another staircase and got into bed. We slept that night in vest and pants, not knowing where we were, too tired to care, and hundreds of miles away from our families. In the morning I looked out of the window, it was lovely, like a fairy tale palace, all glistening pink stone.[57]

Vera Liniham still recalls the kindness of one Mrs Barlow at Woodville Hall in Cheshire:

My two younger sisters and I, along with my best friend and her younger sister, were collected by Miss Groves who was the Housekeeper at Woodville Hall in Marple. We were taken by chauffeur-driven car, no less, to meet Mrs Barlow. It was the beginning of an experience I have never forgotten.

Mrs Barlow was waiting to welcome us. She was a sweet lady, of average height, slim with snow-white hair. Her clothes were very Twenties style. We met Jean who was from Carlisle and Violet who was from Glasgow – the House/parlour maids. Mrs Barlow had her own lady's maid, which was a slightly elevated position in the order of the staff. There was also a cook, a scullery maid, two gardeners and Mr Cheyney, who was the chauffeur.

We were taken to our bedroom and were amazed to see five single beds in this enormous room with a dressing table for each and a couple of wardrobes for our use. We later discovered the room was actually the ballroom! Mrs Barlow always came to say 'Goodnight' each evening when we had milk and biscuits for supper. We were treated like we were her own but as you can imagine it was a very different life to what we were used to as children of working class parents.

Although the war was such a long weary slice of our lives with more than one sad incident to live through, my stay at the Barlow family home was a time I remember with lots of happy memories. I am 87 years old now and the only one of the five of us left. I will always remember Mrs Barlow and her daughter for their kindness to five frightened little girls.[58]

Chapter 6

'I Hope You are Safe and Well'

Contact With Home

Anumber of former evacuees still possess the treasured postcards and letters that were sent to or from their families during the war. When schools were evacuated, anxious parents had to wait for a postcard from their child to confirm their safe arrival and new address. As part of this, prior to evacuation, the schools had given each child a pre-stamped postcard, bearing their parents' name and address. Children were instructed to send these cards to their parents when they reached their new billet.

George Osborn remembers writing his postcard:

> We were given a postcard before leaving Portsmouth for the Isle of Wight. We had to send it home to our parents when our new address was known. *The Portsmouth Evening News* said later, 'Between the lot of them they wrote the first human documents of the war.'
>
> The postcards, crumpled and tear-stained, which arrived through parents' letter-boxes, show that they probably did. I was not given a postcard because it was assumed that a five year old boy would not be parted from his sister, so her card would suffice for the two of us. Unfortunately this was not the case and we were sent to different billets.[1]

Younger children were instructed, by their teachers, to write messages that would not upset their parents, such as 'Dear Mum and Dad, I am living with nice people. I like it here and am very happy. Don't worry about me.'[2] On one occasion, this had tragic consequences for one little boy and his family. He had left his new billet, placed his postcard, with the same message, in the letter box then went for a walk. Sadly he fell into the canal and drowned. His family were advised of his death that evening, but the next morning his postcard with its tragic message arrived at their home.[3]

James Roffey remembers sending his postcard home:

> Soon after I arrived at my billet near Pulborough, I wrote my postcard and took it to the postbox just down the lane. Years later my mother reminded me what I had actually written, which was 'Dear Mum and Dad. We have lost John and the stinging nettles got me on the way back to the hut they call the lavatory.'
>
> Fortunately I was with my sister, who would have sent a much more reassuring message; well, she was five years older than me.[4]

Allan Barnes' postcard home began with a rather blunt message. It simply noted, 'I have gone', though he did go on to state that his address was 'c/o Mrs Blackman, 11 Madeline Road, Petersfield'.[5] In some cases it was the host family who took the time to confirm an evacuee's safe arrival. In Maidstone, for example, the family who took Dorothy King into their home sent a telegram to her parents: Dorothy arrived safely at 10 Beech Drive Maidstone.'[6]

Terence and Jack Frisby's mother devised a brilliant scheme for their postcard. It was their own secret communication code to make evacuation exciting for the children and to reassure their mother that they were being well cared for. Terry recalls:

> Just before we left home our mother had said, 'Now listen, both of you. Look what I've got here. It's a postcard. And it's in code. A secret code. Like the Secret Service. Only this is our own secret code. Read it, Jack.' This was exciting stuff, the postcard was stamped and addressed to our parents. Jack started to stumble through it. 'Dear Mum and Dad, arr – arr – arrived safe and well. Ev – ev – every.'
>
> I snatched the postcard from him and rattled off, 'Everything fine. Love, Jack and Terry.' Mum was furious with me. 'Give that back at once. I told Jack to read it, not you. He is the older one, you do as he says. Always.' 'I don't see why.' 'Always,' she repeated. The word was flung across the room at me cutting through my disobedience, telling us both on a deeper level just how serious all this was.
>
> Jack completed the reading of the card, uninterrupted. There was a pause then Jack ventured nervously, 'But what's the code?'
>
> 'When you get there,' Mum continued, 'you find out the address of the place where they take you, then you write it on the

card there.' She had left a space. She continued to both of us. 'Then you post it at once. All right? Now listen, I've only got one card so you've got to stay together or I won't know where one of you is.'

It was her final shot on the other subject that was eating her. We were disappointed. 'But that's not a proper code.' 'No. Now <u>this</u> is the code. Our secret. You know how to write kisses don't you?' We agreed with 'eargh', 'yuck' noises to show our distaste for such things. She waited for the ritual to subside. 'You put one kiss if it's horrible and I'll come straight there and bring you back home. Do you see? You put two kisses if it's all right. And three kisses if it's nice. Really nice. Then I'll know.'

In the anxiety and horror of this major crisis in her life – our lives – our mother, and perhaps our father too, had come up with something for them and us to cling to in the chaos.[7]

Soon after they arrived at their new billet, the moment came for Terence and Jack to fill in the card to send home – as well as making use of the secret means of communication agreed with their mother:

In bed on the first night in our new home we stared at Mum's postcard by candlelight and considered our code. Jack held the pencil. 'How many kisses shall we put?' Suddenly our new – surrogate – mother was with us. Jack slipped the postcard under his pillow – too late. She had seen it but said nothing.

She asked us to call her Auntie Rose then said 'I'm going to put out the candle if you're ready?' 'Could you leave it please? We got to do something. We got to send a card to Mum and Dad' 'This one?' She had moved round and produced the postcard from under the pillow, saying 'Is that your writing? It's very grown-up.' 'No it's Mum's. We've got to put your address on it,' we replied. She said, 'Well you've done it haven't you. Yes that's more like your writing. That's not how you spell Liskeard. I'll do you another card in the morning. A nice new one with a picture. How's that?' 'No, no. We got to put something else on.' 'What's that?'

She was met with silence. 'Well?' she asked gently. 'Er – kisses. We want to do it. By ourselves.' She stared at us, reading something special and prepared to give us our heads now that she knew we were up to no mischief. When she spoke again the voice was even more gentle, more reassuring than she had sounded so far.

'All right then. You do it by yourselves, is it? That's right. You got something to write with?' 'Yes. Here. Pencil.'

She left us. 'How many kisses?' said Jack. 'I vote three.' I had no doubts. Jack continued to take his older brother responsibilities seriously, saying, 'There's no taps in the house, no electricity. And no lavatory.' At last he said what we were both feeling. 'It's like being on holiday only there's no sea.'

We agreed three but I had an idea. 'We could put four kisses. The more we put, the happier Mum and Dad will be.' We ringed the card with kisses and posted it next morning.[8]

One London family did not receive any postcards from their children. Concerned, one of the parents wrote to Buckinghamshire Council – though we can guess at what the response actually was:

> My four children left John Hopkins School, Croydon, Wednesday, 2 October 1940 to your county, we do not know whether they are kidnapped or starving or sent somewhere else. I think it down right dirty and disgraceful to keep us waiting for news, there is no excuse.
>
> My boys have stamped addressed envelopes and papers to give to the lady who is in charge of them and they have not even dropped us a line. It is now days. As for my two little girls, I have not the slightest idea where they are. If the people in your town are so mean I had better have my children home at once.[9]

When evacuees wrote to their parents, some wanted to explain how unhappy they were. However, they were aware that their letters might be read by the family they were living with. One girl recalled, 'If I wrote to Mum saying I wanted to come home, I would be told to write another letter and say I was happy where I was.'[10]

John Mathews was unhappy in his billet. He was underfed and locked in his bedroom when not at school with no toys or books. He sent two letters home:

> It was obvious that our letters were going to be censored, so in the first one I wrote the sort of thing one should – 'Having a wonderful time, wish you were here.' Then the following morning I somehow managed to steal an envelope and stamp and wrote a rather more truthful letter home. The gist of it was that if something didn't happen quickly, I was going to run away. Two Saturdays later my mother turned up at the door to collect me.[11]

Not all communication home was tinged with sadness or unhappiness. Evacuees' letters often contained a wonderful mixture of everyday life, family affection and news of the war. As the historian Dr Claire Halstead Ph.D points out:

> Wartime evacuees' letters are valuable historical records. Not only do they reveal the impact of evacuation and familial separation but they also enable historians to examine how evacuees themselves, perceived their new circumstances and surroundings. While diaries and memoirs naturally include one's recollections or memories, evacuees' letters are time capsules and offer a window into the mind of a child.

Phyllis Hanson was seven years old when she was sent from the family home in Forest Hill, London to Newdigate in Surrey, where she was cared for by Mrs Ada Tullett. In common with many wartime households, neither the Hansons nor Mrs Tullett owned a telephone. Making calls was a lengthy process which involved setting a time and day by letter, then waiting at a telephone box for the call. Arrangements were duly made for Phyllis to receive calls from her parents at a call box in Newdigate. Perhaps it is because of such complications and difficulties that most of Phyllis' communication with home was, as in the case of most evacuees, by post.

In one letter, Phyllis revealed that she was aware of the bombing of cities and towns that was taking place – this, of course, being the reason for her move to rural Surrey: 'Dear Mum and Dad, thank you for the sweets. I received your parcel safely thank you. I hope you're not bombed out. I hope you are safe and well. I am.'[12]

When Allan Barnes was evacuated, his first letter home described his journey and the billeting process in Petersfield:

> We came in an electric train, the journey took us about an hour. My hands are jolly sore though from carrying my case.
>
> It is a very nice place I have got, there is a boy (9) and two girls (8 and 11). We were counted 11 times in the course of the journey. The evacuation people here are daft because the person in the house offered to take 2 small children so that I could go in a house with a friend of mine but the daft people wouldn't let me. You can guess we were tired when we got there and they kept taking us round in circles (daft lot). Mrs Blackman has just told me to tell you that she will do all she can to make me comfortable and happy, she thought this would stop you worrying about me. Write often, it will make me feel nearer you and more at home.[13]

Dorothy King was eleven years old when she was evacuated to Maidstone. She wanted to assure her mother that she was safe, despite the air raids on Maidstone:

> Dear Mummy, I received the letter and parcel. We had a lovely French lesson on Saturday. Miss Hinton taught us some little French songs. Does Daddy know 'Frère Jacques'? We have been doing square routes with Miss Davies. I think they are most interesting. I can play 'There is a lady sweet and kind' on my pipe! PS. I have not been hit by a bomb yet. PPS I have not been gassed yet. PPPS I have not come in contact with an air gun yet.'[14]

The letter also contained three of her drawings – a child with a bomb over her head, a child being shot by a gun and a child wearing a gas mask. Looking back at her letters today, Dorothy explains how she felt whilst writing them: 'When I read the letters that I wrote during the earlier years, I find little reference to the war, except occasionally in a rather jokey way. I wrote home regularly. The letters sound chirpy enough, but I know that sometimes I sat over them crying alone in the dining room.[15]

Some of the letters sent by Mrs King to Dorothy, whilst she was billeted with Mrs Lees in Bedford, also survive. The following letter was sent just after Dorothy had paid a short visit home:

> Thanks for your card, glad to hear you arrived back safely. I returned all the way with Mrs Perrell which was much nicer than returning alone. I hopped on a tram at Abbey Wood because I wanted to get to the stores and it was nearly 5 o'clock.
>
> I suppose you wore your new coat today? Just in time because it is turned bitterly cold here. I haven't had a chance to go to John Lewis's as yet but will do so as soon as possible and see what I can get. We are in the middle of air raid at present. It is very quiet but we have had a series of bumps. Your shoes will be ready Saturday week. Daddy took them, I had to work or I might have got them finished before.
>
> Well dear, must stop now. Cheerio for now dear, Kindest regards to Mrs Lees, fondest love, Yours, Mummy.[16]

Mrs King's second letter shows she and Mr King were missing their daughter's presence at home:

> Seems very lonely here without you especially teatime. Just when we get used to it you'll be home again. Let us know in good time

won't you? Daddy has a nasty chesty cough and has felt a bit dizzy. I hope it is only a cold. Must stop now dear as I have a lot to do, Fondest love, Mummy.[17]

In early September 1939, a Newcastle family, the Hodges, were torn apart by evacuation. Mrs Hetty Hodges was evacuated to Carlisle as a voluntary helper, with her youngest daughter, Mary, and thirteen other children. Her husband, Sydney, worked for the Board of Trade and remained behind, whilst their eldest daughter, Betty, was evacuated to Keswick. Their letters tell an emotional tale of family separation and also outline the practical arrangements that had to be made during wartime. A few days after his wife's departure, Sydney wrote to her in Carlisle:

My dear Hetty, I know you were very upset the morning you left and worrying about Betty, but I think it will be quite all right as Betty will be with nice people and receive some education. In any case I think you could easily go over to see her later on. Keep your chin up and keep yourself as interested as you can looking after the kids. By the way there was a telegram on the gates of the Central High School from the Mayor of Keswick, stating that the people of Keswick were determined to do all in their power for the children who are quartered there. As regards myself, I have been working very late. I was there till 2 am this morning and I've just started again. As regards the house I haven't decided anything definite but I shall probably try to get the furniture into store and tell the landlord that I have to give the house up. The streets are so dark at night that it is difficult to get home.

I may try to get accommodation somewhere but haven't made my mind up yet. I can get all the food I want in the canteen here. Owing to the late hours I work I cannot look after the cat [Tinker] and I'm sorry but he will have to be destroyed. I think it will be the best dear. Mr Spence was hoping to get a car and take me to Carlisle today but he couldn't do so. If he had I was going to bring the cat over to you. Don't worry about me. I shall take every precaution I can. Perhaps things won't be so bad as we think. My job is here in any case. I think you had better write to the office here in future so that I can always be sure of getting your letters. Well dear that's all for now. Keep smiling and don't worry. All my love dear to you and Mary your loving Syd.[18]

A few days later, Syd wrote to his daughter Mary:

I received your nice letter this morning and it was lovely. I thought you would like the teddy bear and I hope to be able to send some other things for you. I don't know whether I can come over on Sunday with Mr Smith as I think one of us will have to work and Mr Smith can bring over some more things in his car. I know you will be happy where you are and you have nothing to be afraid of so try to be cheerful and brave and look after Mummy for me.

If I can't come on Sunday I will come another day, when the railway service is more settled. Mummy can buy your new doll at Carlisle but not now, but a little later on. I will let you know when to buy it. I hope Tinker will be able to stay with you. I am quite all right and looking forward to seeing you all again. Lots of love from your loving Daddy.[19]

Mrs Hodges then wrote to her eldest daughter, Betty, who had been sent to Keswick:

My dearest Betty, Mr Smith brought a lot of our clothes over in his car as Daddy has closed up the house and put everything into store. Mr Smith also brought Tinker so he has been evacuated too, and the lady here loves cats and has made him very welcome. I hope you are comfortable in your billets and are being good and doing everything to help the people you are with. The people in Carlisle are being very kind to the children of West Jesmond! We are in a very nice billet, Mary and I together, but I have a lot to do with 14 children to look to. I have to take them out when they are not at school, which doesn't start until next week.

Well dear, all we have to do now is to pray that this will soon be over and we shall be altogether. I have your Girl Guide uniform here so I will send it over with some new pyjamas when I get some money from Daddy. Do write soon. I hope you'll start classes soon, that will give you something to do and think about. Daddy says he is quite alright so keep as well and happy as you can. Take care of your money and don't spend too much – especially sweets – you don't want to get bilious. Well darling, I must stop. We are always thinking about you. Lots of love from Mary and I, your ever loving and devoted Mother.[20]

Betty quickly wrote back to her mother:

I am quite at home in my billet and I make the bed in the morning, wipe up all the washing up, peel the spuds and do various jobs about the house. Auntie Peggy doesn't let me go out by myself at all so you see she is taking great care of me. The people in Keswick are being very kind to us all as well. How on earth did you get hold of 14 children. I nearly fainted on the spot when I saw it. Nine would have been enough, but 14 – phew!

I don't spend much except on stamps and postcards and you will be pleased to know that I've only had one penny Crunchie so far. Miss O'Dell told us that we were to give all our pocket money to our form mistresses. Most of the girls, Enid tells me, are grumbling like anything about it, we are allowed four pence a week for ourselves and if we want any more we have to tell our form mistresses why. I'm having my hair washed in a minute so I must stop. Give my love to Tinker five times over. A kiss to yourselves 10 dozen times, from your loving daughter, Betty.[21]

She also enclosed a letter for her sister:

When your letters came about 9 o'clock and I read the news I nearly cried with happiness … I'm glad you are happy in your new home. I'm as happy as I can be without you. I'm afraid I must close now too as I am writing a letter to Mummy. But Mummy will read it to you I am sure. Give Tinker a big kiss from me, you are lucky having him with you. But I shall see him soon I'm sure. Don't fret about the news dear, we will pull through and the Poles have done a lot haven't they? And take no notice of what the Germans say, they only do it to try to frighten us. So goodbye for now, your ever loving sister Betty.[22]

Terence Frisby remembers writing his weekly letters home:

Our weekly ordeal was the letter home and Auntie Rose was adamant. We were never allowed to miss. I regarded it as a chore to be endured.

One winter evening I sat at the table chewing a pencil whilst Auntie Rose mended socks with a letter from her son, Gwyn, on her lap. She was upset and not inclined to be indulgent to my whinges. 'I can't think of anything to write.' 'You say that every week.'

I was as foolish as ever and said, 'You've read that letter from Gwyn hundreds of times.' She replied, 'And I shall probably read it hundreds more. They said he was only going training back home in Wales. Now they send him abroad. Abroad. Where? Haven't they ever heard of embarkation leave?' Her voice had risen to a querulous high and she stared at me as though it were my fault and I had the answer. Auntie Rose continued. 'In the last war Jack was the only one who came back alive to our village in Wales. The only one. It's why we left; every woman staring at me as if it was my fault.'

She shuddered and returned to the present, waving Gwyn's letter accusingly at me again. 'Ink on paper instead of a person here in your life. That's all there is: letters. And every letter from Gwyn is one page long.'

'Two sides,' I tried helpfully. 'It's not enough. You write two pages home to your mum and dad this week. Two. Do you hear?' This awful sentence took my breath away. 'That's four sides.' 'I know how many it is.'

'That's not fair,' I replied. 'We shouldn't have to write at all. It was her who sent us away.' As soon as I had said it I wished I hadn't. I tried not to catch her eye and muttered, 'Well, she did'. 'What?' she said quietly. 'I didn't mean it.' …

Three years later, when Auntie Rose's son Gwyn was killed in action, Jack and I thought very carefully about our letter home to advise our parents. After a great deal of deliberation, we wrote: 'Dear Mum and Dad, Just a line to let you know that Auntie Rose and Uncle Jack's son Gwyn has been killed in Sicily. They are very unhappy. Auntie Rose keeps crying and Uncle Jack keeps going to the bottom of the garden and just sitting there instead of going to work. We thought it would be a good idea if only one of us came home and one of us stayed here with them and became their son. Then you've both got one each. That's fair. We were going to toss for it but Jack said I've got to go back to Dartford Grammar School. Jack doesn't mind not going to the Poly and he can stay here and work on the track with Uncle Jack. He says he would like that. He could come and visit with a privilege ticket.'[23]

Geoffrey Wright, was evacuated with other pupils and staff from Kelvinside Academy to Tarbet, Scotland. A few days after his arrival he sent this letter to his mother:

Dear Mummy, I can't find my identity card. Mr Murie wants it now but I have looked everywhere, it must be at home. Matron isn't so nice as I thought but we have two Nannies – Nansky and Bessy. I make my own bed and I think I have to send things to some laundry.

7.45 wakened, 8.30 breakfast, 9.00 prayers and school. 1 o'clock dinner, free at 3. Tea at 6, prep. 6.45 – 8, supper 8.30, lights out at 9. Good bed, not very homesick! Railway runs so that I can see a bit from my window – I like it.[24]

One young girl, evacuated from Earls Hall School in Southend to Derbyshire, enclosed some picture postcards with her letter:

Dear All, I hope you are all well at home. We arrived at Chinley at 3.30 Sunday afternoon and when we got out of the train some boy scouts gave us all a half pint bottle of milk. After waiting about twenty minutes we got on a bus to Whaley Bridge. We went to a hall and had a cup of tea and a piece of cake. After about one hour they started to put the children to their new homes.

First the farmer came and said we could go there but the teacher would not let us. Then the vicar came and asked us to go to the rectory but then something happened. After all we were put with Mrs Bailey. As soon as we got home she got tea and when we had finished, Winifred and Yvonne took us to the post box. These postcards are some of the lovely places here, and my bedroom window looks out on a lovely hill. Please send my shorts and my music book. We are all very well. Give my love to grannie, please send this round to Ian, Love Kathleen.[25]

June Somekh received regular letters from home: 'My father used to write to us either every week or fortnight and enclose money for our foster carer. Mother sent us parcels of goodies. Father did not feel that the allowance for children was enough to feed us adequately, so he sent extra money.'[26]

Lily Dwyer also received gifts: 'At Easter we got parcels from home – Mum sent an Easter egg for me and also one for Mary. Mum also sent me a Holy Communion dress which she must have had to save up for as she had no money. The Bishop came to Gresford for our communion.[27]

Len Page received a memorable parcel from his parents:

One day I received a card from Chipping Norton station to collect a parcel. It was a full size bike which had belonged to my sister May who was still in London. That bike was the best present ever, for no more the mile and a quarter walk to school. Sometimes it was a source of revenue as one boy at school would give me three pence to ride it about for the school dinner time. But this came to a stop when Mr. Knight who was on point duty outside the town hall caught the boy on my bike (it being a girl's sports bike) and he thought he had pinched it![28]

Patricia and Peter Campbell received this letter from their father:

DON'T do it, Mother —

LEAVE YOUR CHILDREN
IN THE SAFER AREAS

ISSUED BY THE MINISTRY OF HEALTH

LEAVE HITLER TO ME
SONNY — **YOU** OUGHT
TO BE OUT OF LONDON

ISSUED BY THE MINISTRY OF HEALTH

Above left: 'Don't Do It Mother' is the message as Hitler whispers to a mother to bring her evacuated children back from a safe area – one of a number of evacuation posters produced before and during the Second World War. (Author's Collection)

Above right: One of a series of evacuation posters produced by the artist Dudley S. Cowes. An illustrator of children's books, Cowes also worked for the Ministry of Information during the war. (Historic Military Press)

Right: A Ministry of Health poster supporting the work to find billets for evacuees. (Historic Military Press)

She's in the Ranks too!

CARING FOR EVACUEES
IS A NATIONAL SERVICE

ISSUED BY THE MINISTRY OF HEALTH

Above: Waiting for the actual time to arrive, Portsmouth evacuees conduct an evacuation drill. (George Osborn and Home Front Museum, Llandudno)

Right: As their journey into the unknown begins, two young evacuees, complete with their gas masks in boxes, speak to the crew of the train taking them away from their home town or city. (Historic Military Press)

Left: The evacuation of school children from Gateshead gets underway in 1939. (Courtesy of Gateshead Libraries)

Below: Porters at a London railway station present bars of chocolate to children being evacuated from the capital to the West Country during 1941. (Historic Military Press)

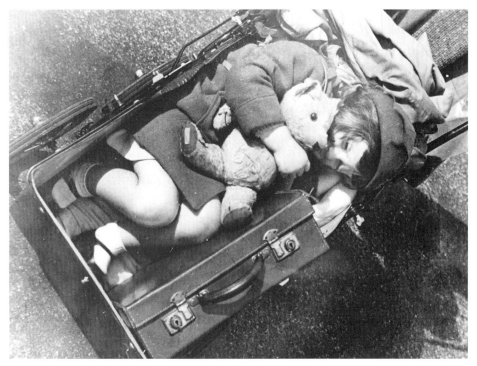

Above: An evacuee finds comfort with teddy bear in an open suitcase. (Courtesy of the Kent Messenger Group)

Below: These twins just filled the chair, and also themselves, as they partake of a snack before their departure for a safety area from a London railway station, February 1941. (Historic Military Press)

Above: Grimsby evacuees relax with their teachers in the Tower Gardens in Skegness. (Courtesy of Peter Hopper)

Below: Westcliff High School evacuees arrive at Chapel en le Frith, Derbyshire. (Courtesy of Whaley Bridge Library)

Above: A large group of evacuees, all with their tags hanging around their neck, wait with a female Police Officer for the train that will take them away from London. (Historic Military Press)

Left: These evacuated children are pictured leaving a clearing house depot of the Women's Voluntary Service on the first part of their journey to safety away from London's bombs. The Matron, accompanied by a nurse and two WVS workers, is escorting the youngsters to the bus that will take them to a safety area. (Historic Military Press)

Above: The moment of departure: a boat full of evacuees departs from the Channel Islands bound for Weymouth. The passenger ship in question, pictured here in St Helier Harbour, Jersey (note Fort Regent on the headland in the background) on 21 June 1940, is the SS *Brittany*. (Courtesy of Damien Horn; Channel Islands Military Museum)

Below: A group of evacuees from one of Guernsey's schools pictured together at a railway station in the UK. Hazel Knowles, recalled: "For the first time I saw a train. It was quite a frightening sight to see this huge monster with clouds of steam hissing from it. We then set out on a journey which seemed to take forever." (Courtesy of CIOS Guernsey)

Above: Horsforth prepares to receive Guernsey evacuees at Southlands. (Courtesy of Horsforth Village Museum)

Below: 'Auntie Rose' was a wonderful foster mother to Jack and Terry Frisby during the war. (Courtesy of Terence Frisby)

Above left: When Micky Archer arrived in Bideford, the family he had originally been allocated to would not take him in. (Courtesy of Val Morrish)

Above Right: This label was attached to parcels sent to children through the Foster Parents' Plan. (Muggeridge Family Papers)

Right: The original caption, dated 31 December 1940, states that this image depicts British evacuee Joan Bradley, aged 7 years old, recording a Christmas message in the USA for her parents in London. Joan was the daughter of a British employee of the Warner Brothers film production company. Her group sailed to the US from Southampton. (Historic Military Press)

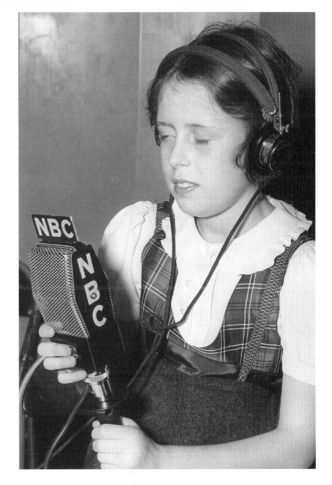

Left: Hazel and Mavis Duquemin were separated during the Guernsey evacuation. (Courtesy of Hazel Duquemin)

Below: Channel Island evacuees enjoy a Christmas meal in Cheadle Hulme, Cheshire. (Author's Collection)

Above: The first meeting of Channel Island evacuees in Stockport's Reform Club. (Author's Collection)

Below: Alderney Headmaster, Philip Godfray, with some of the Channel Island pupils he brought to the UK mainland. (Courtesy of Anne Mauger)

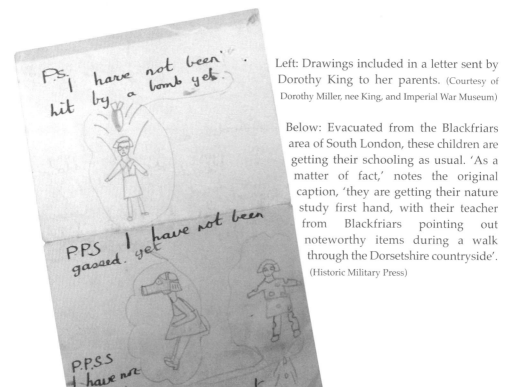

Left: Drawings included in a letter sent by Dorothy King to her parents. (Courtesy of Dorothy Miller, nee King, and Imperial War Museum)

Below: Evacuated from the Blackfriars area of South London, these children are getting their schooling as usual. 'As a matter of fact,' notes the original caption, 'they are getting their nature study first hand, with their teacher from Blackfriars pointing out noteworthy items during a walk through the Dorsetshire countryside'. (Historic Military Press)

Left: Sadly, not every evacuee returned home. Richard Tipping, a 15-year-old evacuee from Liverpool, died on Anglesey in July 1944. This is his grave in St Mary's Churchyard, Llanfairpwllgwyngyll.
(Courtesy of Eric Jones; www.geograph.org.uk)

Below left: Faith and Stella Shoesmith who suffered at the hands of Mrs Woods.
(Courtesy of Faith Catchpole)

Below right: The evacuees return home. Here John Helyer is pictured leaving Bury, Lancashire, by train in 1945. He had an unhappy homecoming. (Courtesy of John Helyer)

Hampstead Nursery,
22nd May, 1945.

Left: The letter sent on behalf of John Churcher to his American foster parents at the end of the war. (Courtesy of David Churcher)

<u>Your Foster Child</u>: No.6476 - John Churcher

Dear Foster Parent,
    The war is over and he had a big nice party with flags and flowers. My Daddy is soon coming home,
                    Love from
                        JOHN.

Below: One of the many homes, buildings and camps that were used to house evacuees and which can still be seen today. These structures are the remains of Dunaird Camp (Camp No.8) at Broughshane in Northern Ireland. As the sign states, it was built to house Gibraltarian evacuees during the war. (Courtesy of Robert Ashby; www.geograph.org.uk)

Above: Evacuees thank those who cared for them in Britain at Liberation Day parade in Guernsey, May 1946. (Carel Toms Collection, Guernsey)

Below: One of many memorials located around the UK, the plaque on this stone in Pentre Road, in St Clears, a small town on the River Tâf in Carmarthenshire, recalls the arrival of 168 child evacuees and twenty-four adults, on 23 June 1940. (Courtesy of Chris Whitehouse; www.geograph.org.uk)

Above: Blue Plaque at Stockport railway station marks arrival of Channel Islanders in 1940. (Author's Collection)

Below: On 10 May 2015, three new memorials were unveiled in East Park in Kingston upon Hull to mark the 70th anniversary of the Second World War. The memorials comprised stainless steel cut-outs of a Merchant Navy sailor, a soldier, airman and sailor, and, on the right, evacuees. (Courtesy of Chris Whitehouse; www.geograph.org.uk)

I am real glad to know that you and all the others are so happy and that you are settling down in your new surroundings all right. It's great to hear from you and to know that you are all getting on so well. Both Mammy and I miss you all very badly indeed, especially at the week end.

I saw from the *Folkestone Herald* that you got a great welcome in Wales on your arrival, I see Peter's photo there, perhaps Mammy will send you on the paper for you and Ivy to see. I understand you are not too far away from the boys, I do hope you will look them up now and again and see that they are all right. I see they have all written to Mammy and quite good attempts they were too, they all say they are very happy and have not mentioned about coming home, well that is the way to be. After all, you are all in a very safe place, safe from all the dangers of Air Raids, etc, we have had quite a lot of 'sirens' for the past few days, nearly every night they visit us, guns and searchlights too.

We have not heard from Ivy for the first couple of days and Mammy was getting a bit worried about her, but I see she has now written and that she is settling down as well as the others. I'm afraid I will have to go away very shortly now to Hammersmith, but it won't be for a week or two yet anyway – if and when I do go I am taking Mammy and Grandad and all and we shall make a new home there – so that when the war is over and you all come home again it will be to London you will be coming home to, not Folkestone.

Now, Pat, be a good girl, do what you can to help the boys and Ivy, also do what you can for the lady who is looking after you all, and don't forget to remember your prayers at all times, especially for Mammy and me. So 'little girl' Ta Ta, I'll be writing again some other time. I am, Your old Dad.[29]

In 1942, Ron Gould, the evacuee from Guernsey who was living in Cheshire, wrote to his mother, who had been evacuated to Bradford, Yorkshire:

Dear Mum I am sorry to hear about your being ill, was it a serious operation? I hope you will be able to get out soon. Have you any idea when that will be? I went for a cycle ride yesterday to Pick Mere, that's a big lake about 6 or 7 miles out. It was a lovely ride. Is the weather nice down there, its boiling up here, well I think that is all for now so cheerio, from your loving son, Ron.[30]

In Cheshire, another Guernsey child, Frank Le Poidevin, also contacted his mother, who had been evacuated to Glasgow with his brother.

Whilst waiting for the family to be reunited, he sent her a note and enclosed some sprigs of wild flowers. His mother kept that note and the dried flowers until the day she died.

When William Crawford's school was evacuated from Belfast to Port Rush, his parents were employed in the colonial service in Ceylon. William's son, Bruce, states:

> Dad's contact with his parents was very seldom during the war years, about once a year or so, and only by post. Even then letters were very short, little more than a postcard-sized page, and subjected to heavy censorship especially from the East where the war against Japan was getting going. Dad wrote once a week to Granny in Dublin, and to his parents, again, very short, censored letters. Dad says that the only time he actually missed his parents was at Christmas, but he tried to push the feelings to one side by trying to learn to play the piano.[31]

Brenda and George Osborn were evacuated to the Isle of Wight and in late December 1939 many of the evacuees received an unexpected Christmas letter. George recalls:

> Brenda received a letter from the Mayor of Portsmouth but mine never turned up. 'The Lady Mayoress and I want to wish you a very very jolly Christmas and Happy New Year. We only wish that it was possible for us to be with you and to tell you this ourselves instead of writing to you. We know you are most grateful to those kind people in whose homes you now live and who have given you so much care and attention. All those who love you would, we know, wish to join us in sending them our warmest thanks as well. We look forward to the time when you will be with us again, but for the present it is much better that you should all remain where you are. We hope that you will all keep well and happy and that this Christmas will be every bit as enjoyable as those you have had in the past. Goodbye and God bless you.'[32]

Marion Wraight received letters from her mother but had no contact with her father:

> I thought about Mum a lot and missed her and my sisters. Mum wrote letters to me perhaps one a month and my sister Jean sent me a £5 note once. My mum sent me a photo of me, which I still have. It has a handwritten note on it which says 'my little Marion.' Mum

and my sisters went to Ireland to do seasonal farm work and I have a photograph of them doing this. My Dad deserted from the Pioneer Corps – he had shot a corporal during an argument and was in prison for a while. He also attacked a woman in 1943 and beat her nearly to death. This was reported on the front of the local newspaper, and my sister Lilian saw it when it was delivered through her door, this was the first my family knew of it![33]

Roisin Toole (née Carney) recalls an activity that was undertaken by homesick evacuees in Kettering: 'We would write messages to our mothers on tiny scraps of paper and go to the railway bridge near the end of the Headlands and wait for a London train to pass under and try to drop the message on to it, thinking of it getting to home even if we could not.'[34]

In late September 1939, the postage costs incurred by evacuated children was raised in the House of Commons. The Postmaster General was asked whether he could allow one free post, weekly, between parents and evacuated children, in view of the heavy expense caused to families by evacuation. After some consideration, the Assistant Postmaster General replied: 'The difficulties involved would make it impracticable to operate such a concession. Moreover, if such a postage concession were granted, similar claims would be received from other groups who feel that they are equally entitled to special consideration.'[35]

During their first few days in England and Scotland, Channel Island evacuees were able to send letters to the islands and some even received replies. Frank Le Poidevin sent this cheerful letter to his father:

> I am enjoying myself very much, are you? I hope that you are. We were travelling in a train all night Friday the 21st. There are a few Guernsey here already and also babys and women. All the Forest school children are here but not in the same room. I wasn't at all seasick on the boat. We have just been given books, crayons and a lot of toys.[36]

When the islands were occupied by Germany on 30 June, the postal service ceased and telephone lines were cut. However, five months later, a lifeline was provided when evacuees were invited to send British Red Cross messages to the islands. Initially, they were only allowed ten words per message but this later increased to twenty-five.

It was not until March or April 1941 that evacuees received replies to that first batch of messages and Ruth Alexandre wrote in her diary: 'What a thrill, the first messages arrived for me from home!'

For child evacuees separated from their families, a family visit was a memorable event. However, as some stories reveal, the parting at the end of these visits could be hard to bear. Some towns and villages set aside certain dates for visits, whilst in others, parents could visit whenever they wished. When Derby School was evacuated to Amber Valley Camp on Wooley Moor, Derbyshire, the Headmaster organised the first visit: 'Buses will be available for parents who would like to visit the Camp on June 6th. The fare will be 2 to 3 shillings in accordance with the number who use the buses.'[37] Thereafter, though, parents had to make their own arrangements – as Gordon Lancaster recalls:

> I went home to Derby at half term and my parents visited me at the camp a couple of times. It was quite difficult to visit us if you didn't have a car. The nearest railway station was Stretton, two miles away, so it was quite a walk. I was quite homesick really but it wasn't too bad. We had a tuck shop at the camp for sweets and bought things with the spending money received from our parents.[38]

When Catford Central School was evacuated to Sayers Croft Camp in Surrey, special buses transported the parents:

> The parents came once a month, on the last Sunday. Single decker London Transport buses arrived in convoy, sometimes as many as ten or twelve of them. It was a testing time for these parents, particularly when it was time for them to return to their unknown perils of war in London. On the whole the parents made light of the air raids which was natural in their desire not to worry the boys, but their powers of endurance were being severely tested after spending many nights in the air raid shelters.[39]

After visiting their children, a group of London mothers placed a letter in a newspaper to thank the Truro families who were caring for their children:

> After visiting our children on August 3 we must send at once our heartfelt thanks and appreciation for all that the mothers of Cornwall are doing to mother our children. We all noticed how clean, well-kept and happy the children were and how well they looked. We also wish to thank the foster mothers for the kind way they welcomed us into their homes and looked after our welfare until we had to leave. We are sure the time will come when we can

repay the hospitality. Mrs AR Martin. On behalf of the mothers of East Ham, London, E6, August 8, 1940.[40]

Dorothy King lived with several different families and received visits from her parents:

My parents were invited for a meal when they eventually came to visit me and Mrs Merrifield arranged for them to stay with a neighbour so that we could all spend Christmas together. And, at my mother's request, Mrs Merrifield sympathetically broke the news to me that my beloved dog, Trixie, had died! My second home was with Mr and Mrs Tapley in Bedford, but I stayed there just three weeks. I remember one blissful day before I left them – my mother came with a friend and took me to Canterbury for the day.

We saw round the Cathedral and I had my first Knickerbocker Glory. Events like that compensated for a lot! I then moved down the road to the home of Ivy and Bert Waller and when my mother first visited me there, she and Ivy established an immediate and lasting rapport.

During 1944-1945 I didn't go home regularly. The Doodlebugs had started appearing during one of my holidays at home and the house had been damaged just after I had left home to return to Bedford. My father returned from seeing me to the station to find my mother and grandmother covered in dust and sweeping up glass. He was most unwilling for me to come home after that.[41]

Peter Staples made special arrangements when his parents came to Norfolk:

The local signposts had been removed, so when my parents visited, I wrote 'Old Rectory Lane' on pieces of paper and placed them in hedges so my parents could follow them and find us. Mr Scarff and my Dad got on very well and they took several of us kids to the cinema at North Walsham, with Mr Scarff asking my Dad to do 50mph on roads where it would have been suicidal to do more than 30. Besides which I don't think his car could reach 50. When my parents returned home again, I cried, but was soon fine as there was so much to keep me occupied.[42]

Richard Singleton's parents travelled from Liverpool to Wales to see their sons:

Every time our parents paid us visits Aunty would ask Sian, a girl from the farm about a mile away, to clean the house up. One day when Dad, Ron and myself were in the hay field. Mum came to Dad and said 'Do you know how many fleas I caught in the boy's bed?' 'No' said Dad, 'How many?' 'Thirteen' she replied. 'They're not heat lumps our Richie has, they are bloody flea bites.'

Mam must have got over the fleas as she wrote to Grandma saying Ron and I looked well. One time when they came they took Ron and I to Aberystwyth where we had a meal then the four of us went on board a boat with other people. Everyone was given a fishing rod with bait then we all cast our lines. Everyone must have caught at least a dozen mackerel. Then Dad took us to an arcade, he must have gone through a bit of cash but we never won anything. The chap must have felt sorry for us as he gave Dad a teaspoon with 'Aberystwyth' on the handle.[43]

Barry Fletcher remembers one family visit which ended badly:

My mother was not able to visit Feckenham very often, public transport only brought Mom from Birmingham to Astwood Bank and a two-mile walk in all weathers made it a long and slow journey. Each visit about every 6 to 8 weeks was awaited with eager anticipation bringing sweets, cakes and a little pocket money and each visit passed all too quickly, ending in sadness.

During one visit Mom brought me my Dad's watch recently repaired - he had died in May 1939. I was thrilled to have his watch on my wrist. All during Mom's visit I kept checking the time, it was a wonderful feeling. Later in the afternoon it was time for Mom to walk back to Astwood Bank to board the bus. On these occasions I would walk halfway before returning on my own. I said goodbye to Mom and set off back to Feckenham. Almost by Barrett's, I realised the watch and strap was no longer on my wrist. Retracing my steps I searched until dark but couldn't find the watch.[44]

Phyllis and Pat Hanson received occasional visits from their parents and Mr Hanson would often cycle the fifty to sixty mile round trip from London to Dorking to see his little girls. The family still have the letter which contained arrangements for visiting days:

For the convenience of parents and friends of the evacuated children in Newdigate, the village school will be open on the first Sunday in the month from 12:30pm to 5:30pm to coincide with the arrival and departure of buses. Cup of tea 1d, slice of cake 1d, will be available and picnic lunches brought by the visitors can be eaten in the school. There will be an extra visiting day on Sunday, March 16 to start the scheme, when it is hoped that parents will be able to come.[45]

Mr Hanson was not the only parent to cycle a great distance to visit his child. One mother cycled from London to Oxfordshire to see her child: 'It had taken two days for her to get there. She expressed great satisfaction at what she saw, and wished that other mothers and fathers could see the surroundings in which these children are.'[46]

Jim Davey remembers his first parental visit:

> Mother and father came down to visit Betty and I just before Christmas 1939, this was the first that we'd seen of them since September. They came down for the day, left our Christmas presents and returned home in the evening.
>
> Later I was evacuated with my school to Rossall, Lancashire, and we were allowed to go home at the end of each term. We had a specially chartered train which took second place to all the goods trains, troop trains and regular trains.
>
> The first time that I came home for the holiday was Christmas 1943 and the train was four hours late. Our parents had been waiting at Euston station all that time. It was a strange sort of evacuation as we were able to come home for several weeks at the end of every term but it was also a big wrench going back to school again.[47]

Philip Doran remembers a 'secret' day out arranged by his foster mother:

> One day Mrs Roberts announced that we'd be going on a day's outing, the destination was to be a secret. We boarded the bus full of anticipation, the bus took us to Caernarfon where we transferred to a train; we still had no idea where we were going. It was a complete surprise to us when the train drew into Central Station; we were back home, home in Liverpool. Mrs Roberts had managed to glean certain information from us and so she knew that the number three bus would take us to the Dingle, just a short walk from where we lived.
>
> We were only able to stay for the day but it was such a happy day for us all. Mrs Roberts had arranged the trip through the goodness of her heart; little did she know that despite the joy we all felt, it would have a very negative effect on our lives. We returned after a

very long day, all of us tired and worn out. That brief spell at home meant that from that moment on, nothing in North Wales could be substituted for our real home and our real family; the pangs of homesickness were now stronger than ever.[48]

Jean Griffin (née Pare) received regular visits from her parents. 'Once a month a Midland Red coach, from Digbeth coach station, came to Lydney bringing families to see their sons and daughters,' she remembers. 'My mother came every time and got on well with my wartime foster parents, Auntie Lil and Uncle Bill.'[49]

Marjorie Parker's family visited Glossop where she and her sister were living with Lady Partington: 'Mum, Dad and Alan came to stay with us for a fortnight each summer. It was very emotional when they arrived but more so when they left. They always took us to Manchester to buy new clothes and we would go out for walks.'[50]

Brenda Paulding's mother made great efforts to visit her children:

Despite working on munitions and having a war-disabled husband and lodger to look after, my mother spent many weekends visiting her far-flung evacuated daughters. She endured the well-known experiences of war time trains, some cancelled, many, often very cold with long waits in tunnels whilst troops or more important cargo went ahead. I remember her arriving on a Saturday and after a cuppa and a snack we went off to the local shops to find me some shoes. Then before leaving she measured me for a dress which she made by hand, with glass buttons. It was to be worn on 'the walks', an annual parade with banners around the streets of Macclesfield in which we Sunday School children took part. However due to the postal delay it did not arrive until two days after the event.[51]

Terence Frisby will never forget his mother's first visit:

A few days after we arrived, I was watching a train from Plymouth pull into the station. One or two people strode up station approach. I stared in wonder. My mother – my mother, lugging a heavy suitcase – was actually trudging up from the station towards me. She had received our card all right but turned up anyway. I did not rush to greet her; instead, I turned and raced to Railway Cottages. I ran breathlessly indoors. 'Auntie Rose, Auntie Rose, Mum's here. My mum is here. She is outside.'

I gulped, excited beyond belief. I didn't see her reaction, though she must have been flustered, because having delivered the news I turned around and ran straight back to Mum. My mother has often since reminded me of that moment. Her blue-eyed boy recognised her, turned and ran away. Whatever was wrong with him? It had clearly upset her.

She said that all sorts of anxieties took over in those few minutes before I came back. Nothing was wrong at all, of course. I had simply run to tell Auntie Rose. Had Auntie Rose become, in under a week, the first person in my life to share such things with, leaving my mother in the road outside? I don't know what Auntie Rose thought of Mum but Mum must have trusted Auntie Rose immediately because she told her about the kisses code and our judgement of her. I hope it gave Auntie Rose the pleasure she deserved. After Mum's first visit Auntie Rose and Uncle Jack were given express permission – if they needed it – to treat us exactly like their own children and punish us when we deserved it. I can think of no better expression of the trust Mum had in them from the word go.[52]

George and Brenda Osborne were able to visit their mother in Portsmouth for a few days at Christmas, as George later recalled:

It seemed ages since we had seen our house in Portsmouth and when Brenda and I returned to Wootton after the Christmas break, there were fewer than half a dozen of the original fifty evacuees at school. Most mothers had decided to keep their children with them rather than suffer the misery of being parted again. We went back to Wootton because it suited our mother. With us away and father permanently in hospital, she could easily find work. She was delivering milk to the doorsteps of smart houses in the Southsea area and being paid a regular wage which was more than she had ever dreamed of earning before the war. Once every six weeks she came to see us for a week-end.

I remember her visits well because it was the only time we were given egg and bacon for breakfast. She always brought us lots of nice things, like sweets and chocolate, and I was often chastised for asking for these things before kissing her, or even saying 'Hello'.[53]

Jean Bell was afraid that she would not recognise her own mother when she visited:

My brother and I were told that our mother would be coming to see us and would be arriving on a train, due to arrive in the early evening. We were sent along to the station to meet her and I was very worried because I did not think I would recognise my mother as we had not seen her for such a very long time. However, she missed the train from Paddington and caught the next one which meant that she arrived very late at night when we were in bed, thereby solving the problem of me not recognising her.[54]

On one occasion, Lily Dwyer's parents visited her then took her brother home with them:

One day my mum and dad came to see me. Dad was a merchant seaman so he must have been on leave. It was a sad little visit. They both looked ill at ease although Mrs Bee made them welcome. I was very shy in their company, but I remember feeling really sad when it was time for them to go. They were going to visit my brother in the village. I followed them all the way down the hill and waved to them until they were out of sight.

When I went to school the next day I looked for my brother everywhere. I was taken into the staff room and they told me that my parents had decided to take him home to Liverpool. I missed him so much. Even now when I think about it, I have tears in my eyes.[55]

John Glasgow occasionally received a visit from his father who was in the Army:

My father would occasionally get a weekend leave and come to take me out. A great treat was a visit to Hythe on Southampton Water. From Winchester, this could be done using four forms of transport. Bus from Winchester to Southampton Common where we would alight and I would go in the children's paddling pool. Tram to the Bargate, into the penny amusement arcade then on down to the Royal Pier where we would get on the steam ferry across to Hythe Pier. Then onto the pier railway to Hythe itself to a cafe where my father could have tea and I would enjoy a bottle of pop, lemonade or cherryade being a favourite with cake. A great day out.[56]

Nellie and Reg Cutts cared for Joan and Marjorie Hart in Bletchley and their niece Jean recalls:

The girls' mother and sometimes father used to visit on the train from Euston. Things were very crowded in the house with Joan and

Marj sharing that small bedroom and all of us living in the back room downstairs. The front room was turned into a bedroom for these parental visits, which were always of at least one night's stay. Despite the crowding, the parents were always made welcome. They brought treats when they came and my uncle, being a butcher, made sure they didn't leave empty handed![57]

A visit from John Payne's grandmother was followed by tragedy:

In 1944, Grandmother decided to travel from London to visit us and a telegram followed her arrival. Telegrams usually meant bad news and this was no exception. It informed her that one of those flying bombs, doodlebugs, had hit the flats where she lived. She returned home immediately only to find that she had lost her home, everything. The shock brought on a stroke and tragically she died. We returned to London for the funeral and stayed for two or three days. Whilst we were there, doodlebugs came thick and fast. The next noises were ambulances, police and fire engines. We were so glad to get back to the peace of the countryside.[58]

Anne and Jean Holmes were very unhappy in their Blackpool billet and Anne remembers a simultaneous visit from their grandmothers:

Anne and I were both weeping and begging to go home, so they promised us faithfully they would see what could be done about getting us back to Manchester. As we were seeing them off, on the bus, to go home, I suddenly realised that Jean had crawled out through this little tiny window. She lay down on the tram tracks on Lytham Road and wouldn't move until they promised to take her home. She lay in front of the trams, stopping the traffic!

Eventually our Grandmas were so embarrassed that they went back to where we were staying, got our things and brought us home that night.[59]

Jean was not the only evacuee to lie under a vehicle in protest. John and Rose Hawkins remembers one particular Sunday visit from their mother:

These visits were welcomed by all the children but proved to pose a terrible strain when the time came for parting. On one occasion a small, tearful boy resorted to lying prone under the wheels of the bus, in a determined effort to delay the parting that he had dreaded

97

so much since his Mother had arrived earlier that day. On one particular day, Rosie and I were waiting for the bus to arrive.

We saw Mom step down and turn with a ready smile in response to our exultant shouts. She hugged us both very tightly then we all turned to make our way up the lane to the farm. We both seized that opportunity to frantically pour out our endless tirade of troubles to her. She looked with quiet concern at our anxious young faces, now pleading to her 'Please Mom, please take us back home with you. We can't stand no more of it here, honest.' We displayed a welter of vivid mauve chilblains, callouses and roughly chapped hands to support our tearful plea.

Seeing our desperate unhappiness, which must have matched her own at being so abruptly parted from us those months before, she replied, 'But you don't know what it's like at home now. Even without the raids, we have blackout every night and you can't see your hand in front of your face. The rations they give us now are so small we have to go hungry for most of the time.' I replied, 'They've always had a black out here Mom. When there's no moon out here, you can get lost going to the lavatory. We'd rather starve to death in Brum with you.'

Our impassioned pleading tore cruelly at her heartstrings and made her mind up for her. She sighed, 'Well, I suppose if we've got to go, then at least, we'll all go together.' And so, calling on the Billeting Officer then rather nervously informing our surprised and rather indignant foster parents of her intention to remove us, two overjoyed children hurriedly packed our belongings and happily bade our grim-faced hosts and their farm, a very cheerful farewell.[60]

For many evacuees there were no family visits. The cost of wartime travel was prohibitive, a matter that was raised in the House of Commons. 'Some children have been taken a very long distance ... some of the parents are far too poor to pay the railway fare for the whole of that distance.'[61] Bob Cooper was one who did not receive any family visits: 'My parents couldn't visit me as it was just too far away from London and they could not obtain train tickets.'[62]

Although the majority of Channel Island children had left their parents behind, some received visits from evacuated friends and relatives who were billeted in other towns. After one family visit, Hazel Hall wrote in her diary, 'Today my brother Rex, who is now in the army, visited me, bringing with him my younger brother Ken whose evacuee school is in Cheshire. It was a lovely surprise and we had a photograph taken!'[63]

In April 1944, Harry Ingrouille (a resident of Guernsey) and a friend escaped from Alderney in a motorised fishing boat. A German guard was supposed to accompany the fishermen each day, but on that of the escape, Harry told the guard that the presence of a German in the boat might attract the attention of a British Spitfire and they would all be killed.

The journey across the Channel in a small fishing boat was difficult but the men eventually reached Weymouth. They were taken into custody and transferred to London for interview. After their release they visited numerous Channel Island evacuees in the UK, including the Ozanne family in Croydon. Joan Ozanne recalled the event: 'It was my birthday that day and his visit was a wonderful present as he could tell us about home.'[64]

Harry also paid a visit to Mr Percy Martel's Guernsey school which had been re-established in Cheshire and Percy wrote in his diary:

> His visit was a marvel, yes a marvel! Harry went into every classroom, and the children's names were called, one by one. He said, 'Yes I saw your father and mother just before I left, they are well' and 'Your parents are living at …' 'Your father is working at …' and so on.
>
> One boy asked, 'We had a litter of pigs at our house before I left. Are they still alive?' to which Mr I replied, 'No, we have eaten them!' Afterwards we had lunch with him and he gave us lots of up to date information about conditions on the island.[65]

It was four years before Lorraine and Lloyd Savident saw a member of their family because of events that occurred on their first evening in Manchester:

> We children and our teachers were taken into a big hall and during the night, the air raid warning sounded. We became separated from our school group and spent the night in a shelter with elderly people. The next morning we discovered that our Guernsey school had been moved to another area without us! They assumed we had been killed in the air raid and had sent a message to our parents in Guernsey – just before the Germans invaded the island.
>
> So for four years our family thought we were both dead. In the meantime, we were chosen by Mr and Mrs Fitton, who lived in Hulme. They really only wanted a girl as company for their daughter Brenda, but we told them we didn't want to be separated so they took us both. They cared for us very well but there were no cuddles.

In 1944 we were in a Manchester park helping to 'dig for victory' and a young man in Navy uniform approached us, saying 'You are Lloyd and Lorraine aren't you?' He was our cousin and had somehow found us through the Red Cross! Now our family knew that we were alive![66]

Chapter 7

'God Keep You Safe From Harm'

The Kindness of Strangers

During the war, certain organisations and individuals made a huge difference to the evacuees' lives, not just physically, but also emotionally. When evacuees arrived in the reception centres, people of all ages and from all walks of life flocked there to welcome them, feed them and make them comfortable. Organisations worthy of mention are the Women's Voluntary Service (WVS), Salvation Army, British Legion, Girl Guides and the Scouts. However, mothers, teachers and hospital staff also turned up to help.

In Stockport, Kathleen Potts found beds for evacuees:

> Mum and I went to every road in our area, knocking on doors and asking 'Are there any people here whose children have gone into the forces?' Then when someone said 'yes', Mum said 'Please can we borrow their bed for the evacuees at the Town Hall?' Scouts took the beds to pieces with a special key, labelled each piece of each bed with the name of the person who owned it and then put it onto the Scouts Trek Cart. My brother and I then put the bits onto the Trek Cart and pulled it up to the Town Hall, back and forth. People also gave us spare pillows, pillow cases and blankets, they were happy to give to the evacuees even though they didn't have much themselves.[1]

Bernard Elsdon rushed to help evacuees at his Sunday school:

> I went along because help was needed to receive beds and bedding and other things including kitchen ware. We also found some large

curtains to put up at the windows to give some privacy to the evacuees. We had expansive kitchens which included two huge gas fuelled copper water boilers, each capable of heating enough water for one thousand cups of tea![2]

Marion Greenhalgh visited Stockport town hall to help hundreds of Channel Island evacuees:

> I was a Girl Guide and remember us going up the marble staircase, picking our way through all the women and children sitting on the stairs. We spent time mixing feeds for the babies and nursing them whilst their mothers went for a wash. We played with young children and read to them to stop them crying. I can still see those wretched mothers looking so frightened.[3]

Newspaper appeals asked readers to help evacuees who had no possessions. One announced, 'Boots and clothing are required for 90 boys who are now billeted in Hale. They are separated from their parents, their home and their friends. Gifts in cash or kind will be gratefully received.[4]

The response from local communities was outstanding. Firms sent gifts of food, clothing and fruit to evacuees, whilst in Lancashire, slippers and sandals were donated to evacuated orphans.[5] The employees of the Bury Felt Company made free mattresses for evacuated children during their lunch hours, without being paid for this work.[6]

A Flintshire newspaper announced, 'Blankets, camp beds, food supplies and rations have been prepared but there is still a shortage of blankets and camp beds.' On 1 August 1940, The *Stockport Advertiser* appealed on behalf of evacuated mothers:

> They have been placed in empty premises in our town. Between them they have only beds, a few chairs and an occasional teapot. Readers probably possess furniture and household utensils for which they have no further need but which would be a Godsend to evacuees who have been unfortunate enough to lose all their goods and chattels.

Peter Hopper remembers the clothing that was donated to evacuees from Grimsby:

> The Evacuation Officer in Skegness was Elsa Barratt, who was a kindly woman with an ever-ready smile. The local newspaper

commented, during December 1939, that many of the child evacuees who came to Skegness were insufficiently clad to face the rigours of winter. Readers were asked to notify Mrs Barratt if they had any clothing to spare. She was popular with the local community, and there was a great response.[7]

Lourdes Galliano was evacuated from Gibraltar and remembers the kindness she received from a London volunteer:

Mrs Donaldson had a daughter named Theresa who was my age. Now and again she brought me comics which Theresa kindly sent. One day she said her daughter wanted to meet me so she took me home with her to lunch. I was delighted. She drove me to her house in Holland Park where I met the generous Theresa who was a lovely girl. I so enjoyed her room of dolls and books and later, lunch, in a beautiful dining room served by a maid in a white apron. It was like a dream. After that I was to be invited by them quite often and Theresa and I got on beautifully together. Unfortunately after we left the evacuee reception centre in the Empress Hall, we lost touch completely.[8]

In Worthing, West Sussex, Joan Strange's mother provided afternoon tea to five elderly evacuees from London who had been bombed out of their homes. She wrote in her diary:

The five arrived today! All to tea here. Poor Mother - they arrived two hours earlier than was expected and Mother had to entertain them all. Two were stone deaf which wasn't to be wondered at as they were eighty-nine and eighty-five! The two others were very jolly seventy-nine and seventy-six and the other fifty-odd. After tea we dispersed them - four to Schofield's landlady and one to Dorothy MacPherson - with hopes that all would be well. The two very elderlies had not been out of their house for two years till they were bombed and the elderly gent looked like death. They are very old and helpless.[9]

One evacuated mother praised the people of Oldham for their kindness:

We will never forget those who have been kind to us in our sorrow, for the invitations to their homes for a break and lunch. For the treats, for the cricket matches and cinema trips organised, for the sweets and strawberry teas. For the kindly help from everybody in the Co-operative hall where we have been billeted. For the policeman at the door who never failed me from getting times of buses to various places, bringing me the morning paper and the daily cup of tea.[10]

A letter published in the *Leek Post and Times* on 29 June 1940 praised the kindness shown to London's evacuees:

We feel it is our duty to express our gratitude to the inhabitants of Leek for the kindness and hospitality shown to us on our arrival. We write on behalf of the evacuated children, who have found comfort and friends in this beautiful country town.

When we alighted at Leek Station we were given a hearty welcome and the scene will always live in our memories. We are known as 'visitors' which makes us feel more at home than if we were called 'evacuees.' Once more, we express our sincere thanks for your most friendly welcome and care. Yours truly, Iris Skells and Joan Macdonald, Edmonton Higher Grade School.

In June 1940, the arrival of over 25,000 Channel Island evacuees in Britain, swiftly followed by the news that their islands had been occupied by Germany, was met with an outpouring of sympathy and generosity. A reporter from the *Weymouth Daily Echo* had witnessed the evacuees' arrival and told readers the following on 22 June 1940:

First to come were the youngest tots. With dolls in their arms and their possessions in pathetic bundles they came off the boats. A schoolmaster told us, 'We were packed like herrings. The children had behaved like true Britishers and so had their parents who were left behind.'

Channel Islanders formed a Refugee Committee in London to assist evacuees. When the committee placed a letter in *The Times* appealing for help, the story was broadcast by the BBC and touched the hearts of the British public. Sacks full of letters and donations poured into the committee's office. They had no idea that the public response would be so overwhelming and, by the end of 1940 alone, they received over £24,000.[11]

One Channel Islander still remembers the generosity shown to them. Mrs Eva Le Page recalled: 'I left Guernsey with my baby and only a pound note in my purse. The Bolton people were very kind and if they helped you they did it with good hearts.'[12]

Len Robilliard was standing outside his evacuee reception centre when, 'A policeman came along and handed me a 10 shilling note, a lot of money in 1940 and told me to buy sweets for the Guernsey children'.[13] Irene Hawkins arrived in Bury, Lancashire:

> I was evacuated to Bury with my school friends and some of our teachers. The WVS came round in a van to give us free hot meals. When we Channel Island children strolled around the streets, people used to stop and ask us 'Are you those evacuees?' When we said 'Yes' they gave us pennies for sweets. They said that they had read about us in the papers. They were so very kind to us. I will never forget that! One person even asked me for my autograph![14]

Mrs Agnes Scott moved into an unfurnished house in Manchester:

> The neighbours knocked at the door with all kinds of household equipment, which was most useful as we had nothing! A coal man came with two bags of coal, with the compliments of Mr and Mrs Milligan who lived across the road. I will never forget the kindness! I found work at a factory in Northenden and had to work a week in hand before getting paid. I had no money so I walked to and from work. The foreman, John Dewhurst, noticed that I never went to the canteen and wanted to know the reason. He gave me a loan of 10 shillings. I was delighted, it was so unexpected.[15]

Yvonne Russell's family encountered a similar level of generosity in Halifax:

> We would come home to find all sorts of things had been left at the house for us. Beds, mattresses, sheets, blankets, crockery, saucepans, cutlery, furniture, even rationed foods. Anything and everything was left for us to find, from packets of tea to bottles of sauce. Some people left notes, so we were able to thank them but a lot of things just appeared. Fairies were at play in that house! We were amazed at the kindness of Yorkshire people.[16]

When Marlene Whittaker arrived in Glasgow, she was helped by a Yorkshire woman. 'I did not know it at the time, but my parents had managed to get to England with my two little sisters. They arrived in Yorkshire and expected to see me there; they were very upset.'

In the hunt for his daughter, Marlene's father put this notice in the district newspaper:

QUEST FOR MISSING CHILD: An evacuee couple from Guernsey, who originally lived in Barnoldswick, are anxiously awaiting news of their nine-year-old daughter who set sail a day in advance of her parents. They are Mr and Mrs Horace Whittaker, now staying with Mr Whittaker's parents at 10 Lower West Avenue, Barnoldswick. Two younger children are with them.

The missing child is Marlene Whittaker who was evacuated from Guernsey a week ago with the scholars of Amherst school. Mr Whitaker said he and his wife felt confident that Marlene is somewhere in England but the entire absence of information was very disturbing.

Marlene wore a label giving a future address at Barnoldswick and it is rather surprising that we have not seen or heard anything of her. Of course my wife and I appreciate the tremendous amount of work that has fallen to the evacuation authorities – no doubt it will take time to get in touch with all the parents and if they work in alphabetical order our name will be pretty low down on the list.

The description of the child is as follows: age 9 years, height 4 feet, fair hair, blue eyes, light complexion; clothing includes a navy blue raincoat.[17]

Remarkably, the appeal yielded results. Marlene takes up the story and reveals what happened next:

A local lady saw the advert and called on my parents telling them she was on her way to Glasgow and would be most willing to call on the authorities and ask for my whereabouts.

One day I was called into the teacher's room, and was told a lady had come from Barnoldswick and she was going to take me to Mum and Dad. I was over the moon, she helped me pack my clothes and I said goodbye to my friends.

We arrived at a little railway station in Yorkshire and there on the platform was my Dad. I remember grabbing his hand for dear life. As we walked down the road it seemed I was 12 feet above the ground. As we turned on the avenue to go to my Grandma's house everybody was at their doors saying 'hello' to me as I passed and waving flags. What a lovely day, in my memory forever and ever![18]

One family owes their thanks to the thoughtful staff of the *Stockport Advertiser*. Soon after arriving in the town, five-year-old Stanley Bienvenu contracted pneumonia and it was not known whether he would survive. Nobody knew if his mother had managed to reach England from Guernsey before the occupation of the island. When a local reporter heard Stanley's story, he launched an appeal in the *Advertiser* to find Mrs Bienvenu. This was picked up by the national press and she was found in Southampton, practically penniless.

The press provided her train fare to Stockport where she was reunited with her son:

> For days, little Stanley Martin Bienvenu, the five-year-old Guernsey evacuee, has been lying seriously ill in a Stockport hospital. His parents could not be found. It was feared that they had been caught in the Nazi invasion of Guernsey. Appeals were sent out and as a result Stanley's mother was happily reunited with her son yesterday and a jovial, if not altogether tearless reunion, took place between mother and sick child in his little cubicle.[19]

In many of the towns and villages that contained a large number of evacuees, social clubs were often organised for them. These clubs gave adult evacuees a chance to meet up and to give emotional support to each other. Social activities were also provided for adults and children.

In November 1939, the Reverend George Henderson of St Ninian's, Stirling, described how his church was reaching out to evacuees from Glasgow:

> The first thing we did was to establish contact with the mothers and infant children in their new homes. Through the kind co-operation of the Headmasters of the local school we got a complete list of their addresses, and without exception the Church Sisters were cordially welcomed. This visitation afforded opportunity to assure the mothers of the Church's friendship and help, and to invite them into the fellowship of the Sunday services and weekday meetings. The next thing was to establish contact with the children of school age who had been sent without their mothers.
>
> There were regular visits to the mothers and unaccompanied school children in the homes so as to maintain personal contacts. We began a Guild of Friendship, which meets on Tuesday afternoons. During this time, a staff of workers entertain the children so that the mothers may be free to enjoy this fellowship. We also have a supply of garments which they may find useful for themselves or their children. For many years we have had a Women's Fellowship, which

met on Thursday evenings. This winter it will meet in the afternoons, and we have arranged for the Church Sisters and lady workers to take charge of the children to permit the mothers to join the Fellowship.

On Sundays a considerable number of parents come from Glasgow to visit their children. We have, therefore, opened one of our halls and invited parents to meet their children there from 2.30 to 4 o'clock. It may be found desirable to augment these arrangements, but during the short drab days of winter three afternoons each week will be lighted up for mothers and children by the friendship of the Church.[20]

In Ramsbottom, Lancashire, clubs were organised for evacuated mothers from London and Manchester:

The committee have created a real 'home from home' atmosphere, many friendships have been formed and sorrows lightened by the little chats and conversations with those less fortunate. Some of the mothers have formed a small choir, and letters from mothers who have returned to London were read out. Miss Blake, a blind evacuee from London, provided a recitation in a jolly Cockney style. This was proof of the value of such a meeting room where local and evacuee mothers can meet and be of considerable help to each other.[21]

Roisin Toole attended evacuee meetings in a church hall in Kettering:

On Saturday afternoons the girls had their club with the hall divided into three sections – tea, biscuits and cakes served in the first which also housed the table tennis for the boys – dancing and general socializing in the second – a discussion group in the third, or listening to music when the record player was not wanted for dancing. Father Jones would come and go as duties allowed and in this way he got to know the young people of the parish and also could impart to us some of his ideals and enthusiasms. We had very many interesting discussions on all sorts of topics and he broadened our minds a lot.[22]

The Women's Voluntary Service was particularly active in setting up social facilities for evacuees. In East Sussex, for example, evacuee clubs were provided with magazines, toys, a gramophone and records. On 18 August 1944, the *Leek Post and Times* advised readers that,

The Women's Voluntary Service propose to start a club for the ladies from London. They have engaged a room at the British Legion in

Russell Street to open on Friday evening August 25th, from 7 until 10pm. There are facilities for playing cards and table tennis, etc. The W.V.S will start the ball rolling by providing tea and light refreshments on the opening night. They feel that the visitors will appreciate an opportunity to chat together or play games. The W.V.S will be pleased to receive gifts in the way of cleaning or cooking utensils, old furniture not in use, or any article which will help in providing for the evacuees.

Evacuees came together in other ways too, often through sport. When Guernsey evacuee, Reg Fallaize, played for Oldham Football Club, Channel Islanders flocked to support him, gaining an opportunity to meet and chat to other islanders at the same time.

The Christmas holiday, normally a time of family celebration, could be a time of heartbreak for evacuees, but communities made great efforts to include evacuees in festivities. David Forbes remembers his first Christmas in Dunning, Scotland:

My mother, myself and my brothers and sisters had been sent to a cottage, quite near a Castle where the Queen Mother's relations, the Bowes-Lyons, lived. We're in this lonely cottage and suddenly this knock comes at the door! It was the people from the Castle, they came up and gave us toys. And they gave my mother perfume. Probably my mother never knew what perfume was at that time. And they gave the other evacuee family the same things.[23]

Stella Marlow had a wonderful Christmas in Downham Market, Norfolk:

Despite being away from my family at such a special time, I could not have enjoyed myself more. The table at every meal was loaded down with Christmas fare and I managed to forget that there was a war on. I went to Christmas parties and my hostess arranged one for me too. Nine of my friends were invited and we played games, and there were small presents for everyone. It was such generosity that made our stay such a pleasant one. I remember Christmas 1940 as one of the happiest I ever had.

They were keen to ensure that those who had been forced to leave their homes would not have a miserable festive season. They invited 200 London mothers and their children, who had been billeted in Downham, to share a Christmas dinner at the Town Hall with their husbands.[24]

Marjorie Townsend remembers Christmas in Derbyshire: 'In Baslow, the Dowager Duchess of Devonshire had parties for all the village children at Christmas. We got lovely presents and she also gave me a savings certificate.'[25] In Leek, Christmas parties were organised for children, mothers and babies:

> Members of the Leek Welfare Committee entertained about 660 evacuated children and Leek school children to a party on Monday afternoon. The parties were made possible as a result of public subscriptions, and the members of the Committee are deeply grateful to all who subscribed to help make the parties such a huge success. Those over nine years of age attended the Town Hall and those under nine were catered for at the New Assembly Hall of the Britannia Street Senior School.
>
> The proceedings commenced with a tea, and the meal included potted meat sandwiches, pork pies, jellies, mince pies, slab cake, fancy cakes. The long tables were heavily laden with these good things, but with so many little 'Oliver Twists' present wanting more, it was not long before 'the cupboard was bare.' Christmas crackers aroused wild delight, and their contents, paper hats, added a further festive touch. The adults' party at the Salvation Army Hall proved equally enjoyable. Twenty mothers and little children and babies were present. Games were played for an hour and a steak and kidney pie meal was then partaken of, with pudding, mince pies, cakes, jellies and other good things to follow. Mr. Jarman of Ashton Old-road School, distributed toys to the children on behalf of the Welfare Committee, a grant of 1s per child having been made by the Manchester Education Authority.[26]

On Christmas Day 1942, Pamela Le Poidevin found herself in hospital:

> I was ill in Stockport Infirmary. I told the nurses I was an evacuee from occupied Guernsey and they realised that I was not going to receive any Christmas presents. There was a scramble to find some things for me from Father Christmas! We received a visit from the Mayor and Lady Mayoress of Stockport and I had my photograph taken with them.[27]

Evacuees often describe the generosity shown to them by the British, American and Canadian servicemen who were based around Britain. Roisin Toole, for example, recalls the kindness shown to evacuees by Eighth Army Air Force personnel based in Kettering:

The effect the arrival of the Americans had on our lives was immense – they were so fresh to the war, so optimistic and full of fun – somehow we felt that everything would be all right. The chaplains used to bring some of their men in to visit the local families who were ready and generous hosts to them. We found them very different and exciting and they were also very generous guests, bringing in foods which were real luxuries in war-time Britain and of course plenty of chewing-gum!

Their chaplains used to arrange to take groups in army trucks back to their bases and, on one occasion they showed us the huge B17s and their chapel and gave us a lovely tea. They also arranged Christmas parties with Father Christmas arriving in a jeep on to the dance floor at the George Hotel! I think of how brave those men were, going out on dangerous missions by day, from which some of their crews had perhaps not returned, then coming into Kettering, trying not to think of tomorrow by relaxing with a family such as they might have left in the States.[28]

Dennis Camp experienced kindness from a group of injured soldiers in a Blackpool hospital:

Mum and I (I was aged four) had been evacuated from Guernsey to Stockport. I caught pneumonia and was sent to a hospital where injured British soldiers from Dunkirk were undergoing treatment. The hospital contacted Mum, in Cheshire, to say that I was on the verge of death. She visited me as soon as she could, then sadly told me, 'I can't stay here with you, Dennis, as I have no money to pay for a boarding house.'

When the soldiers heard about Mum's situation, they handed me all their pennies and two pence pieces, which I gave to Mum so she could stay in Blackpool. The soldiers constantly prayed for me and I firmly believe that it was with their help that I survived.[29]

Evacuees also received help from America and Canada. The Canadian Red Cross was important to evacuees for many reasons, but most remember particularly the warm clothing, quilts and blankets which were distributed to evacuees. Alice Thornton recalls, 'The Canadian clothing was in very bright colours and stood out when you were out in the street, but it was so warm, we were so glad to receive it.'[30]

Raymond Carre never forgot the assistance of the Red Cross and after the war he travelled to Canada and presented the staff with the Red Cross quilt that he had been given in Halifax, Yorkshire, during the war.

Likewise, evacuees in West Sussex received Christmas gifts from school children in the United States: 'The gifts came from New Jersey and the boxes contained the sort of presents American children thought English children might like – marbles, balls, hair ribands, pencils, pens, india-rubbers, writing pads and picture books.'[31]

When news of the occupation of the Channel Islands reached the ears of 500 Channel Islanders living in Vancouver, Canada, a sense of shock swept through their community. Realising that the evacuees in Britain would need clothing, shoes, cash and medical supplies, they formed the Vancouver Channel Islanders Society. They raised funds and by February 1942, they had sent $3,254 to London for the evacuees and over a hundred crates of clothing.[32]

Some Canadian housewives placed personal notes in the pockets of the coats they donated. A boy in Cheshire found this note in the pocket of his coat, 'To the little boy who receives this parcel. Please write to me at the above address and let me know how you like it. May God Bless you, and keep you safe from harm. Sincerely yours, Mrs C J Collett.'[33]

A number of British evacuee schools and nurseries survived during the war because of the financial support of the Foster Parent Plan for Children Affected by War (FPP). The FPP was formed in 1937 by John Langdon-Davies, a journalist, and Eric Muggeridge, a social worker and brother of author and journalist Malcolm Muggeridge.[34]

The original aims of the FPP were to help children whose lives had been disrupted by the Spanish Civil War. On more than one occasion, Eric Muggeridge had led groups of terrified children, on foot, across the freezing snow-bound passes of the Pyrenees to the safety of the French border. In 1939 the FPP became a chartered New York organisation and gained access to fund raising opportunities in the United States. It began to help children from all countries whose lives were affected by the war in Europe. The FPP letterhead was amended to include the motto, 'To help children of the UN and the little victims of Nazi oppression receive food, shelter and loving care through the Foster Parent Plan.'

The FPP searched for people who would support children by sending a monthly cash donation and becoming their virtual 'foster parents'. These supporters were also asked to write letters to the children to show that someone cared about them, creating what we call today 'child sponsorship'.

Eric Muggeridge's daughter, Maureen, proudly recalled her father's efforts:

[He] father used to talk in front of huge crowds of well-off Americans, pleading for sponsors for these suffering, European children. He obviously did quite well to attract some very well-known people who are proudly displayed on the Sponsor List. He was very persuasive about the things he was passionate about, none more so than helping desperate children.[35]

Eric was clearly very successful because the list of FPP sponsors includes some well-known names from the 1940s. Sponsors in England and America included Bing Crosby, Ira Gershwin, Jack Benny, Dean Martin, Robert Donat, J.B. Priestley and Dame Sybil Thorndike.

One evacuated school owed its very survival to the efforts of the FPP. In June 1940, the pupils of Guernsey's La Chaumière School were evacuated to England under the care of Father Patrick Bleach. The children arrived in Knutsford, Cheshire where they were billeted with local families. However, Father Bleach believed it would be best for the children if he could re-open his Guernsey school in England. He was offered Moseley Hall, a large mansion with beautiful grounds and two tennis courts. The owner gave the building to Father Bleach, rent-free, rather than allowing it to be requisitioned by troops.[36]

The children were delighted to be reunited with their friends and teachers under the same roof. However, Father Bleach had little money to work with and his time was consumed with searches for beds, linen, toys and school equipment.

In 1942, the school's fortunes changed for the better when Father Bleach discovered the existence of the FPP. Within weeks, the children of La Chaumière School became an 'FPP colony'. Every month, funds arrived to support each child and letters and parcels arrived from America. Pearl Saltwell received letters and parcels from the students of Tranquility Union High School in California. Mavis Fitzpatrick bought cakes for all the children with her birthday gift of five dollars from Mrs Joseph Harchow of Columbus, Ohio.[37]

In November 1942, the FPP added an extraordinary name to its list of sponsors. Eleanor Roosevelt, wife of the American President, visited the FPP in London and sponsored three evacuees. One of those children was Paulette Le Mescam, a pupil at La Chaumière School. Paulette now became 'Foster child 306' to Mrs Eleanor Roosevelt, 'Foster Parent 200'.

Mrs Roosevelt duly received a summary of Paulette's life and a photograph: 'Paulette is about five feet tall and is in fine health. She is fond of school, and does especially well in Religious Instruction and English. She is fond of singing, and is almost always humming a merry tune!'[38]

Prior to receiving letters and parcels from Mrs Roosevelt, Paulette had not had any communication with her parents for five years. She was actually born in Paris in 1932 and had one sister, Monique. When Paulette was 18 months old, her mother died. In 1936 her father sent Paulette to live with her maternal Grandmother in Guernsey. In June 1940, Paulette was evacuated to England with La Chaumière School.

When Paulette began to receive letters from her 'foster parent' at The White House, Washington the address meant nothing to her. 'I was only 11 years old and there was no television in those days, so we didn't hear a lot about famous people. To me, she was just my "Aunty Eleanor".'[39]

Paulette's first letter to Mrs Roosevelt described her life in Knutsford:

> We are living in one big house altogether. Moseley Hall is a beautiful house and it was given to us by a kind man. My Mother is dead and my Father is a sailor. I do not know where he is now. My sister is somewhere in France but I do not know where. God bless you and keep you safe. Your loving foster child, Paulette.[40]

Mrs Roosevelt provided Father Bleach[41] with ten shillings a week for Paulette's care, paid for clothing to be sent to her and wrote several letters. Paulette was delighted to receive parcels from America which bore the distinctive Foster Parent Plan label: 'She sent me some lovely clothes. I particularly remember receiving a lovely red dress and some Lux soap which had a lovely smell.'

In October 1943, Mrs Roosevelt discovered that Paulette had been sent a dress which was too large. Her Secretary wrote to the FPP in New York: 'Dear Sirs, It seems to Mrs Roosevelt that the method of selecting clothes for these children might be improved if, as this child states, the dress sent her is so large that she must wait to grow up to wear it. This seems to Mrs Roosevelt inefficient and foolish.' The FPP offered an explanation:

> In checking our records we find that Paulette, who is small for her age, received a size sixteen dress, instead of a twelve. It was certainly never meant that a child should receive a dress so large that she would have to put it away until she grew into it. We regret very much that this should have happened in connection with Mrs Roosevelt's gift for Paulette and are having the correct size sent to the child at once.[42]

FPP founder, Eric Muggeridge, realised that Eleanor Roosevelt's sponsorship could bring a great deal of publicity to the FPP. Now

Paulette discovered who 'Aunty Eleanor' actually was and, in May 1943, she and Eric travelled to London to deliver a BBC radio broadcast. Paulette spoke in both French and English about the work of the FPP, about her family in France and her sponsor, Mrs Roosevelt, who actually listened to the broadcast.

In April 1944, Mrs Roosevelt sent two dresses, a muslin slip, pyjamas and socks and Paulette wrote to thank her, adding, 'I hope this dreadful war will soon be over so that I may return to my beloved native home Paris, with my father and sister, then I could tell them how kind you have been to me.'

Paulette sent a picture postcard of Guernsey to Mrs Roosevelt in July 1944: 'Dear Aunty Eleanor, I am sending this beautiful view to show you how pretty our little island is. We are all waiting to return and see all these beautiful places again. I have now started shorthand and I like it very much. Your loving foster child, Paulette.'

To this day Paulette still has the letter which Mrs Roosevelt sent in reply. She was advised to persevere with her shorthand lessons. Mrs Roosevelt added: 'It is a splendid thing to know, and one can almost always obtain work in it.'

Paulette received her final letter from Mrs Roosevelt which included an invitation to visit the White House but she was unable to accept this offer: 'I was only young and hadn't the money or support to enable me to do this. To this day it is a journey I would have loved to have taken.'[43]

Another evacuee who experienced the kindness of the FPP was three-year-old Londoner, John Churcher. At the time, John's mother had tuberculosis and his father was serving in the Army. John was sent to New Barn, Hampstead, Essex, a country house for young evacuees run by Anna Freud and Dorothy Burlingham.

New Barn was financially supported by the FPP, so John became 'foster child number 6476' and was sponsored in America. The nursery staff sent monthly letters to the American foster parents, to share the personal story of each young child. They also used John's story to raise funds because it tugged at the heart strings of potential sponsors. John's son, David, has some of the wartime letters that were sent to the foster parents who financially supported John. The first letter described John in detail:

> Dear Foster Parent, John is a very charming little boy who has just turned three. He enjoyed his birthday party thoroughly as he does everything now. What a change to the Johnnie who came to us two months ago. He was completely detached then, showed no signs of

pleasure and very few of sorrow at any particular happening. But mostly he looked very sad.

His mother is in a T.B. sanatorium and Johnnie has been through so many hands since he has had to leave her. His life seems to have been bound by all the things a little boy may not do and all his initiative had disappeared. His father, who is in the Army, came to see him once and was very pleased at the change in him. 'He used to be such a carefree little boy,' he said. And we are pleased to see that he is becoming as happy again as he must have been when the family was united.[44]

In May 1942 the nursery staff sent John's foster parents some sad news:

Johnny adores his Daddy more than anybody else. Unluckily he could only come to see him very seldom as he is in the army. He gets leave every three months. He used to come and spend the time with his wife who was so very ill. A fortnight ago she died and poor Johnny lost his mother. We are all very sorry for him especially as his father has to go abroad, and so this leaves this little boy quite homeless. We all try to make him as happy as possible and hope that we will be able to keep him here a long time, certainly until his father can make a home for him again. Little John is still too small to thank you for your help.[45]

The next letter was more cheerful:

John is looking forward very much to meet his Daddy here. He is going to have his army leave and we have invited him to stay a few days with us. Johnny has already got a little soldier cap and often asks me: 'Do I look like my very own soldier Dad now?' He simply adores his father and we will be very pleased to have him here for a few days as he has to go abroad and he will not be able to see his little son for a very long time after this.[46]

Throughout 1944, numerous letters and parcels passed between John and his FPP contacts. The nursery's final letter to John's foster parents cheerfully announced: 'Dear Foster parent, the war is over and we had a big nice party with flags and flowers. My Daddy is soon coming home. Love from John.'[47]

Chapter 8

'She Was Supposed to be Sent to Safety'

Out of the Frying Pan

The aim of evacuation was to send children and adults to safety until the war was over, But the war took many forms, and few places in the UK were completely free from danger. Air raids, unexploded bombs, military vehicles, guns and minefields posed risks to the children, wherever they were posted.

Some did not even reach their destinations, the most notable and tragic instance being the sinking of the SS *City of Benares* in September 1940 which, amongst other passengers, had been transporting ninety British evacuees to Canada.

After the fall of France, the British Government had developed plans for evacuating one million children to the United States, Canada and other overseas Dominions. The scheme was administered primarily by the Children's Overseas Reception Board (CORB), a British government sponsored organisation. It began its work on 17 June 1940, when Under-Secretary of State for Dominion Affairs Geoffrey Shakespeare was tasked with implementing this evacuation programme. The same day, negotiations opened with the travel agency Thomas Cook & Son for the new organisation to be housed in its Head Office at 45 Berkeley Street, London.

Speaking in the House of Commons on 2 July 1940, Shakespeare outlined to MPs the 'main elements of the scheme which we are charged to administer':

> In the case of all children who have reached the age of five but have not reached the age of 16, parents can make application for their

children to be sent overseas, to the Dominion of their choice. The benefits of the scheme are open to school children within those ages, wherever the children are now situated, or whatever the circumstances of the parents. For easier administration, we have divided all children into two categories, namely, those who attend State grant-aided schools such as elementary and secondary schools, and those who attend other schools.

No mother is eligible to accompany her child overseas, but an exception may be made in the case of the widow of a man who has lost his life in active service in the present war. If parents are excluded, it is clearly necessary to organise a system of escorts or helpers, to look after the children on the journey.

No charge will be made for the railway journeys or voyages, to the parents of children from grant-aided schools but they will be asked to contribute, week by week, the same amount as they are now contributing, or as they would contribute under the United Kingdom evacuation scheme …

As regards the quota, we have decided on a fair quota in respect of the two kinds of schools. In England and Wales, 75 per cent. of the children will come from grant-aided schools, and 25 per cent. from other schools. In Scotland, 49 out of 50 children will come from what are termed local education authority schools, and one out of 50 children from other schools. These quotas follow roughly the proportions of children existing to-day in the respective kinds of schools. It may well be that if we cannot satisfy the quota in respect of either category, we shall be forced to select children on some other basis. Hon. Members will see that there is no ground for the constant reiteration by Lord Haw-Haw that the benefits of the scheme are exclusively for the rich.[1]

The Under-Secretary of State for Dominion Affairs then went on to provide a little more detail of the mechanics of the actual journey itself:

We are also securing the services of teachers from the schools in these areas who will travel with the children to the port of embarkation, and further, we are securing the services, both centrally and locally, of those who belong to the Women's Voluntary Services Organisation … The children will be detrained in the vicinity of the port of embarkation, and will sleep for at least one night in hostels there provided. We have already provided suitable hostel accommodation near enough to the ports of embarkation but far enough away to ensure the children's safety. The escorts and helpers who will take the children on the voyage will join the children at these hostels. Hon. Members will be interested to know that we are working to a scale of one helper to 15 children, in addition to nurses and doctors …

Each child will have been given a luggage label with its C.O.R.B. number and as each child embarks it will be given an identity disc with its C.O.R.B. number. There will be an expert staff to check the final list of the children that embark on any ship; one copy of the document will go to the Dominion, another copy will come back to us at headquarters, and the third copy will go to another place of safe keeping in this country, in case our records should be destroyed. We shall know actually and absolutely the number of children that embark on any one ship.

As to the voyage, the Admiralty, the Ministry of Shipping and my Department have been conferring as to the best means of providing protection, and I will say no more about that. During the voyage, the escort leaders and helpers will get in touch with the children and talk to them about conditions in the Dominions to which they are going. There will be doctors, nurses, and a chaplain on each ship. I should like to emphasise that children, from whatever school they come, will proceed in the same ship without any distinction. It will be, as it were, a boys' club or a girls' holiday camp proceeding overseas under the proper supervision of experienced persons who have done this work all their lives.[2]

As part of the westbound Convoy OB-213, in which she was the flagship of the convoy commodore, *City of Benares* had sailed from Liverpool on 13 September 1940, bound for the Canadian ports of Quebec and Montreal. The journey was relatively uneventful until late on the evening of the 17th, when the liner was spotted by the crew of the German U-boat, *U-48*. Its commander, *Kapitänleutnant* Heinrich Bleichrodt, fired two torpedoes at the British ship at 23.45 hours – but they both missed. Just after midnight, Bleichrodt fired a third. This time the German U-boat was on target – the torpedo struck *City of Benares* in the stern. She sank in just thirty minutes. Seventy-seven children and 187 adults were killed.

Sonia, Derek and Barbara Bech represented the only evacuee family to survive the disaster intact. Sonia remembers only too well the events that fateful night on the icy waters of the Atlantic:

Little did we know at 10 o'clock that night that a U-boat had spotted us and was out for us. We rushed out onto the deck and the lifeboats had already been lowered into the sea which was very rough and we were on a sinking ship with no lifeboat and we wondered what was going to happen next.[3]

Barbara managed to climb a rope onto a lifeboat, while her mother, Sonia and Derek spent six hours in the Atlantic before being picked up by the destroyer HMS *Hurricane* – but not before despair had set in. Derek recalled that, 'Our mother told us "Let's just undo our lifebelts and we'll go to sleep in the water'. It was Sonia who refused to let the family die and urged them to keep hoping until the lights of rescue vessels appeared out of the dark. Safely on board and recovering from hypothermia, they waited for news of Barbara, as Derek continued:

> My mother kept on calling 'Has anyone seen Barbara?' A report came in that some people had died in their lifeboat and then another report came in that everybody had died in another boat. It went on and on and my mother was virtually giving up hope until in the last minute a sailor came down to my mother and said 'Here's your Barbara'
>
> It is one of those stories that never fades in the retelling and is a stark reminder to all of us of those dark days of the Second World War when terrible things happened to men, women and children.[4]

Fifteen-year-old Bess Walder was being evacuated on *City of Benares* along with her younger brother Louis, then aged nine. Bess was asleep in her bunk when *U-48*'s third torpedo struck. Accompanied by another evacuee, 14-year-old Beth Cummings who had been in a neighbouring cabin, Bess headed out on deck to find a lifeboat:

> Lights flickered and dimmed, then went out. Freezing water cascaded into the stricken ship's interior, and bodies bobbed past.
>
> Bess Walder and Beth Cummings managed to scramble on deck and into lifeboat No.5, which was lowered into the blackness of the ocean but took in water almost at once. It bucked wildly on the waves before upending, throwing both girls into the sea.
>
> By the time they had swum and clawed their way back to the lifeboat, it was upside down. In the darkness and through the spray and rain – the liner had been attacked at the height of an Atlantic storm – Bess Walder could just make out Beth and, beyond her new friend, a line of wrists, fingers and whitened knuckles where at least a dozen people were clinging on the other side to the lifeboat's upturned keel …

For nearly 20 hours during the night and day that followed, Bess Walder and Beth Cummings, with only their adrenalin to sustain them against cold and exhaustion, clung to their overturned lifeboat in the stormy seas; they were clad only in pyjamas and dressing gowns.

At first about 20 other passengers hung on, but one by one they let go and drifted away, eventually leaving only Bess Walder and her friend.[5]

'Our bodies were very badly bruised,' Bess later recalled. 'Every time waves came we were lifted up and flung down again against the side of the lifeboat.' The pair's ordeal, though, was not yet over and, exhausted but unafraid, the two girls concentrated on staying alive by clinging to a rope wrapped around the lifeboat's keel. Afterwards they could not open their hands for two days.

In time, Bess passed out. When she came too, she found she was onboard HMS *Hurricane*. Beth had also survived. Bess' good luck, though, was initially tinged with sadness for she was under the impression that her little brother had drowned:

> After her rescue by *Hurricane* ... she [Bess] was summoned to the captain's cabin: 'He banged on the door and he said he had a surprise for me and pushed my brother into the room ahead of him.' Louis, rescued from another lifeboat, had seen his sister's wet dressing gown hanging in *Hurricane*'s boiler room to dry.[6]

Passengers such as the Bechs and Bess and her brother were the fortunate ones. In total, 260 of the 407 people on board *City of Benares* were lost. This included the master, the commodore, three staff members, 121 crew members and 134 passengers. Out of the latter, seventy-seven were child evacuees. Only thirteen of the ninety child evacuee passengers embarked survived the sinking.[7]

Following on from the earlier attack on the SS *Volendam*, which had been carrying child evacuees (though they all survived), the CORB programme had already been subject to official scrutiny. The *City of Benares* disaster sealed its fate. The government soon announced the cancellation of the Children's Overseas Reception Board's work, and all children who were preparing to sail were ordered to disembark and return home. It had, up to this point, evacuated over 2,600 British children. They were sent mainly to the four Dominion countries of Canada (a total of 1,532 individuals in nine parties), Australia (577; three parties), New Zealand (202 in two parties), and South Africa (353; again two parties), with also some to the USA. Official overseas child evacuation efforts came to a halt with the end of the CORB, but large-scale private evacuation of a further 14,000 children continued until 1941.

Of course, an evacuee did not have to be at sea to be killed through enemy action. Four-year-old John Stobart, for example, died when a pair of semi-detached houses in Gower Street, Newcastle-under-Lyme received a direct hit from a bomb on 26 June 1940. 'Planes were heard and several bombs fell in a residential suburb within a radius of 50 yards,' ran a report in the local newspaper. 'One hit a bungalow and demolished the living rooms, but left the bedrooms, occupied at the time by a family of three, intact.' John Stobart was not so fortunate as the bomb that struck the house of the two semis where he was staying crashed through the bedrooms to the ground floor. 'The dead boy and most of the people injured were trapped in the two semi-detached houses, which were completely wrecked … Rescue and fire squads worked heroically to release the victims.' Though most of those inside the two houses were injured, only one woman was hospitalised and poor young John was the single fatality. He had only arrived in the district a few days earlier from his home in Romford, Essex.[8]

Child evacuees from London were amongst eleven people killed when high explosives fell on a Devon town in January 1941. 'The baby sister of two children who died was saved and their mother was admitted to the local hospital suffering from cuts and shock,' reported the *Western Times* on 24 January 1941.

The bombs, though, did not necessarily have to be German. Florence Webb, originally from Carshalton in Surrey, had evacuated to Friends Green near Weston. At about 09.00 hours on the morning of 26 August 1944, the skies overhead the Hertfordshire village were full of USAAF bombers as they headed out from their bases to targets in Europe. Amongst this aerial armada were the Bowing B-17s of the 390th Bombardment Group which had taken off from Framlingham (Parham) in Suffolk.

Disaster struck as some of the bombers passed over Weston. One B-17 from 568 Squadron, nicknamed *Ding Dong Daddy*, collided with another from 569 Squadron. *The Sunday Post* of 27 August takes up the tragic story:

> Florence Webb … was killed by a bomb which crashed through the roof of a bungalow in Hertfordshire but did not explode. The tragedy occurred when two United States bombers came into collision in the air near Hitchin. Four members of the crew escaped by parachute. In total, fourteen United States airmen, a child and the evacuated mother died.

Cathy Hammond lost her baby brother during an air raid alert in Bolton, Lancashire – though it was not a bomb that was the cause:

> One of the air raid wardens came to help my mother by carrying my baby brother whilst she looked after Pamela and me. Unknown to my mother he dropped my brother on the way to the shelter.
>
> On arrival he handed him back and did not say what had happened. Nicholas died during the night, leaving my mother shocked and devastated. She later learned that the warden had been too afraid to say anything.[9]

The death of a young evacuee from Southsea, was reported in the *Portsmouth Evening News* of Saturday, 5 April 1941:

> John Ferrari (16), from Portsmouth, was killed last night when assisting to extinguish incendiary bombs at a South of England village. His death is believed to be due to his being struck by a shell fragment of an A.A. shell.
>
> He was originally at school in Portsmouth, but with his brother Peter, who is two years younger, was evacuated to the village some months ago.

Though there was danger for the children wherever they had been removed to, the reasons why they had been evacuated from the London area was made all too painfully aware, as revealed the bleak headlines in *The Times* 'Returned Evacuees Killed By Flying Bombs Launched From Aircraft' of 20 September 1944:

> Children who had only just returned from evacuation were among those killed by flying bombs which were sent over the southern counties, including the London area, early yesterday. It is believed that the flying bombs were discharged over the North Sea from aircraft based on aerodromes which may be in the island of Sylt or even farther away. An intensive A.A. barrage was put up. Vivid flashes were followed by two explosions, and it is claimed that the A.A. gunners, including mixed batteries, shot down two bombs. The whole action lasted under 20 minutes.
>
> Two months ago, when flying bomb attacks showed no sign of slackening, a little girl named Margaret, aged five, and her two sisters were evacuated from their home in a southern England town to Birmingham. Then a few days ago the menace seemed to be ending, and the parents, who had now also a baby boy, decided to

bring the children home. On Friday there was a family reunion. Now only Margaret is alive. The others were all killed while they slept. When their house was demolished early yesterday rescue workers dug for two hours. They could hear Margaret crying for help, and found her with her mother's arm around her. It was feared that nine people were killed in this incident, including members of the family next door.

A large number of houses were seriously damaged. At another place four people were killed and eight seriously injured. Some of them had been sleeping in their houses, having discontinued going to their shelters when they thought the raids were practically over.

During the Second World War, a total of 14.5 million acres of land, 25 million square feet of industrial and storage premises and 113,350 holdings of non-industrial premises were requisitioned by the British Government.

The War Office alone requisitioned 580,847 acres between 1939 and 1946, much of it for training purposes.[10] Such activity came with its own inherent risks, not least the question of unfired or unexploded munitions left littering the ground.

The armed forces were urged to ensure the dangers were minimised. 'How would you like your son or your young brother to take home a 'dud' grenade as a souvenir?' noted one set of instructions. The same document went on to add:

When ordered to search for or mark down or destroy 'blinds' [unexploded ordnance] make a clean job of it. Leave nothing to chance and leave nothing lying about for other men's children to find. Remember that children pay even less attention to warning and out of bounds notices than soldiers do. No fencing and no notices will keep out small boys.

Do not leave explosive articles lying about where children can get at them. If you think you have found a 'blind', leave it alone, mark the spot, arrange for a friend to guard it if possible, and report it to an officer at once.

A 'blind' goes off sooner or later, and if it goes off because a child treads on it or picks it up when bird's-nesting or blackberrying or hunting for souvenirs, someone's child is killed.[11]

In 1943 alone no less than 118 civilians, 'including many children', had been killed and a further 390 seriously injured directly, or indirectly, as a consequence of military training.[12] Some of the casualties were evacuees.

In Cardiff, Philip Anthony Fry died when he accidentally hit a detonator with a stone. He lost a hand and a leg in the blast.[13]

Similarily, John Bartlett died of multiple injuries due to the accidental explosion of a rifle grenade. Mirroring the military instructions quoted above, at the subsequent inquest it was stated that proper precautions should be taken by the Army to clear up at the end of their training exercises.[14]

Fixed anti-invasion defences also posed a very real risk – though the intended victim was supposed to be an invading enemy. Sophie Rosenthal and her friend were killed when two land mines exploded in the West of England:

> A witness said that the young woman appeared as the smoke of the first explosion cleared away. He shouted at her to stay still but she could not have heard him. She stumbled on about a hundred yards, another mine exploded and she was blown up.
>
> The jury asked that the military authorities should take steps to prevent any further occurrences. A police officer said that it was possible to walk from the sands onto the minefield as there was only one warning sign.[15]

Danger from ordnance was all around, as the *Western Daily Press* reported on Saturday, 24 April 1943:

> A 10-year-old boy, named John Peter Bartlett, of Forest Road, Walthamstow, London, who was evacuated to the country nearly three years ago, was killed on April 7, through the explosion of a rifle-grenade.
>
> At a West Country inquest the jury returned a verdict that death was due to haemorrhage and shock and multiple injuries to the accidental explosion of a rifle-grenade. They considered that no blame [should] be attached to anyone. They however expressed the opinion that proper precautions should be taken when clearing up after firing had taken place.

Another fatal explosion occurred on Sunday, 30 July 1944, when six boys climbed through barbed-wire fencing into an anti-tank minefield on a beach near Gunwalloe in Cornwall. The only witness, an Auxiliary

Coastguard, saw the boys climbing through the wire from his lookout post about half-a-mile away. In his statement to the inquest into the death of two of the boys, one of whom was a local lad and the other an evacuee which was reported in the *Cornishman* of 3 August 1944, the Auxiliary Coastguard said that when he saw the boys trying to enter the minefield he waved a red flag and blew his warning whistle. One of the gang, eleven-year-old evacuee, Peter Michael Reed said:

> The two deceased boys and four others, including himself, went towards the minefield. [Harry] Dale and [Donald] Munting entered by getting through and over the wire fencing, and shortly afterwards the explosion occurred.

When asked by the Coroner if he had not seen the danger warning notices, Peter Reed replied that, 'The only notice I have ever read is the one which stated that there is danger when a red flag is flying and planes are exercising.' The father of Donald Munting believed that, 'the place was not sufficiently protected and the nearest warning notice was not facing in the direction the boys approached the minefield. The evacuees had not been warned about the minefield.'

In response, Major Ernest Harvey Jarvis, Royal Engineers, declared that: 'The minefield was protected by various forms of wiring, of a width of six feet. The wiring was periodically inspected, and was in good order. The fence was put there as a deterrent and not with the intention of making it impossible for anyone to get through. The number of warning notices was larger than the official instructions required to be placed there.'

The Coroner summed up the sad episode with these words: 'Boys of such intelligence must have known that they had no right to be inside the fence. The result was extremely sorrowful for all concerned.'

An equally reckless, or one might say, senseless, act was reported in the *Aberdeen Journal* that same summer, 26 July 1944:

> Three boys, including a South of England evacuee, were killed and two others seriously injured, in an explosion on the Lancashire Moors last night. They were playing with an explosive missile when it exploded. The three were killed instantly.

Aside from enemy action and ordnance, there were, unfortunately, so many different ways in which an evacuee could come to harm. With the increase in military traffic, the roads could be dangerous places for young children. This was the case with Patrick Pearson, a fourteen-year-old, who died in Spilsbury Hospital, Lincoln, after being knocked off his bicycle by an RAF lorry at East Keal. He suffered severe head injuries and died without regaining consciousness. A similar story was reported in the *Bucks Herald* of Friday, 22 September 1940:

> A little boy named Alan Mearing, aged six years, an evacuee from the Metropolitan area, was picked up dead on Saturday afternoon after a military motor lorry had passed Brook Cottages, Soulbury, where his mother stood talking to another woman on the roadside. Neither the mother or the neighbour or driver of the lorry saw the accident happen, and no one saw the child in the road at the time …
>
> George Henry Mearing, a lorry driver, of 44, Priscilla Road, Bow, London E., said that he was father of the child, who, with his mother, had been evacuated … Mrs. Phyllis Edith Mearing, the mother of the boy, stated that … she was outside her house and was talking to Mrs. Ella Norman. She saw a military motor lorry coming towards Soulbury from the direction of Linslade. The lorry passed her, and before she saw this lorry her little boy was a little distance in front of her, and there were other children playing near; but her son was not very far from her; and she had not noticed a stationery motor car on her side of the road. After the motor lorry had passed her a military motor lorry went by, and after it had passed she saw her son lying in the road.

She went over to her son and when she picked him up she saw he was seriously injured. He was covered with a coat by a soldier as they waited for a doctor to be summoned. The woman that Mrs Mearing was talking to, Ella Norman, likewise did not see the accident.

Private Philip Malcom McKillop, RASC, was one of the passengers in the military lorry, which he said was being driven at a normal speed. He was in the back of the lorry and saw two women waving their hands. He shouted at the driver to stop, before jumping out to see what assistance he could offer. The next statement was given by the driver, Private Reginald William Lambourne, RASC. He said that he was driving at a normal speed and that he knew the road:

> Near Brook Cottages the road was somewhat bent and he was just gathering speed when he had to pull in to pass a stationery car on the side of the road. He did not notice the two women standing by the side of the road, nor did he notice any children, and his attention was not distracted by anything. The road was only about 17 feet wide. He heard shouting from the back of his lorry and stopped

gradually. He got out and saw a little boy lying in the road a little distance back. He did not go down the road to the child, but his passenger did … He examined his lorry but found no marks whatever on it.

Young Alan Mearing was taken to the Royal Bucks Hospital but was pronounced dead in the ambulance. Dr Patricia Gertrude Cooper said that she examined him and her findings appeared to contradict the driver's story. She found,

A large laceration on the left side of the head, and a fracture of the skull. The injuries were such as would result from a direct hit. There were no signs that a vehicle had passed over the child and death was due to fracture of the skull and laceration of the brain.

A similar incident took place in the summer of 1941, which was reported in the *Western Daily Press* on Monday, 9 June:

A verdict of 'Accidental death' was returned at an inquest at Taunton on Saturday, on an eight-year-old evacuee boy – one of the first to arrive in the Taunton district – who was knocked down by an Army staff car, on the Bridgewater-Taunton road, at Bathpool, and was killed instantly …

The car involved in the accident was driven by Driver George Turle, R.A.S.C., who did not give evidence. An eye-witness stated that the boy halted part way out in the road, looked in one direction, and then took a step forward. But for this the car, which carried the boy along, might have avoided him.

In pronouncing the verdict of accidental death, the Coroner said that there was no evidence of criminal neglect on the part of the driver.

This was not the case in an incident witnessed by evacuee Terence Frisby in Doublebois, Cornwall:

Soldiers were always billeted in the grounds of Doublebois House and we children constantly hung around them, cadging rides, wearing their forage caps and swinging upon the big iron gate at the entrance so that cars, lorries and even Bren Carriers could rumble in and out. The gate was deemed by the military too much of a bother constantly to open and close, so was taken off its hinges and leant against a wall to be removed. Instead of swinging on it we just sat on it.

The smallest of us all was five-year-old Teddy Camberwell, evacuated with his mother and baby sister. He was not one of the Welling crowd. I call him Teddy Camberwell, but I don't remember his surname, just that he was bombed out from Camberwell in the Blitz. Teddy, his mother and little sister were billeted at 3 Railway Cottages and he tagged along with us in most of our play.

On this particular day he was at the end of a row of us sitting on the gate, when a lorry came round the corner, caught the gate, tipped it forward and left us falling backwards into the bushes – except for Teddy. He was thrown forward and went under the gate and under the lorry.

I clambered out and looked at the scene before me: the driver, staring aghast at the result of his tiny error; the unbelieving sentry; three other children, one with his hand in his mouth, all beyond tears. Teddy's crushed body under the gate, leaking blood and other things.

I turned and ran for the only help I trusted. 'Auntie Rose, Auntie Rose. Come quickly. Teddy Camberwell is dead. He's dead. Teddy Camberwell's dead.'

She stared at me, shocked. 'What are you talking about?'

'A lorry went over the gate.'

We ran back up the main road and met the sentry, accompanied by the bemused driver and three children, carrying Teddy's tiny, crumpled body to his home at 3 Railway Cottages. Auntie Rose shouted at them, 'What are you doing? What are you doing, man?'

'Are you the mother?' asked the sentry, probably dreading the answer. 'No, where are you taking him?'

'The boys said he lives in the cottages here.'

'What are you trying to do? Give his mother a present, you bloody fool? Take him back to the camp.'

The sentry, no more than a teenager, was hopelessly out of his depth. 'I didn't know where to –'

Auntie Rose practically pushed him. 'Go on. Take him to your medical officer. His mother will be out any minute.'

I next saw Auntie Rose taking Teddy's mother into our house, where she lay collapsed and sobbing on the sofa, watched by Jack's and my detached, curious eyes until we were driven out.

So much emotion seemed more than one person could contain. Her body jerked and heaved as her grief tore its way out of her. The next day a soldier appeared in the courts: a private, Teddy's father. He was accompanied by an awkward-looking army padre, an officer, and stood mutely, arms pinned to his side by his wife as she clung to him and sobbed anew. What guilt she must have suffered besides her simple agony. To have brought her son to Cornwall for safety and then to have this news for his father.

Driver error was also the cause of another evacuee being killed which was reported in *Taunton Courier, and Western Advertiser* of Saturday, 15 February 1941.

> Irene Joyce Wells, aged eight, was fatally injured when an Army truck crashed into the Unitarian Church on Friday afternoon. A witness stated that the lorry came round the corner quickly and with a very big sweep towards a car, then it shot right across the road towards the church, crashed into the railings outside and knocked the child over. She had been standing at the doorway of the church … The railings outside the church were smashed and were wedged inside the cabin of the truck. There was a bicycle entangled with the broken railings.

The cause of Irene Joyce's death was shock from multiple injuries, 'consistent with the child having been pierced by an iron instrument and pinned against a wall.'

The driver of the Army lorry explained what went wrong. He had backed into one street and was going forward again:

> As I was pushing the clutch pedal in with the intention of changing into second gear my seat slipped back. This caused my foot pedal to fly out and my right heel to slip back. This caused acceleration and the truck went forward, mounting the pavement. Then I hit the rails. I found the little girl lying just inside the gates. I picked her up and carried her into the church.'

The final comment on this case by the Coroner gives an indication of just how dangerous the roads of Britain were in those days with Army vehicles rushing around the country, when because of rationing there were less civilian journeys being undertaken: 'Mr Christopher Rowe, at the Hospital on Monday, expressed the view that something must be wrong for so many as 300 a day to occur.' Clearly one of the unrecognised statistics of the war.

Chapter 9

'The Most Wicked Woman we Had Ever Met'

Mishaps, Misdeeds and Murder

For some children, being left in the hands of strangers resulted in neglect, physical and mental cruelty and abuse, some of it sexual, at the hands of their foster parents. In the worse of cases, the helpless evacuees would die at the hands of those who were supposed to keep them safe. These stories make very difficult reading, but they need to be told in order to provide a full picture of the British evacuation experience.

In some instances, evacuees did not even survive the journey to their destination unscathed. Pauline Burford's sister, Sylvia, was the only evacuee to die during a Channel crossing from Guernsey to Weymouth:

> My mother and I (I was four years old) sailed on an English ship but my sister Sylvia and brother Brian were separated from us, going on a different boat with their school classes. None of us knew which boat the others were on. Father saw us off then went back to work at the Guernsey prison.
>
> Sylvia, seven years older than myself and five years older than Brian, had been rather ill after a tonsillectomy. She was really too ill to travel and it should never have been permitted by the medical authorities, and my mother had not been allowed to travel with her. Sylvia was prone to stomach upsets and the boat had no stabilisers as is usually the case today.
>
> Due to her seasickness and of course the aftermath of the operation, she haemorrhaged and became dangerously ill. She kept

calling for her parents and wondering why they didn't come. I understand that she died in hospital in Weymouth two days after landing, having been carried off the ship on a stretcher. My mother had no sooner arrived at her parents' home in Rugby, Warwickshire, when the police called with the sad news of Sylvia's death. Leaving me with a grandmother who wasn't at all welcoming, she hurried back to Weymouth with my grandfather for identification and burial.

My father was given special permission to go to Weymouth for the funeral but then was not allowed to return to Guernsey. As he was English born, he would no doubt have ended up in a German prison camp, probably Biberach, where many British born residents were interned.

Sadly my parents' ways parted after that due to the problems of accommodation in the Rugby home and the need to seek work in wartime. The effects of these traumas have remained in the background all my life and obviously left my mother traumatised right up to her death in the 1980s.[1]

Beryl Blake-Lawson, a First Form pupil at Westcliff Girls High School in Southend-On-Sea when she was evacuated to Chapel-en-le-Frith in Derbyshire, recalls how one of her friends had a fatal accident whilst returning to her billet:

There was one tragedy. One day, running down the hill from Bank Hall for lunch at her billet, Christine Markham, it is assumed – tripped and fell against the stone wall – and was found by two senior girls. It was a great shock to them as she had broken her neck and was dead.[2]

On 8 November 1941, the *Hull Daily Mail* reported the tragic news of the death of a Hull evacuee which occurred within hours of the youngster's arrival in the market town of Driffield in the East Riding of Yorkshire:

Alfred George Parsons, aged 4, and his brother were evacuated to Driffield and later to the sick bay at Filey for treatment. A nurse said that she found Alfred with his nightclothes on fire in the corridor. From another child she learned that he had pulled aside the fireguard, placed paper on the fire and his clothing become ignited.

Recording a verdict of death from shock following extensive burns the Coroner said, 'I do not think it can be reasonably suggested that there was any negligence – however it is recommended that in places and institutions where there are children, fixed fireguard should be in place'.

It was the parent who lost her life as tragedy befell Brian Russell's family when they were evacuated to Cheshire:

> I was just two and a half years old when my brother and I were evacuated from Guernsey with my mum, Miriam. Dad had said we should leave and he went to join the Army. Mum and I arrived in Stockport but within three weeks, Mum died of meningitis.
>
> Dad was allowed some leave to sign her death certificate, but could not look after my brother and I because he was in the Forces. My brother and I were then placed in a Children's Home in Styal, Cheshire, where we were separated. This caused me great distress at such a young age.
>
> Apparently I was asking for my Mum all the time and my brother said that I went berserk. After we had been in the home for two months, Dad managed to persuade his brother, who had married a Dorset woman, to look after us. They looked after us and fed us, but there was no affection whatsoever.[3]

Jenny Horne's parents lost their infant son during the evacuation – to somewhat unusual circumstances:

> My parents, Verna and Marshall Edmonds, were evacuated from Guernsey to Cheshire. With them were my three year old brother, Glen, and my Aunt, Brenda Mould, who was in her teens. Tragically, Mum and Dad lost Glen because a local farmer gave him unpasteurised milk to drink. Mum and Dad had not planned to have more children until the end of the war, but the loss of Glen changed their minds. They went on to have my brother Pete in 1944 and I was born after the war when they returned to Guernsey.[4]

Maurice McCall died a few months after arriving in Portland. He had been playing with friends in a worked out quarry when a large stone fell on his head from twenty-five feet above him.[5]

On one occasion, the *Cheltenham Chronicle* informed its readers of the death of Helen Margaret Whittaker. 'Helen was balancing on a plank placed on top of a sheep pen then fell onto the iron rail round the pen, then onto the concrete floor. In spite of everything that could be done, the child died the next morning. The girl's father said that he had not seen either of his daughters since they left London six months ago.'

Numerous evacuees died through drowning, and on 29 May 1941 the *Hartlepool Mail* reported on two Sunderland evacuees who had drowned in the Tees at Eaglescliffe: 'One fell in when playing on the riverbank, the other grasped the branch of an overhanging tree and made an attempt to reach him. The branch gave way and both were carried away. One of the boys had only arrived the previous day.' Perhaps uncertain of new surroundings, Helen Parsons also drowned soon after her arrival – in this case in the mill lade at Port Elfinstone, Aberdeenshire, where she had only been for five days.[6]

Two Glasgow children drowned when they were swept out into the Solway from the Gretna shore, near the mouth of the River Sark. They had been in the district for twelve days.[7] A month later, the drowning of another Glasgow evacuee was reported in Dundee:

> Mrs McCracken of Glasgow and her children have been resident at Knockbrex for four weeks. On Wednesday, Campbell McCracken aged two years and seven months was reported missing. A search was made through the woods and along the course of the burn which runs through the estate to the shore. The body of the boy has been found at the mouth of the burn which was in heavy flood.[8]

When these incidents were reported in the press, the Government feared they might affect morale and cause parents to panic by bringing their evacuated children home:

> There should be greater supervision in these areas to see that children do not suffer … supervision is absolutely essential. Here is a case which I saw in the *Daily Record* today. Two little Glasgow children who were evacuated a fortnight ago were drowned yesterday.
>
> Fancy that type of news coming to the father of children who have been evacuated. It is bound to arouse in the minds of every mother in Glasgow the thought that her child might be in danger and it will have the effect that many children will be brought back from these evacuation areas into Glasgow.[9]

Even though vehicle ownership was far lower in the war years and this factor, along with the lack of fuel due to rationing, meant fewer cars and lorries on the roads, the risks to children from civilian traffic was just as great as that from the armed forces. In Cirencester, by way of illustration, Barbara Andrews was killed whilst walking with her mother. A goods lorry, covered with a tarpaulin, was travelling in the same direction as Barbara and her mother when 'the tarpaulin sheet billowed out and wrapped itself around Mrs Andrews. It swung her round and the three-year-old child was flung under the rear nearside wheel of the lorry, which passed over her.'[10]

Evacuee Charles Farmer, aged seven, was killed whilst posting a letter in Honiton, Devon: 'He and his sister were billeted with a Mrs Turner who told the coroner that the boy went to post a letter for her at the bottom of the road and ran off whistling and singing. That was the last time she saw him alive. He died almost instantaneously when he was crushed by a lorry against a wall at the junction of Mill Street and King Street. The driver said it was necessary for him to manoeuvre the vehicle close to the wall near the letterbox.'[11]

A gun is, of course, a deadly weapon – and never more so than when in the hands of a child. On 1 July 1940, the *Gloucester Citizen* published news of one incident involving an evacuee: 'Ten-year-old Leslie Whitaker, of Bermondsey was accidentally shot dead by L …, aged 13, when they went to a cherry orchard to scare birds. L … found the gun in a shed. It went off whilst he was reloading it and killed his companion.'

Just seven days after arriving in Market Harborough, another boy was shot in similar circumstances:

> Michael Moscow, aged 6, had been staying with his brother at the home of Mr Neil, the village postman. The two boys went into an outhouse where they found a gun which was used for shooting birds. The elder brother was playing with the gun when it exploded and Michael received a wound at the back of the head. He died within a few minutes.[12]

Although the majority of evacuees received loving care from their wartime foster parents, others did not. In some instances, children even endured physical and mental cruelty at the hands of unsuitable hosts. In some cases, this may have been the result of the authorities being overstretched, with the result that billets were not always fully vetted before children were placed there. Even if an official did visit, it may have made no difference, as Sheila Whipp recalled: 'When a Billeting officer visited any of my foster homes, he never asked me if I was happy or even spoke to me. It was as if I didn't exist.[13]

In the event that an evacuee was ill-treated, they were often 'rescued' because a neighbour observed the situation and contacted the authorities. In other cases, teachers noticed bruises and marks then gently questioned the child.

The authorities organising evacuation often failed to appreciate the psychological repercussions of evacuees being moved into the homes of strangers. Faith and Stella Shoesmith, aged six and nine respectively, were evacuated from Lowestoft to Glossop, Derbyshire. Faith remembers the harsh treatment the two sisters received in their billet:

> We were the last to be picked and grudgingly collected by a Mrs Jessie Woods. Our stay was very unhappy as she treated us like slaves. Every Saturday we had to clean all of the bedrooms from top to bottom and we also had to polish the hall floor on our hands and knees. Mrs Woods inspected our work thoroughly afterwards to make sure that we had done a good job. We were not allowed into the dining room, and if we wanted to go upstairs, we had to ask permission. I would say 'Please may I go upstairs?' or 'Can I please go upstairs?' but it was always wrong and Mrs Woods would stand and laugh at us. We had to mind our manners, stand with straight backs and walk a certain way!
>
> Our Dad had joined the Army. Mum was in Lowestoft and every now and then she would send us parcels of sweets but we never received them. She did visit us when she could, and always brought sweets and toys with her. Our one victory was that we found a large square tin of biscuits hidden behind Mrs Woods' wardrobe. Every week when we cleaned her bedroom we helped ourselves to one biscuit.[14]

Eventually, after about two years Faith's and Stella's mother found accommodation in Sherwood and removed them from their foster home. Likewise, Philip Doran's experiences with Mr and Mrs Burgess led to him being removed from their home, also by his mother:

> It was my job to go and buy the potatoes and vegetables from a farm about half a mile away. The farmer was a kind old man who always presented us with three or four windfall apples, a rare treat.
>
> One day, I was sent along on my own; as it happened, on this particular day the farmer was not around so his wife dealt with me but she didn't supply me with any windfalls. My best friend, Joe Ducket, had been evacuated to a farm some distance from me. On my return from the farm with the vegetables, I passed Joe's house, he was sitting on the garden wall eating an apple. After a brief chat, Joe gave me the core of his apple to finish off on my way home. As

I got to Mrs Burgess's house I had just finished the core and threw the remains into the hedge. I was unaware at the time that Mrs Burgess had witnessed this. I walked up the path and handed over the potatoes and vegetables; Mrs Burgess asked me where the windfalls were, I replied that the farmer had not been there and his wife had not given me any.

Mrs Burgess exploded with rage and started to punch me like a woman possessed; all her pent up resentment seemed to come out in that moment. She was screaming, 'I saw you eating the apples coming up the road, you little liar!' By now blood was streaming from my nose and mouth; I knew I had to get away. I made my escape and ran back to Joe's house, he got me a flannel and helped me to clean up but the blood continued to flow.

I asked Joe to find me some paper, an envelope and a pencil. Together we went down to the canal and I wrote a letter to my Mother, telling her of the unhappy episode. As I wrote, blood dripped onto the paper, proof if it was needed that I was telling the truth. I didn't have a stamp but just prayed that the post office would deliver the letter anyway. Heavens knows what my Mam thought when she opened the blood stained note!

I told Joe that there was no way that I would be going back to Mrs Burgess; he suggested that I come back to his house. When we arrived, the kind old lady with whom Joe was staying was just returning from a trip to town; when she saw the state of my face she said, 'Well, you're going to have to stay here until your mother arrives.'

With that, Mr Burgess arrived to take me back to the house; he too looked shocked at the state of my face. He begged me to go back, saying that his wife was deeply sorry for what she had done. The kind lady reluctantly agreed to let me go and off I went back to the house with Mr Burgess.

On arrival I ran straight up to my bedroom, fearful of repercussions. All I heard from downstairs were raised voices; at last Mr Burgess seemed to have stood up to his wicked wife. The next day my Mother arrived and left Mrs Burgess with no doubt about how she felt about the treatment I had received. She told her that, as far as she was concerned her son would be a lot safer in Liverpool despite the falling bombs. Within a few hours I was back home in Liverpool. The smell of the Mersey never smelt sweeter.[15]

Because their parents did not want them to live with strangers, Jean and Bern Noble were sent to the home of their grandmother's brother, Frank. It was not, Jean recalls, the place of sanctuary they expected:

Frank had a bad temper and his maxim was 'spare the rod and spoil the child'. Frank's daughter and son in law, who also lived in the house, tried to protect us from Frank's anger but for much of the time they were not at home.

On one occasion my brother helped me turn a somersault in the backyard which, because of my previous illness, (rheumatic fever) was forbidden. Seeing it, Frank turned on Bern and started beating him with a stick. Frank's son in law, a much smaller and less aggressive man, intervened to stop him and Frank then attacked him and was punching and threatening to kill him. I ran screaming into the toilet and locked myself in. This was my first experience of a man being a tyrant in the home.

We were not given keys to the front door either which meant if everyone was out when we got home from school we had to wait for someone to return before being let in. Arriving home one afternoon from school I had the urgent need to relieve myself and rang the doorbell, hopping anxiously from one foot to the other. The curtains in the window twitched and Frank looked out to see who was at the door.

I waited for what seemed ages for him to open the door and rang the doorbell again and again, wondering what was keeping him. By the time he eventually opened the door the relief and need was such that, humiliatingly, I wet myself. He looked down at the doorstep with a disdainful and disgusted look on his face and said 'What dirty little dog has done that on the doorstep?' The need rose again on another occasion but rather than go through the same humiliation I walked up and down the street weeping in distress until a kindly neighbour came to my aid and allowed me to use her facilities.[16]

Sisters Peggy and Betty White were evacuated to Oxford. They were very happy with Mr and Mrs Murphy but had to move out when Mrs Murphy was due to have a baby. Their second billet was very different, as Peggy recalls:

We moved in with Mrs Fisher who turned out to be the most wicked woman we had ever met. From the very next day we were beaten and made to do all the housework before going to school. We had to get up at five each morning and we were sent to bed as soon as we got in from school. As an extra punishment we would be shut, one at a time, in a dark coal-shed all night. We hated that as there were huge spiders and it was bitterly cold – you could see white frost on the top of the coal when she let you out in the morning.

The most cruel thing Mrs Fisher did was when her little Scottie dog couldn't get outside since the back door was closed and messed on the kitchen floor. In her rage she took the dog upstairs and threw it out of the bedroom window. He landed on the rockery below. Betty and I ran out and picked him up; he was still alive and whimpering. Mrs Fisher snatched him from us and we never saw the little chap again.

We lived with Mrs Fisher and her husband (who was also frightened of her) for about a year, which to us seemed like forever. However, one day Betty's teacher saw the terrible bruises on her. She questioned us both, and we said that Mrs Fisher would kill us if we ever told anyone. The teacher, whose name was Mrs Payne, took us back to the house and told us to pack our belongings in a suitcase while she had words with Mrs Fisher. Then we all left.

As we walked along the road in the gathering dusk with our battered suitcase balanced precariously on Mrs Payne's bicycle, she said, 'Where would you like to live most of all?'

Betty and I cried in unison, 'With Mrs Murphy.'

She replied, 'That's just where we are going.'

We skipped the rest of the way there. Mrs Murphy cried when she saw us and so did we.[17]

Jennifer Williams was starved and beaten in her Somerset billet. In fact, her treatment was so cruel that even to this day she still bears the scars:

We had a boiled egg for breakfast but were not given lunch to take to school. I got by with an extra bottle of free milk and an apple or pear that a London evacuee gave me as he lived on a farm. In the holidays my sister and I survived by stealing from the watercress beds or taking carrots from the ploughed fields.

My mother visited us from Bristol once in two years, at Christmas 1943. It was a five mile walk from the bus and five miles back to the bus stop to Bristol. We walked the five miles to see my mother catch the bus and walked five miles back. Tired, I was crying for my mother and my 'reward' was a beating with a black stick. I still have the wheals on my back.[18]

Financial gain may have proven the incentive for some individuals to foster an evacuee. Rosemary Hall and her brother endured harsh treatment in Birkenhead:

My brother and I stood in the church hall for ages, people wanted me but not my brother as well. A woman said, 'I will have the little girl' but she was told that we didn't want to be separated. The woman said, 'I don't want two of them' and the Salvation Army lady said. 'But if you take them both you will get nearly 20 shillings a week to keep them.'

The woman quickly changed her mind! We spent a horrendous four months sleeping on camp beds in her hallway behind the front door. We weren't allowed in any other part of the house except the lavatory in the backyard and we were constantly hungry. She clearly took us in just to get the weekly 20 shillings.

After four months our Mum tracked us down. She knocked on the door of the house, saw the state of us and removed us from the premises without waiting for the woman to come back from the shops.[19]

Eileen Parker and her brother were sent from Swansea to an unwelcoming family in Whitland:

My Mum had just had her kidney removed and could not look after us. We were sent to a farm where the people were not very nice to us. Every day we were given fish paste sandwiches and goat's milk, which tasted awful. My teacher saw that I was not drinking my milk so she swapped it for her cow's milk. We had very little to eat at other times and had to work on the farm after school and at weekends.

When Mum was well enough to travel, she came to visit us. As we met her on the railway station platform, she was horrified at how thin we were. She said we looked like a pair of urchins and decided to take us straight home with her, despite the dangers in Swansea. I was so relieved to be going back home! She firmly believed that the couple who took us in only did so to get the billeting allowance.[20]

Rose Hawkins, aged eight, was evacuated from Birmingham to Aston Ingham in Herefordshire, in September 1940:

My brother Bill was badly injured when the factory he worked in was bombed, so Mum sent my brother John and I to the countryside. We moved in with a husband and wife who had no family, and no intention of sparing the rod or making allowances.

Everything was regimented, our letters sent home were censored, or destroyed if they contained requests of 'Please can we come home?' We walked two and a half miles each way to school and if we were late back, there was no meal, straight to bed.

When I first arrived I wet the bed as I was so scared. The woman told me 'If you wet the bed again, I will boil a mouse and make you drink the liquid!' So whenever I ate and drank anything after that, I always checked it for pieces of mouse.

Fifty years later, we attended Aston Ingham's first evacuee reunion, presenting the village with a biblical picture with this inscription; 'Suffer the little children to come unto me, and forbid them not, for such is the Kingdom of Heaven.'[21]

George and Brenda Osborn, aged five and six, were sent from Portsmouth to Wootton Bridge on the Isle of Wight. They were placed in separate billets. It was George who suffered the most. Unsurprisingly, he still recalls his ill treatment:

She had been forced to take in an evacuee. She was never cruel to me physically but the mental torture was just as bad.

I was almost ignored, being sent out to play in the garden or told to sit quietly with a book. Any noise was criticised and the family stepped over me with a 'tutting' sound. Every other mouthful of food was accompanied with comments about how grateful I should be, or how many brave men had died bringing it to our table.

Finally, she told me that if I had not been moved by Friday of that week, then she would throw me out. True to her word Mrs. Wilson packed all my things in a small suitcase and bundled my dirty clothes up in a towel. She told me to call back from school at lunchtime and take everything to the house of Mrs Gallop, where my sister was living.

Mrs Gallop (Auntie Annie to me) had no idea I was going to turn up, but placed me in the care of her lodgers, a young couple with no children.

I didn't tell anyone what happened when I was alone in the house with them. Brenda noticed some marks on my body one night when I was undressing and asked me what they were. Eventually I told her that the lodger had done it, hitting me with his leather belt. She ran down the stairs, wide eyed and red faced, her lips closed tightly together in anger and told Aunty Annie what had happened.

When she didn't believe her – probably her defence for not knowing how to handle the situation – Brenda stormed into the front room, which the lodgers occupied, and told them she was going to tell our mother, her teacher and everyone she knew. They said I was lying, but she knew I wasn't, and she wouldn't let me near them from that moment. They hadn't reckoned with my big sister – aged just six.

True to her word, Brenda told everybody she saw. She added the village policeman, Sunday school teacher and district nurse to her list. Somebody had to take notice and very soon they did. A man called a 'Child Cruelty Officer' called round and he made me take off my shirt to show him the marks, now fast fading, but some had broken the skin and still showed. He called the lodgers in for their explanation but he wasn't convinced. I was immediately removed from their 'care' and went back to living with Aunty Annie and my sister.[22]

George's happiness, however, was short-lived. He goes on to detail the events that happened just one year later:

The last time I saw Brenda was six weeks before she died, walking with Aunty Annie. She was on the way to Dr. Kennedy's evening surgery, her arm in terrible pain and swollen like a balloon. Brenda looked back once or twice, waving in the way she always did when she was saying good-bye. I didn't bother waving back but shouted after her saying something like, 'You're a sissy, it doesn't really hurt, you're only playing up.'

She was rushed straight from the surgery to the hospital in an ambulance. Mother came to see Brenda often, crossing on the ferry from Portsmouth to Ryde. My sister died at St. Mary's County Hospital Ryde, on 28th December 1941. She died of what was called blood poisoning in those days, caused by an infection after an inoculation at school against diphtheria.

Because Brenda's death was so close to Christmas, letters of sympathy were arriving at the same time as 'Get Well' and Christmas cards. Christmas presents for Brenda also lay forlornly unopened – Mother not knowing what to do with them.

With all my heart I wish my last words to Brenda, as she walked to the doctor's surgery, had been kinder. I should have said, 'Please come back soon Brenda because I shall miss you terribly. For as long as I can remember you've always been there for me; you have not only been my sister but also my best friend, mother and father, all rolled into one. I always feel safe and secure with you and you're the only person who has never let me down. I depend on you for so many things, so come back soon and I promise never to be spiteful or hurt you – ever again.'[23]

'I was completely neglected,' notes Edna Dart when describing conditions in her Devon billet as an eight-year-old evacuee. 'For tea one day I was given a sandwich full of fat and a glass of lemonade with salt in it. I wasn't washed and my clothes weren't washed. In those days, the authorities didn't check on the people they put you with.'[24]

Jean Arthur was three years younger than Edna when she was sent to a billet in Cornwall. Her young age did little to prevent her suffering constant humiliation:

> My brother Sid and I were evacuated to St Albans, I was sent to one house and [my brother] Sid was sent next door. We were used to living in flats so it seemed very posh, the people were really snobby and horrible and considered us dirty and common because we were from London.
>
> They made me feel poor and shabby, and they immediately combed my hair with methylated spirits, it was very demeaning. I slept in a little fold up bed next to their daughter who looked down on me from her bed and sneered at me. When I sat at the dining table there were unfamiliar items there. For example there was a dish with a spoon sitting in a silver plated stand, and I had never seen anything like that before. I asked the family 'What is that?' and they mocked me saying 'Don't you know what that is? It's a jam container' which made me cringe with embarrassment. Mum came to visit and saw how unhappy we both were and took us home.[25]

Francis Rutter was also evacuated to Cornwall – to a monastery. His experiences were not happy:

> I was eight years old and sent to stay with the Benedictum Brothers in Redruth. I found it very hard to live under the Brothers' strict regime and tried on numerous occasions to run away. The only way they dealt with this was to beat me in front of the other boys at assembly, to make an example of me. I missed my family immensely and it still upsets me that I was sent so far away and not even to a family. I thought I would be on a farm or in the countryside, not at a strict monastery where we weren't allowed to play, or even talk most of the time.[26]

When Jean Bell was evacuated to South Wales, she found herself being moved from one billet to another which led to a roller-coaster of experiences:

I was picked out, with my sister, by a Welsh lady and unfortunately she turned out to be very cruel to us. She had a daughter who stamped on my sister's fingers when she was drawing hopscotch on the pavement. Both my sister and I started at the local school without shoes and were laughed at by the local children for being badly dressed. My sister told me later this was because our clothes had been sold. I seem to have blocked out most of what happened whilst we lived with this lady but I do know my sister was admitted to hospital with a back injury and it was at this point that we were removed from this house.

A little later, we stayed with a really lovely lady who was very kind to us although I remember that soon after we moved in with her, I fell into the river and was too frightened to go home. Because of my experience in the previous billet, I feared being severely punished. It was quite dark when the lady found me, still very wet and scared, and took me home, gave me a big cuddle and dried me off and put me to bed. After that, I felt loved and settled down happily with her.

We remained with her for a while but then, unfortunately for us, her daughter, who was in the forces, became pregnant and was sent home. The room we occupied was required for her daughter so once again a new home had to be found for us.

This lady looked upon us as servants and we were kept busy with housework etc. Because I was younger than my sister, I had the lightest chores but my sister had to do the washing by hand and scrub the stone floor in the kitchen. I got away with sweeping and dusting. My sister and I also ate in the kitchen whilst friends and family ate in the dining room.[27]

During the Second World War the separation of children from their parents was viewed in a different light than it might be today. Indeed, the author John Welshman believes that evacuation would not happen today, 'because changes in the way that child abuse has been exposed mean that children would never be sent away to live with strangers'.[28]

Evacuee Jean Arthur experienced sexual abuse during her time with her host household in Cornwall. She, like many others, wishes to share her memories to expose what some evacuees had to endure:

After some time we left our first billet and were evacuated again to the countryside, just outside St Austell, Cornwall. The couple who cared for us had no children and were very cold hearted.

I pined so badly for my Mum that I started wetting the bed, which was a cardinal sin! I got thrashed and each night before I went to bed I would get on my hands and knees and pray to God 'Please don't let me go to sleep and wet the bed' but of course I fell asleep and wet it. The husband tried to interfere with me when his wife was out. The neighbours must have known something of what was going on and felt sorry for us because they complained to the authorities about our treatment.[29]

Ann Smith was evacuated from Liverpool to Anglesey with her school. Although she herself was not abused or harassed, a couple of her friends were:

One girl, who was the same age as me (12 years old) had a tough time as the farmer used to sexually accost her. She was very frightened but she would not let us tell the teacher in case of causing trouble. Looking back now, we should have reported it but in those days none of us really knew what it was all about, there was no sex education in schools.

Another girl was billeted with a butcher and his wife and the butcher would bring the girl to see us in his van. However, when it got time for her to go home, she would beg us to go with her in the van as he always tried to molest her. So we used to go back with her in the van so that she would not be on her own with him. His wife was really nice to us and obviously had no idea what her husband was up to.[30]

A number of the evacuees suffered not merely neglect or mistreatment at the hands of their hosts but were actually killed by them. One of these instances was probably the most harrowing story ever told of ill-treatment of young children. This was the case of the death of thirteen-year-old Dennis O'Neill. It was reported in the *Daily Mirror* of Wednesday, 14 February 1945, and because of the starling nature of the crime, it is repeated here at length. The principal witness was his ten-year-old brother Terence, who was described as a sturdy, fair-haired boy:

Terence stood in front of the witness box by the side of counsel to give evidence.

'We were quite warm in bed when we went to the farm in June,' said Terence, after identifying the bed clothing provided for them, 'but when the winter came we were not very warm. I asked Mr. and Mrs. Gough for another blanket but never got one.'

When Mrs. Gough washed the blanket they had to go to bed without one, and they were cold.

Asked what food they were given, Terence said that they had bread and butter for breakfast, two or three pieces, and tea.

Counsel: Do you remember what you had for dinner? – Bread and butter, sometimes two and sometimes three pieces, and tea to drink. Sometimes I think, we had tinned salmon.

They had apple pie sometimes, but often when they had that they only had two pieces of bread and butter. He did not remember having more than one piece of pie.

Counsel: What did you have for tea? – Bread and butter, sometimes two and sometimes three pieces, and tea to drink.

What did you have for supper? – Bread and butter one piece very often, and tea to drink. We never got sugar in our tea. Fairly often I was hungry and we used to go into the pantry and get something.

At this point Terence started to cry, but he recovered his composure.

'Were you ever caught in the pantry?' asked counsel. 'No' replied Terence, 'but they found out and gave us stripes – very often Mr. Gough and sometimes Mrs. Gough. The stripes were given on our hands with a thin stick and sometimes with a fairly thick one. I don't remember how many stripes we had but it was a lot.'

Terence said that every evening they had to tell Mr. Gough what they had done wrong during the day, and then he gave them stripes – sometimes ten for one thing. 'Sometimes,' added the boy, 'they said they were too tired to give us stripes, but other times we had nearly a hundred on one night.'

The stripes were given for going into the pantry, for taking a long time with the horses, for not cleaning the cowhouse properly, and for getting their clothes dirty.

Counsel: How many times do you think you missed having stripes? – Only a few days.

They were given thrashings on their hands and legs.

An album of twelve photographs taken of the boy after death and described by Mr. H.H. Maddocks, for the prosecution, as 'revolting' was handed to the three magistrates and inspected by them. Mrs. M.W. Cock, the one woman on the bench, shook her head and closed her eyes.

'One evening about two days before I left, Mr. Gough stripped Dennis in the kitchen, took him into the back kitchen told him to get on the pig bench, tied a rope across his back and fastened him down

146

with it. Then he started hitting him on the top part of the back with a stick and Dennis cried and shouted.'

Mrs. Gough was in another room, but he thought she must have heard Dennis shrieking.

Counsel: Where were you when this was going on? – Mr. Gough told me to hold the lantern so he could see what he was doing.

'This thrashing,' said Terence, 'did not take long but Mr. Gough threatened that if Dennis kept on being bad he would put him on the bench again.'

Counsel: Do you know what Dennis had done to cause this thrashing? – I think he had had a bite out of a swede. He thought Gough did the thrashing with a thick stick because the thin one had broken off. The day before Dennis died he got up but kept falling down.

In the evening when Terence returned from school Dennis was in a cubby hole, a dark place in the kitchen. He was locked in as Gough had put a nail in the latch ... He (Terence) did not get any tea that day because when Mrs. Gough asked him to get some dry bracken he said he would not be able to find any because of the snow.

On the Sunday night before Dennis's death he was sent to bed early and left Dennis in the kitchen naked. He heard Dennis crying and when Dennis came to bed he was still without his clothes.

Gough came up later, pulled Dennis away and smacked him across the face. He said that if they made a noise again he would throw them downstairs.

Later, because Dennis was crying, Gough came upstairs and put his knee on the bed, Dennis was lying on his back and Gough thumped him on his chest with both his fists.

Earlier, Dr. Andrew James Rhodes, pathologist at the Royal Salop Infirmary, Shrewsbury, said that at a post-mortem examination on 11 January, 'he found ... that he was very thin and wasted. There were extensive bruises on the chest, the result of a series of blows struck with some violence. There were areas of ulceration on the feet and the back of the right leg was severely chapped and cracked.' Dr. Rhodes said there were other ulcers on the left foot which must have caused extreme pain.

'There was a large number of recent bruises on the back, one five inches long, running towards the right shoulder and crossed by another four inches long.'

'His examination,' he said, 'showed no natural cause for the boy's death'.

The surprising verdict was not one of murder, as one might imagine, but that of manslaughter. However, there was a case of murder of an evacuee, that of six-year-old, Patricia Ann Cupit, and it became front page news:

> Unwilling to risk the dangers of a city in wartime, a young RAF sergeant and his wife searched the country for a haven for their only child, a girl of six. A friend in London told them, 'I will show you the safest place for her. I have a sister in a tiny village who will look after her.' So last summer little Patricia Cupit went to live in the village of Wrigglesworth in the heart of the Norfolk countryside at the cottage of Mr and Mrs Paske.
>
> Patricia died yesterday after being found stabbed in a peaceful copse in the village. Mr Cupit and his wife hurried from London when they heard of the discovery. They arrived at the hospital before the child died but she did not regain consciousness. Her foster mother, Mrs Paske, told me last night, 'Patricia was the most adorable child in the world – all the village loved her. A policeman sat by Patricia's bedside throughout the night hoping that she might give some clue but she never spoke.'

Despite Patricia being unable to identify her killer, the police did arrest the culprit, as revealed in *The Times* of 18 July 1942, under the headline 'Death Sentence for Murder of Child Evacuee':

> Sentence of death was passed by Mr Justice Wrottesley at the Central Criminal Court yesterday on James Wyeth, 21, a Private in the Pioneer Corps, committed from East Haring, Norfolk, who was found *Guilty* of the murder of of Patricia Ann Cupit, a 6½-year-old evacuee, who was found unconscious and suffering from head wounds under some bushes at Wrigglesworth Park, near Thetford, on May 5, and died the following day.
>
> For the defence it was urged that Wyeth was insane at the time he committed the act.

The case then went to appeal, and this was reported in *The Times* on 26 August:

> The Court [of Criminal Appeal] dismissed the appeal of James Wyeth, who was convicted at the Central Criminal Court of the murder of Patricia Ann Cupit … Mr F.J. Alpe [for the appellant] said

that the child was killed on the morning of May 6 last in Riddlesworth [*sic*] Park, Norfolk. There was little dispute as to the facts of the case, and the defence was one of insanity.

The appellant had made a statement to the police authorities in which he said on the day in question he was working as a member of the Pioneer Corps, on a munition shed. He saw the child pass by, and the idea came over him to follow her. He did so and took her by her clothes and dragged her under some trees out of sight and did not remember anything more until he saw her lying on her face in front him with blood all over her face. He returned to his work and later, thinking he had done something very wrong and made a statement to the police.

On behalf of the appellant, a doctor was called at the trial who said that he believed the appellant was telling the truth when he said he did not know what had happened when he attacked the girl. He (the doctor) believed his statement, partly as a result of his examination of him, and partly because he knew that the appellant had two blood relatives who were detained in mental homes.

Counsel said that the ground of appeal was that the judge had misdirected the jury in failing to call their attention to the evidence of insanity in the appellant's family.

Mr Justice Humphreys, giving judgement, said that in opposition to the medical evidence was given by the senior medical officer in the prison in which the appellant was detained, who said that he could not accept the theory that the appellant had suffered from any lapse of memory after the commission of the crime, and that from his daily contact with him he could find no ground for saying that the appellant did not know what he was doing, or if he did know, he did not know that it was wrong. It was for the jury to express their view as between the doctors. It was, of course, further necessary that the law should be correctly stated by the Judge.

In the opinion of the Court there had been no misdirection, and, that being so, the appeal must be dismissed.

Despite this judgement, Wyeth was later classified insane. He was reprieved from the death sentence and instead sent to Broadmoor Prison by order of the Home Secretary.

Perhaps the strangest case of all was that of a host family whose evacuees had driven them to commit suicide and murder! William James Reid, a former Acting-Governor of Assam Province in India, had, it was said in the *Glostershire Echo* of 25 November 1939, since the start of the war 'largely lost his sense of proportion'. According to a neighbour, Mr Reid said that his wife could not cope with the children that had been placed with them.

'He asked me to go over with him, on his wife's behalf,' said Mr Charles Prettejohn, 'to try and get the evacuees taken from the house. Afterwards he was very dissatisfied because I know he got rather short shrift'. He said that the evacuees 'depressed' him. Mr Prettejohn continued: 'It was owing to his intense fondness for his wife that he attempted to get rid of the evacuee children billeted with them … He told me he was quite sure his wife could not carry on.'

Doctor W.L. Scott described what he found: 'Sir William had a gunshot wound in the chest. Lady Reid had a wound in the head, and, apparently had been shot from behind … it could not have been self-inflicted.'

The jury at the inquest reached the conclusion that Sir William 'murdered his wife and shot himself while of unsound mind'.

Chapter 10

'We Will Take Care of Them'

The Wartime Foster Families

M ost of the wartime foster parents have long since passed away, though their relatives are eager to share their family stories. In addition, surviving letters sent by foster parents to the evacuees' parents give an intimate glimpse into their lives.

In some cases, lasting friendships were formed between both parties. Frances Gillies remembers the day that her family took Clydebank evacuees into their home:

> The evacuees were mainly from the Whitecrook and Elgin Street schools. Many of their fathers were shipyard workers and the mothers were torn between staying in Clydebank with their husbands or being evacuated with their children. I was kept well away from the hall where both my parents were working on the day the evacuees arrived, but by evening we had our own quota – a mother and her five children.
>
> We made Dad's study into a living room for them and offered them a couple of bedrooms upstairs, but after the first night they were not too happy with that and chose to live and sleep together in the study – presumably they were not accustomed to so much space. Many of the Glasgow evacuees returned home within weeks only to become victims of the Blitz.[1]

A report in the *Campbelltown Courier*, dated 30 September 1939, supports Frances' testimony regarding the rapid return home of some of Glasgow's evacuees:

Almost half the children evacuated to Campbelltown from Glasgow nearly a month ago have returned home. Out of a total of 445 children, 253 remain in the area. It seems that the mothers are to blame for the return of the children although they have good excuses for doing so. Most of these women had only been used to short trips away from their native city and on very rare occasions did they really go into the country.

It is logical that when they arrived at farms, after the first few days of wonderment in their new surroundings, chronic homesickness should develop and the craving to get home finally overcame them. Letters are passed between husband and wife, each telling of their different troubles, until eventually one or either of them cracks up with the result that the mother goes then the children go and after the families have left, the baggage is sent on after them.

When evacuees from Bristol arrived in Bideford, Devon, Mabel Steer took Micky Archer into her home. Mabel's grand-daughter, Val Morrish, shares the family story:

When seven-year-old Micky arrived at Bideford railway station, he had already been allocated to a local business family. However, because of the colour of his skin they felt unable to take him in. My Gran had lost two of her four brothers in the First World War and was on her own. She immediately stepped in and said she would be happy to have him. I am given to understand that he was the only coloured child at that time in Bideford. She grew to love him dearly and always referred to him as 'my Micky'. I am extremely proud of my Gran as she did recount a few times that there was some surprise at her taking the little boy into her home. Micky remained in contact with my Gran until she died.[2]

Margaret Nolan's family offered a home to two brothers when a group of evacuees arrived in Ramsbottom, Lancashire:

Norman and Ronnie came from Bradford, Manchester and they came with nothing, no pyjamas or anything. Our Lesley and John took them to Bury Market on the first Saturday and bought them pyjamas and a suit. Norman was quite happy about this but Ronnie never really settled with us, although we made them both welcome. They had no idea about setting a table or anything which surprised us as they had come from a family.

One Sunday we decided to take them to visit their home and have a look at where they lived. The little cottage was so small that when their mother opened a sideboard drawer it knocked over a bottle of milk which was on the table. We realised then what a vast difference there was between their life and ours.

Ronnie was not happy when he had to come back with us but after that they settled. Occasionally their mother and sister visited us and eventually Ronnie was allowed to go home. Norman stayed on until he left school and we became fond of him. By then the war was all but over and he had to start work so his mother came to collect him. Sometimes Norman and his pals used to visit, cycling up from Bradford.

One Sunday about six of them arrived, saying, 'We've come for our tea Auntie' and they were absolutely ravenous. We just made them as much as we could. That night, after they'd gone, we didn't have a scrap of bread in the house but we were pleased because the lads were full![3]

Linda Mitchelmore's mother, Bessie Giles, looked after evacuees Kathleen and Marina Skelton at the family home in Wales:

My mother was always a rather stern woman who showed little affection, and I have no photographs of her smiling. Yet in all the photographs taken of her with the evacuees, she is smiling and she looked after them wonderfully. She was a skilled dressmaker, her grandfather had been a tailor and taught her all the skills. She made lovely coats and clothes for the girls even though their own mother could have afforded to buy them clothes. Mrs Skelton came to visit them now and again, by car, at my mother's home in Park Terrace, Sarn, near Bridgend. My mother told me that Kathleen and Marina were very bright academically too. She must have cared very much for Kathleen and Marina because she carried their photographs around with her all her life - through eight house moves and a change of country from Wales to England.[4]

Judy Jones' family provided a home for Roger and Ruth Davy, a pair of evacuees from Gosport in Hampshire:

I was born in 1942 and during the war Mum and I lived at my Auntie's house, between Mold and Denbigh, because our Dad was in the Navy. Roger and Ruth lived in the house with my Uncle and Aunt, Mum, me and four cousins, so there was quite a crowd of us! We had no gas or electricity and only had cold water – any hot water was boiled on the fire. We did not have a bath and the lavatory was in the back yard. Roger and Ruth went to school with my cousins and were treated exactly the same way as we were, as part of the family. They were taken everywhere with us, including days out to Rhyl.

Their mum and dad used to visit them and they too became part of our extended family – Uncle Don and Auntie Betty. When the war ended we used to visit them in Gosport. Ruth was my sister's godmother and she and her fiancé, Harry, often came to stay with us. We attended their wedding in Gosport.[5]

Ruth Harrison remembers the day when her mother chose an evacuee in Cheshire:

My Mum was about to choose a Guernsey girl to take home with her, and was told by a rather posh WVS lady, 'Don't worry dear, we will find you a decent one!' My mum was appalled and I will never forget her reply, 'They are not commodities, madam, they are children!' We then took home a little girl called Winifred and she became like my own sister.[6]

Jean Flannery's aunt and uncle, Nellie and Reg Cutts, lived in Bletchley, Buckinghamshire, and cared for Joan and Marjorie Hart, aged eight and four, when the youngsters were evacuated from London. Jean recalls:

There was a houseful in my Aunt and Uncle's three-bedroomed Cambridge Street home! Along with my mother Kitty, my father (when, rarely, home on leave) and me after I was born, they looked after Joan and Marjorie (Marj). Both were loved and were apparently thrilled when I was born! When my mother went into labour they were sent to stay with a neighbour, coming back to the surprise of a new baby.

Marj was her mother's favourite and she really missed home. However Joan, the elder, loved living in Bletchley. She was very happy there and told me later that she could do nothing right for her mother. Even as a young girl she had to scrub a long tiled hallway on a Saturday morning, along with other chores. Marj was allowed out to play but Joan was kept in until she had cleaned the floor to her mother's satisfaction.

With us, she was allowed to just be a child. After the war Joan did not want to go back to London. She felt quite out of place at home and miserable at school. She said that her days in Bletchley were the happiest of her childhood. Joan always considered herself as part of our family. She came to family celebrations and the funerals of my aunt and uncle, whom along with my father and mother she always thought of as hers, too. The last time I saw Joan was at my father's 90th birthday party.[7]

Fred Jones remembers meeting their evacuee, Joe, for the first time:

Dad read us newspaper reports about kiddies from the Channel Islands needing homes. I didn't know where the islands were and Dad said that they were part of Britain but on a map they were very close to France. He said, 'Maybe we should take one of them, a little boy, so you can play together?'

Mum took me to the church hall and we saw Joe there. He looked so scared. Mum said, 'Would you like that little boy to come and live with us?' and I said 'Yes please.' He shared my bedroom and was like a brother to me. Mum couldn't have any more children after she had me and Joe was like her second son.[8]

Sheila Da Costa's family also cared for evacuees from Guernsey:

I was eight years old and remember the excitement of being told that we would be taking in a family to give them a temporary home. We took in Mrs Hafner, her daughter Nell and her son Ted. My father had a large premises with a barber's shop business so we were able to accommodate them comfortably. Nell was a very small baby at the time and her brother Ted was in his early teens. We enjoyed having them with us and made them very welcome.

Eventually they were rehoused on Wellington Road in Stockport where we used to go and visit them occasionally on a Sunday. Mum kept in touch with Mrs Hafner when they returned to Guernsey in 1945 and we went on holiday a few times to stay with them and tour the island. They made us very welcome.[9]

Phyllis Hanson was seven years old when she was sent from London to Newdigate, Surrey. She was cared for by a widow, Mrs Ada Tullett, who also cared for several other evacuees. Mrs Tullett and Phyllis' mother wrote to each other during the war and Mrs Hanson treasured these letters until her death. Mrs Tullett wrote the following letter soon after Mr Hanson had visited her home:

I was sorry I could not say much to Mr Hanson and his brother when they were down but Mr and Mrs May turning up and had such a cold, felt downright bad that Sunday, and all the next week. I really thought I should have had to give in but there was no one to come and help me as they were all down with the flu. But thank goodness I'm feeling better again now – the children have both had bad colds but they play and eat well so nothing to worry about – the old lady will hang on – up and down – hope you are both well and safe at home, no bombs. We have had a nice quiet time lately. Must close to catch post. Cheerio, all the best to you both.[10]

Whilst Phyllis had been sent to live with Mrs Tullett, her three-year-old sister, Pat, had been sent with Honor Oak Nursery School to Birch Grove House in Haywards Heath, Sussex. Birch Grove House was the home of Lady Dorothy Macmillan and Harold Macmillan – the latter, of course, would become the British Prime Minister in 1957.

On one occasion, the nursery staff wrote to Mrs Hanson regarding Pat's progress:

Dear Mrs Hanson, it was awfully nice of you to send me those cigarettes for Christmas and I appreciate them very much. Thank you. I wonder how you are faring these days. We have had quite a quiet time though we have heard the planes zooming towards London. Pat is well; I have spent the last three weeks in her nursery as different people have been on their Christmas holidays so I've seen quite a lot of her. She was very pleased with her Christmas presents and loves her black doll. We have all had a very happy jolly Christmas and plenty to eat. We had quite a bit of snow down here and for several days the country looked really lovely. I expect you will be down to see us again soon. With best wishes to you and many thanks, much love from Patricia.[11]

In 1942, Pat, who was now five years old, left the nursery and moved into Mrs Tullett's house where she was reunited with her sister, Phyllis. All went well until 1944 when Mrs Tullett sent this urgent letter to their mother:

Dear Mrs Hanson, I am sorry to say that Pat has had another bad throat so I called in the Doctor and he has sent her away to Redhill Isolation Hospital as there is symptoms of diphtheria. So I have to keep Phyllis home from school for seven days. The visiting days are

Wednesdays and Sundays from 3 o'clock until four, I cannot tell you about getting there, not knowing about the buses. I cannot go while the other girls are home. She went off quite happily as there is another little one from their school.[12]

Some children never came home after being admitted to isolation hospitals. On 31 January 1942, the *Leek Post* advised readers of the death of a young evacuee:

Master Alfred Charles Harrison, aged 12 years, passed away at the Isolation Hospital, Leek. Alfred was one of Leek's first evacuees and was residing at 2 Sandon Street, with his Mother. At the funeral, four boys represented the Leek Council School, all of them being evacuees. Floral tributes were received from the following: Mother and Sister; Aunt and Uncle and Family; Friends and staff at the Isolation Hospital.

When British schools were evacuated, the teachers who travelled with their pupils became virtual foster parents to the children. Cut off from their own families, they took on a huge responsibility. They not only educated the children, but kept a check on each child's billet and health. They monitored their behaviour within the community, helped older children to find work and provided comfort. When Derby School was evacuated to an open air camp, the teachers became foster parents to no less than 200 boys. Elisabeth Bowden lived at the camp where her father was the resident Master and chaplain:

When we moved into Amber Valley camp in June 1940, the school numbered around 200 boys. We were the only complete family living in the camp and we lived in a bungalow which was very small for three children and two adults. Mother had a very small kitchen with a stove and hob and she would cook for us, or we would have camp meals. The other masters were billeted around our camp. It was a huge responsibility for those adults in charge of 200 boys. Mother had some petrol because she drove the emergency vehicle. Several times she had to take boys with broken arms, limbs and that sort of thing, to hospital.[13]

In May 1940, a young Ben Howard was evacuated with fellow pupils from Catford Central School to Sayers Croft Camp, near Cranleigh in Surrey:

Our teachers were presented with a serious problem. They were now responsible for schoolboys twenty four hours a day, every day and none of them had boarding school experience. There would be no school holidays. After discussion it was agreed that every teacher would be on duty for eleven days out of fourteen. There would be some sessions off during that time but they would have to remain in camp.

All teachers had a main subject but they had to give instruction on whatever the syllabus demanded. If they had no knowledge of the subject of the lesson, it usually turned into 'Current Affairs.' There were occasional outbreaks of child diseases like Scarlet fever and measles. The healthiest dormitory, having the least illness, was right next to the camp sewage disposal unit![14]

When the Guernsey Intermediate Boys School arrived in Oldham, Lancashire, their teachers visited the billet of every boy. It was important to ensure the boys' good behaviour, to check the suitability of the foster parents and to maintain good relations between all parties. Likewise, when Guernsey's Forest School arrived in Cheshire, their Headmaster, Percy Martel, stayed in constant touch with the families that cared for his pupils. His wartime diary gives an indication of the huge responsibility he felt for his pupils:

> I have acted for the best, no one has been able to guide me. This is where responsibility tells. I have done as I would have done for my own. Duty called, the evacuation was ordered so I left, determined to do all that I could for the children of those who were remaining behind.[15]

Caring for evacuees was seen as part of the war effort, but not every household was willing to take them in. When the Duke of Argyll refused to take in women and child evacuees, the matter was raised in parliament:

> His castle was practically uninhabited, having in it only the Duke and his staff. There were all those bedrooms available but instead of putting the people into it, they were put into a local hall in the most degrading conditions. There was far less sympathy and help from the occupants of that castle than from the poorest members of the community.[16]

Another case arose when a farmer refused to take in three evacuee girls: 'The farmer said, "I am not taking girls. I will have one big boy because he can work on the farm." Let us be clear. These children are not sent out to be drudges in the homes or farms.'[17]

In 2013, Geraldine Barker discovered that her grandmother, Jesse Woods, had treated her two evacuees as unpaid servants.[18] When Geraldine heard of their experiences, she contacted Faith, one of the evacuees, to express her regret. Looking back today, Geraldine states:

> My late mother, Rene, upon moving to Suffolk, unsuccessfully endeavoured to contact the girls. I now understand why Faith and Stella were elusive; they had no intention of speaking to Jesse Woods' daughter. Unbelievably, my grandmother, who was always loving towards me, had been cruel to her charges. Yes she was rather 'showy', always dressed well, and desired a home full of new 'things'. Yes, she was self-centred and perhaps to maintain a harmonious atmosphere was indulged by my grandfather. These factors may have influenced the treatment of the evacuees, but it does not fully explain their experience. Jesse's father aspired to be a member of the Victorian middle class and rising from humbler origins would have been conscious of his achievement and social standing. My grandmother married a self-employed carpenter, perhaps not as socially acceptable and resulted in her efforts to 'keep up appearances'. Moreover, the Victorian idea of self-improvement through hard work was instilled in her via the role model of her father. The toxic mix of both character and upbringing were likely to have created a narrow biased attitude towards the evacuees, indeed she considered them poor, a fact she related to my mother.
>
> However there was one further twist, Jesse did not want two evacuees and this caused her resentment and inability to give comfort or love. To keep up appearances her charges needed to behave impeccably and were overworked to instil Victorian values of hard work to achieve in life. My dear late mother worked long hours and may have been oblivious to the evacuees' treatment. Even if she had witnessed the conduct she could not remonstrate, my grandmother would not be criticised. I cannot provide a definitive answer. After having her own children, the plight of the evacuees would have appeared abhorrent to Mum; the thought of her own six year old daughter being sent away and treated so poorly would have been a burden to her. She probably wanted to say sorry to Fay and Stella on behalf of her mother.[19]

Some families refused to keep the evacuees who had been sent into their homes. After one month, a Cheshire family asked for the removal of a

Guernsey evacuee from their home: 'Can you find another home for her? I simply don't have the time to look after another child as I already have two of my own.'[20]

Wartime newspapers often describe court cases involving families, who, for various reasons, refused to keep evacuees. The *Stockport Advertiser* cited one such instance: 'Mr and Mrs Jones of Offerton were charged with refusing to accept an evacuee. The clerk pointed out to the couple that it was unpatriotic of them and they were fined.'[21]

On 18 January 1941, the *Leek Post* reported on another example: 'For failing to accept two evacuees Mr. William Wardles Sales of Leek was fined two pounds and ten shillings costs at Leek police court on Wednesday. This was the first case of its kind to be heard in a local court.'[22]

There were more cases when hundreds of London evacuees fleeing the flying bomb offensive arrived in Leek later in the war:

> Three Leek people were each charged with failing to comply with a billeting notice and total fees and costs amounted to over £40 were imposed. The defence in each case constituted a plea of poor health and in 2 of the cases lack of domestic help also. Mr Horace Bowcock was charged with failing to comply with a billeting notice on the 25th of July, and with a similar offence on the 27th of July. The Clerk read a letter from Mr Bowcock stating he was unable to comply with the notices during the past 5 years. His wife has been in poor health and has constantly been receiving medical attention. At the time of the billeting notice they were expecting his wife's unmarried sister who was ill to come from Macclesfield on a visit. They had only 2 bedrooms and a small room which was used as a study.[23]

Chapter 11

'I Had Mixed Feelings'

Saying Goodbye

On 8 May 1945, the war in Europe was finally over and millions of evacuees celebrated 'Victory in Europe' in their local communities. Marie and Mona Martel recalled that, 'At long last the great day arrived, the war (in Europe at any rate) was over and there were great celebrations. A huge street party was arranged for everyone, with food appearing from nowhere on a long line of tables.'[1] In Nottingham, effigies of Hitler and Mussolini were burned in the streets, whilst in Glasgow the ships of the Clyde sounded their sirens. Winifred West attended celebrations in Blackpool: 'There were crowds by the North Pier, my sister and I heard Churchill's speech through loudspeakers and we went absolutely mad and shouted!'[2]

Lloyd Savident was at the cinema when he heard the news:

> I was in the Crescent in Moss Side and they stopped the film to say that Churchill had made a speech and the war was over and the Channel Islands were to be freed. I returned to the Fittons, who were looking after my sister and I. They had already heard the news and there were street parties.[3]

On 9 May 1945, one day later than Churchill had hoped, British forces began to liberate the Channel Islands. Thousands of Channel Island evacuees enjoyed another day of celebration and the BBC recorded the liberation of Guernsey as it actually occurred. In Yorkshire, Ted Hamel heard the broadcast: 'To us, this was the greatest broadcast ever! It was moving in the extreme and technically perfect. The lapping of the water could be clearly heard as the launch carrying the German commander

161

drew alongside. We sat there, not knowing whether to laugh or cry.'[4]

A report on the Pike family appeared in the *Burnley Express* and demonstrates just how many evacuee family members had been scattered throughout Britain:

> The liberation of the Channel Islands came as welcome news to the evacuees of whom there are a good number in Burnley. In our photograph, Mrs Mary Pike and five of her children are seen gathered around the radio listening to the good tidings. Though they will be sorry to leave Burnley and the many friends they have made here, Mrs Pike and her family – her husband is working in Manchester – will be ready to return home as soon as they are given the word. The photograph on the top of the radio is of Mrs Pike's eldest son, Herbert, who is a prisoner of war. On the left is 4 year old Barry who was born in Burnley, behind him his 9 year old sister Pamela. Alan is 18. Monica, aged 21, escaped with her father, uncles and grandparents in a fishing boat after the Germans had occupied the island. Pearl is only 8 and she can scarcely remember her home. Two other daughters, Hazel and Odette, attend the Guernsey Ladies College, evacuated to Denbigh. Noella is at school in Cheshire, and Ronald works on a farm in Cheshire.[5]

The end of the war prompted a flurry of thanks from parents to the wartime foster parents and George E. Greenhalgh, writing from 15 Beaufort Avenue in Manchester, sent his thanks via the pages of the *Leek Post*:

> May I express from your column my deep and sincere appreciation of the kindness and affection shown by many people in Leek to my youngest daughter, Estelle, who was probably the youngest unaccompanied evacuee to arrive in Leek at the outbreak of war. She was not quite 4, when she left home with her haversack nearly as big as herself and a determination to carry her own like the older ones. She is now 9 and is due to return home after living with Mr and Mrs Porter of Strathmore, Higher Woodcroft.
>
> Mr and Mrs Porter and their family have indeed done a worthwhile job, and mere words cannot really express our gratitude to them and their many friends who took the child to their hearts and helped to build her up into quite a big girl. She will not forget her Leek friends and will probably pay many a visit in the future to the people she has learned to love. To Mr and Mrs Porter, Joyce and Bert, to her Sunday and day school friends and to all who have

helped Estelle in her long stay in Leek. I wish to say a great big heartfelt thank you.

As a group of London mothers and their offspring was about to depart the town of Bury, Lancashire, one of them made her feelings plain:

> Leaning out of the train carriage window, Mrs N Percival of Deptford expressed the thanks of the 3,000 mothers and children who came to the town last July when the flying-bomb menace was at its height. 'Please give our thanks to the Bury people. During the 11 months we have been staying here they have been most hospitable and we shall never forget the many kindnesses they have shown to us.'
>
> When the last farewell had been said the train steamed away with youngsters and parents leaning out of the carriages waving to a crowded platform.[6]

As shown in this account, newspaper correspondents were often present to capture the emotional moments when evacuees left their foster parents and friends to return home. Their reports also indicate some of the complications surrounding the return home of evacuees. Some had lost their homes or members of their families in air raids. In addition, a new housing act had been passed which dictated the conditions that had to be in place before children were allowed to return to their parent's homes. A Norwich reporter stated:

> The first official party of women and child evacuees belonging to the Metropolitan area to return to their homes left Norwich by special train this morning. They totalled 180 and amongst them were some who had been in Norfolk since two days before the beginning of the war. All in the party were people who had homes to go to. A number of children who came here unaccompanied by their mothers will be escorted back to London a few days later and a number of families whose homes were destroyed will have to remain in Norfolk until the housing situation in their home areas is more favourable. A number of babies born in Norfolk, including six in Norwich, were on a special train which also carried household pets such as dogs and cats as well as a quantity of furniture and personal luggage. A number of the Norfolk hosts gave the party a good send-off.[7]

An article in the *Picture Post* described the scene as evacuees left Llanelly, Wales:

Mrs Megan Morton, a mother of three young children, is leaving. She wants to get to her home in Crofton Park, Brockley, to put it right after its blasting, before her husband gets back from Germany so that things will be the same for him. But it is a sad return to London for her; her parents were killed last August by a flying bomb.

The villagers come out to say how sorry they are to lose the evacuees. Some frankly cry, others smile unconvincingly. One of the village men lifts a foster mother up to the window so that she can say a few last kind words as the bus is about to leave, carrying evacuees to the train. Mrs Bessie Jones of Tycroes, wife of a collier, has six children of her own, but saying goodbye to baby Hall of Shepherd's Bush is painful to her. The baby's father, now stationed in Egypt, has never seen him. One young evacuee, Anne Burns, will stay in Llanelly for a while but she comes down to the train to see her playmates off. The odysseys of London evacuee families are almost over, except for those who have no homes to go to and those whose homes are not fit for children to live in.

The new Act, which controls overcrowding, forbids more than an average of two adults to occupy one room in any house. 7,000 teachers have been assigned to see that the family homes of unaccompanied evacuee children are fit for them to live in.

There are still thousands of children who cannot return at all, because no one wants them, because their parents have been killed, cannot be found or are involved in domestic difficulties that can better be solved without the presence of a child. There are also more difficult cases, which involve moral and sanitary standards of homes, where parents are entitled to the children if they demand them, but where their children are far better off in their present billets. Fortunately the good people who have cared for them are, in most cases, eager to keep them as their own. And the children of course want to stay. Parental consent however is necessary and in many cases the welfare of the child must be sacrificed to the obstinacy of an unsuitable parent.[8]

Understandably, there was a delay to the return of Channel Island evacuees. Homes had been destroyed or rendered uninhabitable and the atmosphere of occupation remained with the existence of fortifications, piles of live ammunition and barbed wire. Evacuees were duly informed that, 'The immediate return to the islands of a large number of persons would create very serious problems of accommodation and unemployment.'[9]

In the meantime, thousands of postcards and letters flew back and forth across the Channel between evacuees and their families. Tony Blampied received one from his Guernsey grandparents: 'Dear Tony, I remember a little fair baby, who did not walk. What is he doing now? How does he like school?' However, these long-awaited communications often contained unwelcome news. Mrs Ingrouille, for example, discovered that her mother had died during the occupation whilst Nick Le Poidevin recalled: 'Sadly the first letter that I received from Guernsey told me of my paternal grandfather's death nine days after the liberation.'[10]

Some parents were afraid that they would not recognise their children when they returned home after five years apart, as one newspaper report reveals:

> These are anxious days for Guernsey parents, they fear that they will not recognise their own children when they return after five years' stay in England. One or two said that they were unable to sleep, thinking that they might be unable to pick their children out ... Some parents have received photographs of their families to help them identify the arrivals. Others have had telephone calls. One father admitted that his son's voice was like a foreign tongue and that he could not understand what he had said because of the accent his boy had acquired after five years in Scotland. Mr R Bichard pins his faith in recognising his son Roy because of his red hair which he had been informed, had not changed.[11]

From late July 1945, Channel Islanders began to return home, although some decided to remain in England, as this Lancashire newspaper reported:

> Bury recently said goodbye to its London and South country evacuees and within the next few months most of the town's Channel Island guests will go back to their lovely sun swept homes on Jersey, Guernsey and Sark. In fact the exodus began on Tuesday when three families began the long awaited journey south. About 100 families and other evacuees are awaiting news when they can return, but not all those who escaped before the arrival of the Nazis will go back. For many have gained employment here while others have decided the wider, more active life of a Lancashire industrial town is preferable to life on the islands.[12]

On 21 July 1945, the *Guernsey Star* described the arrival of children from England:

They cheered as the ship berthed, promptly swarmed on to the quay, shouting and cheering and talking loudly in North country accents. Some of them carried puppies and one youngster had a hen and brood of chickens in a cardboard box – a present for his family. Customs officials pounced on him, gravely explaining that it was forbidden to import livestock, and took hen, brood and box into their custody. More than 500 people gathered near the harbour Clock Tower where emotional reunions took place.

When child evacuees all over Britain returned home, either at the end of the war or beforehand, they often not only had to reconnect with their families but also had to meet new brothers and sisters who had been born during the war. Many also had to leave behind the foster families with whom they had formed strong emotional bonds.

The situation was different for each family, but was almost certainly influenced by factors such as the age of the child when evacuated, the quality of the relationship between the child and its natural parents, and the quality of the care given to the child by the foster parents. Many evacuees were delighted to be returning to their own families whilst others had mixed feelings. For some, it was effectively evacuation all over again as they struggled to readjust to life at home.

Lily Dwyer did not want to leave her foster family in Gresford, Wales:

Memories of my Liverpool home faded, then suddenly my mother came to take me home. Mrs Bee came to me and said, 'Your Mummy is coming to collect you.' She had just bought me a bicycle and I went into the garden, got on the bike and rode round and round, I wanted to scream because I was leaving Mrs Bee and going back to Liverpool. Mum collected me and I wanted to scream as it happened. She was expecting her fifth child and I think she needed me to help with the younger children. I hated leaving Wales and Mr and Mrs Bee and their daughter Mary, but as always, I quietly accepted my fate. Mum took a large suitcase away with us so I assume that the lovely clothes Mrs Bee had made for me were in there. I never saw those clothes again, perhaps Mum had to sell them because she was so hard up? I was back to poverty and a bombed Liverpool. The house I had left in 1939 had been bombed out so we had moved into a place over a fish shop. I didn't remember my sisters either. The first night I got home I had to get into bed with two sisters in ONE bed who I didn't know at all. One of them was crying, saying 'This girl is kicking me!' – as she didn't know me either. I became a sort of housekeeper for Mum.[13]

Keith Llewellyn left his wartime foster parents, Auntie Elsie and Uncle Harold, in Brighouse, Yorkshire, to return to Crayford:

This blissful life eventually had to come to an end and all evacuees in the town were brought to the Town Hall for a farewell tea. We were given an orange and a shilling to come away with. Shortly afterwards I said a very tearful goodbye to my foster parents and got on the train still crying. I now tell everybody that I left Crayford in tears and came back in tears. Looking back, I should have stayed there, but it was not up to me. It was, what J.B. Priestley called, a 'Dangerous Corner'.[14]

Adelaide Harris was deeply upset when she had to leave her foster family:

I really loved living with Mr and Mrs Wright and their daughter Renee. Mr Wright worked on the railways and unfortunately he was killed whilst at work. At the time, Mrs Wright was pregnant with her son Arthur, and she still kept me, despite losing her husband. When our school was sent back to Hull at the end of the war I didn't want to go. I was so used to living with Mrs Wright. When I returned home, I cried for days which wasn't nice at all for Mum and Dad. I also missed Arthur and Renee very badly.[15]

Richard Singleton will never forget the day his mother suddenly arrived at his Welsh billet:

She had come to take me and my brother home to Liverpool but we had been happily living with Aunty Liz for four years by this time. I told her I didn't want to go home. Ron, Aunty Liz and I were crying, so in the end Mam just took Ron and said she would be back for me. I was still crying when Ron left, and I really missed him.

When Mam came to visit again it was just like the last for me, crying and not wanting to go. Aunty gave me a pen and pencil set, plus the New Testament that she had given me when we first arrived. Mam wanted me home because I was coming to the age of leaving school, fourteen. I cannot remember leaving – I was too upset to think of leaving Tancwarel and never seeing Aunty Liz and

Uncle Moses and everything that I loved on the farm. I was being taken somewhere that I never wanted to go.[16]

One boy remembers that the little girl who had lived with them for five years did not want to return to her parents: 'She had forgotten them completely and was dragged kicking and screaming out of our house. It was very upsetting for us all.'[17]

A foster mother in Oldham, Lancashire, remembers the day that her evacuee left her home:

When we had taken little George in, years before, I never thought for a minute how hard it would be for us to let him go. We waved goodbye as long as we could and then turned and walked away, neither of us could speak, we were too upset. We went to the pictures. I don't know what we saw but we couldn't go home you see, his little room seemed so empty.[18]

Terence Frisby remembers leaving his foster parents:

When we boarded the Cornish Riviera train for Paddington I was ten-and-a-half, Jack was nearly fifteen. Auntie Rose and Uncle Jack saw us off. Ten shillings a week per evacuee was the official allowance, and in return they'd given themselves without stint. Was there ever such a bargain? They were without guile and without self-interest. 'The salt of the earth,' is the saying. And if ever the earth needed salting, Auntie Rose and Uncle Jack were there to do it. Amid the huffing and puffing of the engine and the stationmaster we said our farewells. 'Give my respects to your mam and dad, write soon. Oh we'll miss you boys,' Auntie Rose repeated.

Doors were slammed, flags waved, a whistle blew. 'Goodbye, Auntie Rose, Uncle Jack,' we shouted. 'Goodbye, boys. Look after your –' he choked, stopped, tried to grin at us and failed miserably. Unheeded tears ran down his cheeks.

Auntie Rose cut in. 'Oh, now don't cry, Jack, for God's sake. You'll start me off.' And she started to cry. The train moved forward. We hung out of the window, waving furiously, and the train went past Railway Cottages above us, where neighbours were waving at the wire fence. We began to round the curve in the line so we could only just see the platform on which Auntie Rose and Uncle Jack were standing, still waving back: last sight of our own Rock of Ages and her bloody-minded bantam. Soon we were in Plymouth and on our way back to our half-forgotten home.[19]

James Roffey, who later formed the British Evacuees Association, left the West Sussex village of Pulborough, in his case in 1943, well before the war's end:

> I received a letter from my parents saying they had decided that I could, at long last, return home. This was the news I had eagerly awaited for the past four years ... I rushed around the village telling everyone my news, but on the actual day of leaving I experienced feelings of sadness which I did not understand. Within days of returning to London I was missing Sussex. Very soon I was expressing my total dislike of London and its way of life.
>
> In retrospect I realise I must have been a real pain to my parents and I feel guilty about the way I treated my mother. Ever since evacuation day in 1939 she must have yearned for the moment when her family would again be reunited. She probably remembered me as her little eight-year-old boy who used to run around the house singing, but he had gone forever and in his place had come a rather serious, self-reliant boy of twelve who made clear his dissatisfaction with his home and surroundings; who often would say that as soon as he could he would return to Sussex.[20]

During her evacuation, Mavis Robinson's parents had moved to nearby Newport where her father had found work at a munitions factory. For a time, she lived with both families on a rota basis:

> I was not able to live with my own family at first. We had an interim period of time-sharing – weekends here and there – so that my wartime foster parents could get used to the idea of my leaving them. Eventually I did go to Newport to live with my family. By this time all of my family felt that we were part of my foster parents' family and stayed in touch with them until they had all passed away. When my husband and I visited their grave recently, I grieved over their loss but rejoiced that life had become richer for us by knowing them.[21]

Douglas Wood recalls how he did not want to return to his family in Birmingham:

> During my evacuation I had only seen my mother twice and my father once. On the day that they visited me together, they had walked past me in the street as they did not recognise me. On 23 November, 1944, a taxi arrived in Rolleston to take me home to them in Birmingham. It was a very tearful farewell indeed. I did not want

to leave my aunts and they did not want me to go. Going home was a very traumatic and sad experience. I no longer had a Birmingham accent and this was the subject of much ridicule. I had lost all affinity with my family so there was no love or affection. When my father returned home from war service the situation become worse with some violent domestic disputes.[22]

In Portrush, Northern Ireland, William Crawford received a telephone call from his father's friend, Uncle Hubert, in Belfast. William's son, Bruce, shares the family story:

Dad was told to get himself to Belfast as quickly as he could, and to get ready to meet his parents. He didn't really know what the message meant, but was granted permission from his housemaster. He took a train to Belfast, and then trolleybus to Uncle Hubert's house near Stormont.

Dad was met at the front door by Uncle Hubert who urged Dad to be quiet, and to make his way into the living room. As he went into the room Dad saw two people, a man and a woman, his Mother and Father who had his head turned away in conversation with someone else. Dad says he was quite dumbfounded and quite overcome, and recalled tears in his eyes (indeed as he spoke about the reunion meeting his eyes were quite red.)

The woman, his Mother, asked 'Are you William?' Dad doesn't really recall answering as such, but probably just nodded through his teary eyes.

His Mother then said 'Matthew, are you going to say hello to William?' Matthew turned away from his conversation and towards Dad and said, 'Are you my son?'

Dad and his Father shook hands, Dad didn't want to let go. He said that in that moment a void that had been in his life, one that he hadn't really understood, was filled. He sat next to his Mother who held his hand as if she would never let him have it back, and so tightly it hurt Dad, but he couldn't say anything about the pain. He was allowed a few days to stay with his parents, and they all went to Dublin to meet his sisters again. Dad said there were a lot of silences, often quite awkward. I think no one knew what to say or how to say it. There was no counselling for these sorts of events in those days.[23]

When the war ended, Alderney evacuee John Glasgow remained on the mainland, with his foster parents, for a little longer:

My father was demobbed from the Army and came to Winchester to be near me. He lived in lodgings and worked in the Prison service and also carried out sign-writing for a coachbuilder. I remained in the home of my wartime foster parents, Mr and Mrs Grant. I think father felt his war was lost, having lost his wife and home and perhaps felt it too painful to return to Alderney. He then went to Guernsey lodging with people he knew at St Julian's Cafe, St Peter Port. He began working again, as an artist, painting and sign writing and then moved to a single storey chalet style bungalow on the Esplanade. Once settled there he thought I could rejoin him. In the Spring of 1947 I left my foster home and returned with him to Guernsey. My foster mother was heartbroken.[24]

Mrs Ursula Malet de Carteret returned to Jersey to discover, as did many of the returning evacuees, that things were, putting it mildly, a little different than when they had left. Ursula, for one, found that her home had been ruined:

In July 1945, Guy and I got permission to go over to Jersey. We stayed in the Manor which was completely empty except for the Turkey carpet in the Big Dining room. Apparently the Germans came into the house soon after landing in July 1940. It was used for troops but there were officers in charge. The house was dirty, gun racks, bunk beds everywhere upstairs. What happened to all the small pieces, curtains, carpets, linen etc – we shall never know.

There were dumps in the town where items from many houses were taken for people to claim. We only found one picture. In 1942 there had been a fire in the White drawing room, the whole of that wing was gutted. When we had left the island in June 1940, we had left our Ford car at the pier then boarded the boat. During the war it had been used by the Germans and we now had to buy it back from the British![25]

For Dorothy King, the return home to London in 1945 was an unexpected disappointment:

It wasn't the joyous homecoming I'd waited for over all the years. Our school building had been bombed and we had to make do with inadequate patched up classrooms. Our homes were shabby with war damage and neglect. The London suburb I returned to could offer none of the entertainments and activities I had enjoyed in Bedford. My mother was still working and, worst of all, I missed my friends. It had taken me four or five years to adjust to being an evacuee. Now I found the readjustment just as difficult![26]

Some evacuees who were now in their teens were disappointed with their prospects when they returned home. Janet Day was unhappy with employment prospects in London: 'For six years, I had been growing vegetables in my country billet and loved working in the fresh air. When I got home there was only factory work.'[27]

Irene Hawkins was another disappointed former evacuee. 'After all that education in England I ended up scrubbing floors! Guernsey seemed so small after the wide roads in England and the wide open spaces of the Cheshire countryside. After six months I returned to live on the English farm where I had been billeted!'[28]

Peter Aves recalls the uncomfortable two day journey home to Guernsey:

On 24 October 1945 my mother and I, plus her sister Daisy, caught the Boat Train to Southampton - we were booked on the *Isle of Jersey*. When we boarded her we heard the *Hantonia* that had sailed the previous night had returned to Southampton after suffering damage from a large wave. Her 336 passengers were transferred to the *Isle of Jersey*.

We sailed at 10 pm but with conditions deteriorating, the captain decided to anchor in the Solent until daylight. At 6.30 am she ups anchor and steams into the Channel but a decision is made to divert to Cherbourg because of the dangers of trying to enter St Peter Port harbour in such bad weather.

On 26 October at 11 am the anchor was raised and the ship headed to Guernsey in difficult conditions making only six knots at best, she arrived off St Peter Port and berthed some forty-two hours after leaving Southampton. During that time I couldn't eat and any fluid I drank quickly ended up in the scuppers![29]

Guernsey teacher Ruby Nicolle returned home after an anxious four-month wait:

In September 1945, we were asked to take back fifteen boys and girls who had left school during the past five years. They were scattered around the Manchester area and we all met at London Road station, as well as Wally, our cat, in a wicker basket, to start our journey back to Guernsey. We stayed the night in London in a church hall and went on to Southampton the next day, arriving in Guernsey at 3.30

on September 21st. There was a joyous reunion at the harbour, my fiancé, relations, children's' parents etc – a wonderful day.[30]

Bob Cooper returned to his family in Islington in 1943. 'Our old house had been damaged by bombs so we moved to Dalston. I attended a new school and because I had picked up a Cornish accent, I stood out a bit, but I was able to stand up for myself and soon lost the accent again.'[31]

John Noble had a similar problem when he returned home to Lewisham: 'I went home and discovered that I spoke differently to the local children. I was a little Yorkshire lad in South East London and had some playground fights as a result.'[32]

When Jim Marshall returned to Rochford, he left behind the luxurious surroundings of a manor house in Bream: 'It was very difficult. I was now fourteen years old and Rochford was unfamiliar to me, as were my parents. It was a life changing experience as during the war I had lived in the lap of luxury, but in 1945 I had to return to reality.'[33]

Lily Dwyer had also lived in luxury. 'When we left Lady Partington's huge house to return to Lowestoft, it felt awful,' she recalled. 'Mum and Dad felt like strangers and the house was so small, like a rabbit hutch! Worse still, we had to go outside to go to the toilet.'

Lourdes Galliano's family endured a difficult journey back to Gibraltar, only to discover that most of their possessions had been stolen:

On 23 December 1944 the best Christmas present of the world was given to us. We were on the list for the next boat which sailed to Gibraltar in the New Year! We spent the next few days in a state of euphoria, happily making plans for our return. We packed our shabby clothes, scruffy shoes and a few meagre belongings and left to board a ship called the Cap Tourain. We had been out at sea a few days when it was suggested that I should keep my life jacket close to me at all times as there were a number of enemy submarines patrolling our route. We were part of a small convoy and one night, off the coast of Portugal, we were all asleep in our cabins when there was a horrendous crash. The ship jolted and I fell out of my bunk. The lights went out and there was a lot of noise, sirens wailing, babies crying and everyone wanted to know what had happened. We thought we had been torpedoed!

The ship was listing as we groped our way to the saloon which was our meeting point in case of emergency. Some very dim lights came on and an officer appeared to guide the way and to reassure us. He then told us that, sailing in the dark, another ship had collided into us. It had made a large hole in our side near the bow and they were trying to assess the damage. Luckily the hole was just above the waterline and it took twenty-two mattresses to fill it up! When at last we were able to move again, we found that the rest of the convoy had gone ahead. We had to follow them slowly to avoid the water getting into the hole. Would we make it to Gibraltar?

Dawn broke and eventually we saw land through the mist. Excitement mounted as we waited for our first glimpse of the Rock after four long years. It was a most emotional moment. A shout went up and we all exclaimed 'There it is, at last, there!' We jumped for joy, embracing each other and laughed and cried at the same time.

When we had left Gibraltar in 1940, we were told our flat would be requisitioned by the army and to place all personal belongings and small pieces of furniture in one room. This was locked and officials came and put a seal on the door. We were assured that nothing would be touched. However when we returned home, we discovered that the sealed door had been forced open and most of our things had disappeared. There were no sheets or blankets and there was not a single toy or game or book.

Gone was the beautiful doll's house which my grandfather had given to his first granddaughter and to which we had been adding carefully over the years. My parents' bedroom furniture was made of mahogany and we found the dressing table and wardrobe were stuck with huge nails where the service men had hung up their helmets and gas masks. Everything looked shabby and worn out but we were just happy to be back. We had lived through so much hardship that we were ready to accept anything. So we cleaned and polished and put up curtains and started to learn how to take up our lives where we had left off.[34]

Brian Russell's mother had died three weeks after their arrival in England and six years later he and his brother returned to Guernsey with their father:

It was not until 1946 that Dad came to Dorset to collect us, with a lady friend who he later married. They came in the dead of night and they were strangers to us. They took us back to Guernsey where we were introduced to grandparents and aunts that we did not know. It was so confusing. I would ask Dad questions about our Mum but he had no interest in talking about her – and he was suffering from shell shock as a result of the war.[35]

George Osborn returned to his mother in Portsmouth without his sister, who had died of blood poisoning during their evacuation:

> Mother mourned Brenda's death for the rest of her life, which I could understand. But my mother, in her worst moments, blamed me for being alive instead of Brenda, which doesn't make for a close mother and son relationship. I found Portsmouth to be a city almost in ruins and I was a virtual stranger in my own city. I could never do anything right, according to my mother. This undermined my already low esteem and confidence. 'You're just like your father' (he was in a psychiatric hospital) had undertones of accusations of insanity. If I offended her in any way, she would not speak to me – sometimes for weeks on end. I remember on one occasion she never spoke to me from Easter to Whitsun, and that was six weeks.[36]

John Martin's mother was horrified by her son's appearance when he finally returned home to Dagenham:

> In my final billet, I had lived in Burnley with people who didn't seem to know how to look after children and I didn't see my parents at all. When I returned home, my mother didn't recognise me and said that I had turned into a 'dirty, scruffy street urchin'. I also spoke in a way that she couldn't understand as I had developed a North Country accent. The first thing she did was to put me in the bath then she threw away the scruffy old clothes I was wearing and cooked me a proper meal. I had been away for two years.[37]

John Mallett remembers seeing his parents after five long years of separation:

> I was shipped back to Guernsey and upon arrival at the quay we had a long walk from the ship to where the awaiting parents were, behind barbed wire barriers. These had been erected by the German occupiers and had not yet been taken down. When I was about a hundred metres from the meeting point, I could recognise all my family. My Father, who had never been a hugging, cuddly person, somehow got through the barbed wire although he tore his trousers. Then he started running towards me and I started running towards him. I was home.[38]

Many British evacuees never returned to their family homes. Those who had been evacuated as adults decided to remain in the communities in which they had settled. Child evacuees remained with their foster parents because their own parents had passed away or could not provide a secure home for them. Many child evacuees were now in their teens and had found promising employment or become engaged to local people. The Ministry of Health took note of this, stating:

> These young people may be eligible for maintenance grants, or billeting allowances may continue for the present. Authorities should arrange for friendly supervision by some appropriate organisation or individual after this boy or girl becomes financially independent; it is undesirable that young people earning relatively high wages should be left without some guidance.[39]

Peter Hopper did not return home when the war ended. His mother had died when Peter was six months old:

> My father was invalided out of the RAF with tuberculosis, so at the end of the war it was decided that I should continue to live in the Willis household as a foster child. Rose Willis and I always had a good relationship. Her husband, Ted and I had a reasonably good relationship in the early years, but I felt a growing resentment as I grew more independent and rebellious in my teens.
>
> It came to a head when he made a violent attack on me, because of a remark I made in trying to defend his wife (Auntie to me) from verbal abuse. I realised later that I should not have tried to intervene between a man and his wife. However, his behaviour gave me cause for concern and certainly would not have been tolerated in today's society. Ted Willis was bigger and stronger. He pinned me down on the bathroom floor, putting his hands around my throat, throttling me. I could not fend him off, so his son, Douglas, then in his early twenties, intervened to save my life, pulling him away.
>
> The police were not called, but had that incident occurred today, my foster father would have at least faced a charge of assault on a minor. As it was, I was the one unfairly banished from the house for three weeks, staying with a friend while things cooled off. Although I was eventually allowed back into the foster home my continued presence in a house with Ted Willis was a fearful one. There was no apology for the violent incident; somehow it was deemed my fault. Unfortunately, there was worse to come. Auntie was to die, tragically, at the age of sixty-two, taking her own life after husband Ted left the family home following a break-up of the marriage, the

result of his physical and mental cruelty and infidelity. A court case was looming in the very week of her suicide.[40]

When John White and his brother were evacuated from London to Essex, they never saw their parents again:

> It was a great life in Rayne, a lovely, warm cottage in the countryside where Fred and I were always out roaming and soaking in Mother Nature. To us, animals were things we had never seen before. In London we had only seen dogs, cats and pigeons but in Rayne it was a like a different world. When the war finished I was eleven and Fred was twelve and whilst most evacuated children returned back home, that idea was not one that we were too keen on getting on board with. For me, the thought of going back home to Edmonton never arose. I didn't want to go back. I also felt that my mother never wanted to have us back either.[41]

Channel Islander Mr Rumens decided that his family should remain in England as he had a good job with a detached house and garden. In late 1945, they briefly returned to Guernsey to collect their belongings. They found the house intact, containing all their possessions. However, their neighbours asked Mr Rumens for payment for this five-year 'caretaking' service. He had to sell some of their possessions to pay this.[42]

Marion Wraight remained with her foster family after the war:

> When the war ended, I was twelve years old. My brother Bill went back home to Margate but came back again after a day or so, as our Mum couldn't afford to look after him. I didn't go back to Margate in the end as my wartime foster mother, Auntie Millie, asked Mum if we could stay with her. I was fine about it all, they never officially adopted Bill and I; Mum wouldn't consent to it.[43]

John Payne's family never returned to London:

> When the war ended my mother and I and my siblings stayed in Stanton as our home in London had been destroyed during an air raid. Mum did consider going back but decided that Stanton was the best place for us. We were all happy and had more or less adapted to the country way of life. In 1950 we moved to Shepherd's Grove aerodrome where our accommodation was disused Nissan

huts made from galvanised tin, very cold in winter. We remained there for seven years then moved into a brand new council house. I am glad my mother made that decision not to return to London but she never got to enjoy life in our nice new house as she died shortly before we moved in, just forty-nine years old, after a short illness.[44]

Richard Smith had been evacuated from Guernsey to England with his mother's friend, when he was sixteen months old. He was another who never returned to his Guernsey home.

My father, who was stationed in the Isle of Man, had found me in England so during the war I was cared for by his 'lady friend' and her parents. I was too young to remember my mother, and I had always been told that she was dead. Years later, in England, when I was married, my father, who had rarely contacted me, told me that my real mother was alive and living in Ellesmere Port! She and I met in Chester where I discovered that I now had a sister.[45]

Derek Dorey was also adopted by his wartime Lancashire family:

I then became Derek 'Pilling' and I had everything in Bury with the Pillings, a better life than I could have had if I had gone home to Guernsey. I think that's why my mother allowed me to be adopted by them at the end of the war. Sadly, the law said that I could not contact my birth family again, once I had been adopted. I was only young so I hadn't realised that this would be the case. I never saw my mother again.[46]

Chapter 12

'It Shaped My Life'

The Aftermath of Evacuation

How did wartime evacuation affect the lives of all those concerned? John Welshman once wrote that 'the feelings of love and separation experienced by the evacuees had a significant effect on them at the time and in their subsequent lives.'[1]

Some children faced a huge conflict, having a loyalty not just to their own parents, but to the foster families that had cared for them. For some, the evacuation left lasting emotional scars or destroyed family relationships. For others, it offered new experiences, a wider experience of life and increased opportunities for education and employment.

In the post-war years, evacuee reunions have allowed people to reconnect with other evacuees to share wartime experiences and come to terms with wartime traumas. Reunions also allow them to examine how the evacuation actually shaped their lives.

In the 1990s, Grace Fry reflected on five years of caring for a large number of evacuees in Scotland. She admitted that it had deeply affected her life: 'It was the evacuation that decided me, well and all, that I was not going to get married and I was not going to have children. Because during the war I had had enough with all this!'[2] Similarly, Mrs Tippett found it difficult to return to the traditional role of housewife and mother after the war. Her son, John, recalled, 'During our evacuation, Mum worked, paid the bills and looked after us whilst Dad was in the forces. It changed her outlook and ideas on what women were actually capable of doing.'[3]

June Somekh's evacuation left her with lasting emotional scars:

Having been away from my parents for four years, I had become very attached to Miss Smith, her extended family and Winster. I didn't think my parents had neglected or abandoned me. In fact my father always sent pocket money for all of us and my mother, the most generous person I have ever known, often sent goodies for us. Many, I am quite sure, are things she would have enjoyed herself.

We each returned home when we were ready to go to our secondary schools. Mother, especially, was very keen for us to have a good education. I am not sure how this, further disruption, affected my siblings as we rarely discussed feelings, but I felt devastated. My parents must have been heartbroken. I was very bitter and resentful and I know I said some very hurtful things which, even now, I am not prepared to repeat. A lifetime after the event, the scars are still there.[4]

John Helyer's evacuation damaged his relationship with his Guernsey parents. 'First of all, I did not know what my parents looked like, I had no photos. When we met I didn't understand them and they didn't understand me. We had all sorts of problems – it didn't work out like I had expected. And my father died a few months later.'[5]

Rex Carre also returned to Guernsey, leaving behind his loving foster parents, 'Auntie and Unk' Morgan in Oldham:

I found settling in after the return far worse than my parents realised as I kept it all bottled up inside. After the first flush of family feelings, my relationship with my father showed up as far less happy than it had been with Unk. I think subconsciously, I bitterly resented having been 'left to it in 1940' and I have reason to believe I was not the only Guernsey refugee to feel that way. My father did not really want me to continue my education at Elizabeth College for the Higher School Certificate and certainly not university. However my mother had solemnly promised Unk that I would go as he was convinced I would do well. I was admitted to Elizabeth College but did not appreciate the absurd amount of sport or the ridiculous Corps we were forced to join by Major Caldwell. However I tried to keep quiet about all this as my father's reaction to any complaint was always 'Why don't you leave?' I am eternally grateful to Johnnie Martel, Deputy Head of the Castel School, who helped me get into Southampton University.

I kept up regular contact with Unk and Aunty Morgan and my mother and I went to Oldham for the first post war Christmas. Then Aunt and Unk came to Guernsey for two summer holidays. It was just wonderful to be with them again, and they enjoyed the comparative peace and quiet, and the beauty of my island. I passed my 2:1 Economics Degree and Teacher's Diploma and applied for jobs wherever Grammar schools were advertising. I received two invitations for interview – the first in Oldham, the second at my old school in Guernsey. I was offered the Oldham post and my Oldham family were thrilled. Unfortunately Aunty and Unk had moved to Boston-le-Sands but I was able to go over and see them from time to time up to Unk's death. Aunty then went to live with her stepson in Oldham. I firmly believe that fate decided the pattern of my life. As Shakespeare says, 'There is a divinity that shapes our ends, rough-hew them as we will'.[6]

Bonds forged between evacuees and their wartime carers were often hard to break. Sheila Gibson stayed in touch with her wartime foster family until their death. 'I returned home in September 1944, but every year I returned to Derby, to visit Mr and Mrs Croft, their son Nigel and his wife. I attended Mrs Croft's 100th birthday party in 2012. Mrs Croft passed away at the age of 101 but I will always remember her with fondness.'[7]

Likewise, Percy Martel never forgot the kindness shown to his pupils by the people of Cheadle Hulme in Cheshire. In April 1946 as the Guernsey primroses came into bloom Percy sent 1,000 bunches to the villagers as a thank you. Douglas Wood remained in touch with his wartime 'Aunts', Edith and Kate: 'Auntie Kate died in 1949 but I continued to visit Auntie Edith. She came to my wedding and my 25th wedding anniversary. I visited her a few days before she died in 1989, three months before her 100th birthday. Being an evacuee with my lovely 'aunts' changed the course of my life. They will never be forgotten.'[8]

Philip Doran benefited from the influence of his Welsh foster mother, Mrs Roberts:

Of the seven of us [evacuees], I was one of the last to leave Mr and Mrs Roberts. This meant that, for some time, I had the benefit of having Mrs Roberts' kindness all to myself.

When I left school, having signed up as a seaman, I would write to Mrs Roberts telling her of my real life adventures and describing all the wonderful places I had visited. Many years later, after I'd married and had children of my own, I returned to Penlynn Farm. Tom had sadly died; his old war wound finally getting the better of him, but Mrs Roberts was there, still her same old self. Hugs and kisses all around and a sumptuous tea produced from nowhere.

I sat there listening to Mrs Roberts reminisce, I looked around the room and it took me right back to that happy time as an evacuee. I noticed little things that hadn't changed in all that time: there on the shelf was the little butter mould, which ejected the butter into its perfect shape, complete with a beautiful swan imprint. Despite its age and being riddled with woodworm, it still symbolised to me all that was good about Penlynn Farm.

After several hours and lots of chat we said our final goodbyes, not knowing if I'd ever see this woman again. It was a difficult moment saying goodbye to someone who had such an influence on your life, someone who gave us light when all around seemed darkness. My wife and children all thought that Mrs Roberts was a wonderful lady, she was indeed but she was more than that, she was an angel, my guardian angel. I'm sure that if there is a heaven, Mrs Roberts will be there, once again looking after all the little children, whilst poor old Tommy ... well, he's probably flying around in his best suit with 'Watney's Beer' stamped on his wings.[9]

Ron Gould stayed in touch with Miss Yearsley who had cared for him so well in Cheshire and remembers their final meeting:

My last visit took place in October 1984 and she was now in a nursing home. It was a shock to see her. Her only space was a curtained-off corner of a large room which she shared with a number of other old ladies, most also in a very sad state. We said goodbye to her, almost in tears, and she passed away in early January 1986. My wife Hazel and I felt the least we could do was pay our last respects so we flew from Guernsey to Southampton, hired a car and drove up to Hale, through the snow, for the funeral.[10]

Richard Singleton will never forget the Welsh couple who lovingly cared for him and his brother:

When, at fourteen years of age, Mam had taken me away from Aunty Liz and Uncle Moses and their farmhouse, to go home to Liverpool, I had cried bitterly. I next saw Aunty Liz when I took my own family on holiday to Bronant in the 1960s. I took them to Tancwarel Farm to show them where Ron and I were evacuated. Aunty was in the field where we had once reaped the hay and she had a dog with her. I gave her a hug and was going to kiss her on the cheek but I couldn't. She had cancer of the face. She told me that

Uncle Moses had died and she wasn't able to look after the farm.

We didn't stay too long, I was too upset – in fact I feel like crying now writing about it. We left the way we had come, across the fields over the stiles like Aunty, Ron and I did when we went to the village and chapel in the 1940s.

I returned to Bronant again in 1989 for an evacuee reunion and went into the chapel. I cried my heart out. The war was a terrible thing, but to me it didn't exist, I loved being evacuated. The cemetery was so small that it didn't take long to find the graves of Aunty and Uncle. My regret is that I never told Aunty that I loved her for giving me and Ron a wonderful life while we were under her care.[11]

Win de La Mare is still in touch with her wartime foster sister in England:

It wasn't easy to leave England, in fact, the truth is, I have never really settled. When I got back home to Guernsey, my mother had two more children, who I didn't know, and I often felt that I just didn't fit in.

Also I really missed Ruth, the daughter of the family that had looked after me in Cheshire. She had become a sister to me during the war. We wrote to each other when I got back, which kept me going, and we are still in touch now, and visit each other as often as we can.[12]

Dorothy King is another who treasures the kindness of her wartime family:

After the war I went back many times to stay with Mr and Mrs Waller in Bedford, even taking friends with me and really enjoyed being there. They came almost as often to visit our parents in London.

Then Mr Waller died – just as he was about to retire. They had moved to a comfortable little house on the other side of the town and Uncle had equipped an immaculate workshop for himself which should have given him years of pleasure. Mrs Waller lived on for several years, increasingly lonely and even rather embittered. A sad return for their hard working lives. Many years later, long after the war, when I was taken to see Mr and Mrs Waller's old house, empty, mouldering and awaiting demolition, I felt a surge of nostalgia.[13]

Len Page remembers his last meeting with his foster father, Mr Knight:

> After the war, I kept in touch with the Knights. Mrs. Knight died in 1972 and dear old Harry died in May 1987, aged eighty-nine years. Fortunately I went to see him three weeks before he passed away.
>
> By [then] he lived in an old people's home at Bicester, near his now married son Sam and wife Doris. We talked about the war years that I stayed with them; I always thought of him as my second dad and although I never got round to calling him Harry, I don't think I could ever show more respect than calling him Mr. Knight. Harry always introduced me to his friends as 'My little evacuee from London'.[14]

Terence Frisby also has fond memories of his wartime foster parents:

> Auntie Rose and Uncle Jack. Auntie and Uncle. Not father and mother but not distant either, just in-between relatives. In fact, of course, they weren't even that; they were our foster-mother and father, not relatives at all. But even now, seventy-three years later, I still cannot say their names without a full heart and a lump of gratitude in my throat. We stayed in contact with them both for years; indeed they came up to Kent for my brother's wedding. Then Uncle Jack died quite suddenly of heart failure and we lost touch with Auntie Rose who went to live with her son and daughter-in-law in Weston-Super-Mare.
>
> In 1988 I produced a radio play about my evacuation story and received a letter from Auntie Rose's granddaughter. Auntie Rose had told her stories of us both and she said, 'You felt like the brothers I'd never met.'
>
> We became friends with her and her family. She couldn't get to the first production of the stage musical in Barnstaple in 2003 so I sent her a DVD and she was in floods of tears because the actor playing Uncle Jack brought him exactly to life again. She was right, he did. Both my brother and I couldn't watch him and stay dry-eyed. She and her family met my son and his children at my book launch along with her cousin and we all now keep in touch.[15]

With the ties created during the war still strong, and almost unbreakable, Derek Trayler visited his wartime foster family many times:

> After the war my brother and I went back on separate occasions to meet our foster parents in Norfolk and their daughter came to stay

with us for a short visit. However, when Dr Beeching closed their railway line it become more difficult to get there.

By 1967, I had a wife and three boys, and we were on holiday on the Norfolk Broads. I found that we were not that far from the village we had stayed in 1940. I decided to take my family to see the place and hoped we could meet our foster parents again. I drove right though the village twice as I didn't recognise it at first. A place looks much larger when you are walking to school as a seven-year-old than it does in a car as an adult. We knew that the family had moved since we were there but had no new address.

We stopped at the village shop/post office and asked for them by name. The postmistress looked at me and asked if I was one of the evacuees. She directed us to our foster parent's new cottage and we spent happy hours remembering the time we spent together.

Our 'Auntie' mentioned that my eldest son was the same age I had been when I arrived. She also reminded us I had only been there for three weeks and had to go into hospital in Norwich to have my appendix out. This was reported in the National Press as, 'The first evacuee to be taken into hospital'. Three weeks after we came home from holiday my eldest son was taken in to Oldchurch Hospital to have his appendix removed![16]

Several evacuees have revealed how they were not encouraged to maintain contact with their wartime foster families after the war and their return home. Richard Titmuss believed that 'some mothers were afraid of losing the affection of their children to someone who appeared more important or who had more material things to offer'[17].

Alice Greenston wrote several letters to her foster mother in Scotland but never received a reply. 'I was upset,' she recalled. 'But a few years later, my mother me that she had ripped the letters up rather than posting them.'[18]

Jenny La Mare[19] was never allowed to mention her wartime 'Auntie':

My Guernsey mother did not want to hear me talking about my 'Auntie Maisie' in England, such as what she did for me, and how much I missed her. I soon stopped talking about my time in Lancashire, as I could see it upset my Mum. She felt I couldn't love both her and Auntie Maisie – and several of my school friends had the same problem.

Lily Dwyer was discouraged from writing to, or making contact with, her wartime foster family:

In the years following the war, I used to write to Mrs Bee's daughter, Elizabeth, and send her little drawings. One day I was doing a drawing for her and Mum came into the room and saw what I was doing. She took the letter off me and said, 'Don't write to her any more, you don't live that life now, you live here'. I now wonder if she had actually ever posted the previous letters.[20]

Some evacuees have revealed that they feel physically connected to their place of evacuation because of the death of a relative or foster parent. Valerie Sarre's brother died during the family's evacuation to Wakefield:

My mother, father and brother Alan were evacuated to Wakefield from Guernsey in 1940. Sadly my brother, Alan, died of scalding in 1941. My family had made friends with a Mrs Hampshire and her son, John, who were Wakefield residents and when my parents returned to Guernsey in 1945, the Hampshire's looked after my brother's grave for them.[21]

Sixty-eight years after leaving his foster mother, Geoffrey Durrant felt duty bound to restore her grave:

During the war my brother Malcolm and I were evacuated from Lowestoft to Glossop, where an elderly widow, Mrs Booth, took great care of us. When we returned to Lowestoft in 1943, my mother continued to correspond with Mrs Booth and in 1946 she received a letter to say that Mrs Booth had passed away. Malcolm and I would often talk about her and always remembered her in our prayers. Malcolm died in 2001 and in 2005 I was persuaded to join the Lowestoft Evacuee Group. I placed a letter in the *Glossop Chronicle* asking if anyone remembered us at Mrs Booths and received four replies.

After returning to Glossop in 2008 for an evacuee reunion, I began a quest to find Mrs Booth's burial place. It took two to three years to find it with the help of Sam Fielding and Ian Webster in Glossop. When I saw the grave, I was overcome. It would have been the icing on the cake if my brother had been there with me. It was in a sorry state so I asked a local stonemason to repair and restore it. It was a labour of love for a wonderful lady. We visit the grave every year with other evacuees and our good friend, Sheila Webster, places flowers on it at intervals on our behalf.[22]

For John White, the discovery of a family grave, seventy-two years after the end of the war, revealed why he had not been taken home in 1945 – a story that starkly reveals the tragedy surrounding so many evacuees' wartime experiences. John and Fred White had always assumed that their mother did not want them and John recalled:

> Years later I was amazed to discover that my mother had actually lived through the war. I'd always wondered if she must have been killed during the Blitz and that was why Fred and I never heard from her when the war ended. Seventy-two years later a friend tracked down my mother's name as she had remarried. I decided to visit her grave in Edmonton cemetery. I noticed that it was nicely kept and at the bottom of the grave was a rose bush which had just been watered. I wrote a letter and put it in an envelope in a freezer bag, saying 'Read me' and put it under a vase.
>
> My half-sisters found it and rang me. I found out that my father had died in 1943 and that my mother had remarried. I was told that there had been big family gatherings after the war and people would ask, 'When are the boys coming home?'
>
> However, Mum had told her new family that we had been evacuated to Australia, rather than just the countryside, and that we had never been found. Whenever she asked her new husband about us returning, he'd tell her that if we were to show up, he would sell the house and leave her! That explains why we never heard from her again.[23]

Many evacuees believe that through experiencing life away from home they gained a lasting sense of independence. They also realised that there was a different way of life available. For his part, Bill Smith developed a lasting love of horticulture during the war:

> All the gardening that I did whilst an evacuee in Dunning started my interest in horticulture. Before I arrived there I was a proper town lad. Now I'm vice-chairman of the Scottish National Chrysanthemum and Dahlia Society. I've been a committee member there since 1970 and I've shown all over Scotland and the north of England. I've won a gold medal for best vase in the national show, and some of the cups there. All that interest in growing things started right there in Dunning when I was an evacuee.[24]

Peter Hopper's evacuation to Skegness led to a career in journalism:

At the age of twenty, I joined the *Grimsby Evening Telegraph* as a reporter. Being a wartime evacuee actually helped me to get my first job as a journalist on the weekly *Skegness News* when I was only fifteen. I had no educational qualifications whatsoever, just enthusiasm. However, I became lifelong friends with Mrs Elsa Barratt, who had been the Evacuation Officer in 1939 and later became a Councillor, Chairman and Mayor of Skegness. Thirteen years after my unexpected arrival in the resort, I became a reporter for one of the two local newspapers and in 1953, a photograph was taken of me as a gawky, perhaps over-confident youth, dancing with Mrs Barratt at an official function. That year I was in her company almost on a daily basis, reporting on her year of office.

This began a forty-five-year career in journalism, during which I specialised in agricultural journalism. As Agricultural Editor of the *East Anglian Daily Times* for twenty-seven years, I travelled all over Europe; won two national and several regional awards; met several members of the Royal Family and received a presentation from Princess Alexandra of a framed print of the Suffolk Show at Ipswich in 1869. The presentation was for twenty-five years of coverage at the show. For the past eighteen years I have been an Honorary Life Vice-President of the Suffolk Agricultural Association and I even worked for Prince Charles on one occasion, writing an article on his visit to a Norfolk agricultural research station for his Highgrove Estate magazine.[25]

The opposite experience to those enjoyed by the likes of Bill Smith and Peter Hopper is that sadly many child evacuees endured traumatic experiences which still shape their lives. Edna Dart's experiences have left her with agoraphobia and claustrophobia:

The authorities didn't check on the people they put you with and I was physically abused by my foster father. It wouldn't be allowed to happen today. When I went back to my mother, she said she would never let me be taken away again. Those twelve months as an evacuee have shaped my life. I don't travel far nowadays, but when I do go anywhere, the fear only disappears when I'm returning home. Consequently, I haven't been able to go to the places I would've liked, because I wouldn't have felt safe. I've learned to control it to a certain extent, but not completely.[26]

Jean Bell cannot forget the cruelty that she and her sister experienced in South Wales:

It made me very sad to write my story down and I feel sorry for the two little girls that we were. We were very vulnerable at the time having been away from our mother from a very early age. I was very shy and withdrawn when we finally returned to London for good although my sister seemed to cope with everything much better.

My husband was curious to see the village in South Wales to see if it was as bad as I had painted it. I had absolutely no wish to return but a few years ago we were in South Wales when we finally went to see the village. My husband could not get over how run down and dirty it was. The mine had closed so I suppose there was no work for the men there ... I certainly have no wish to visit this village again.[27]

Some of the evacuees who had bad experiences or witnessed the unhappiness of others, began careers in child care when they left school. The dreadful experience of being constantly passed from billet to billet during the war certainly altered Sheila Whipp's future:

I decided to work with children in care because of my experiences during the war. Children didn't have any rights then about where they were placed. None of the billeting officers had ever asked me if I was actually happy. They never spoke to me, on my own, to see if I was OK. I was invisible. As a result, my childhood influenced my future and my career.[28]

Studies undertaken during and since the war have shown that many family relationships were irretrievably broken down because of evacuation. Susan Isaacs examined how the evacuation scheme impacted upon the welfare and education of school children who had left their parents behind.[29] The chief difficulty, Isaacs found, was the break in family life, and the survey concluded that any future evacuations should be planned with 'more understanding of human nature' by the authorities involved.

One report issued in Guernsey, where half the population had been evacuated, described the far-reaching effects:

The parental separation had a long term effect upon the children, persisting after the reunion with the parents. Of the fourteen children who had problems in adjusting to life on return to Guernsey, eight of these made a satisfactory adjustment after the initial difficulties. So for the population as a whole, the numbers of those who could have been permanently adversely affected by the evacuation could be very large.[30]

Marion Wraight's mother could not afford to support her after the war, so Marion remained in Staffordshire with her wartime foster parents. This had a huge impact on her life and on her relationship with her real parents:

> I left school at the age of fourteen and worked full time on my foster parents' farm. I then met a local farmer's son, became pregnant and was told that I had to marry him. It was a bad match and had a massive impact on my whole life. I had three children, then in 1972 John had an affair and our marriage ended acrimoniously. My Dad died in the 1960s in a mental institution and was diagnosed as a paranoid schizophrenic. Mum wrote to tell me about it but I didn't feel anything.
>
> After forty-two years of not seeing Mum, my daughter Christine and I decided to visit her. She lived in Canterbury by then. I was happy to see her but it was not very emotional. I also met my sister Lilian in April 2015, for the first time since 1938.[31]

Lloyd and Lorraine Savident were reported as 'killed in an air raid' on the day they arrived in England in 1940. Four years later, in 1944, their parents in Guernsey received a twenty-five-word Red Cross message telling them that their children were actually alive. Lloyd recalls:

> We returned to Guernsey after five years away from our family. A lady came up to us and said 'I am your mother, these are your sisters and your brother'.
>
> He was quite a bit older than me. I turned to my sister Lorraine and said 'I want to go back!' I felt completely lost.
>
> We went to our house and my Dad couldn't speak to us. Lorraine and I spoke English but the only English Dad knew was 'Hello' and 'Cheerio' – he [only] spoke Guernsey patois. This meant that we could not communicate properly.
>
> In addition, there was no bathroom or running water and the toilet was at the bottom of the garden, which took some getting used to. It took me a long time to get over our return home and Lorraine still says today that she found it quite traumatic.[32]

For Lourdes Galliano's mother, the stress and strain of the experiences brought on by evacuation ultimately shortened her life:

Seven weeks after our family's joyful return to Gibraltar my mother suddenly collapsed in the street and died of heart failure.

She was only forty-nine years old, but the war had turned her into a sick, worn out woman. We were thankful she was granted her wish to die and be buried in Gibraltar.

But once again we were plunged into deep sorrow at another separation, this time permanent. I was seventeen years old at the time. My father never recovered from this blow and became practically a recluse for a long time. It was then that we discovered that things could never be the same again. Gibraltar had changed, each and every one of us had changed. The old ways were to be no more. We began to realise then what a key role Gibraltar had played in the war as guardian to the entrance of the Mediterranean. But this had only been made possible by the Gibraltarians who had sacrificed their homes, their families and their way of life for four long years.[33]

The evacuation deeply affected the lives of Alderney evacuee, John Glasgow and his father. In the spring of 1947, John left Winchester and his loving foster parents to live in Guernsey with his father. For a child, the situation was not ideal:

We lived in a chalet style bungalow but my father soon recognised that he wasn't coping too well in looking after me. I was then billeted at a café, The Café Bon Bouche – the proprietors had a son of about my own age and we shared a bedroom. All was well until I was evicted from the cafe when it was discovered that the boy and I were smoking. Father and I then returned to Alderney where my father was independently able to support us both financially with his artistic painting. He would work without interruption for two or three days before stopping. Mealtimes if they existed were irregular.

Sadly he would sometimes become a victim of the Black Dog or mild depression. I believe this could have been the events of the past, losing his young wife, losing his home and other exigencies of the war. He began drinking. Always beer. In this he would seek oblivion.

This would cause anxiety to me and if he wasn't home I would expect the inevitable and go looking for him. Starting in one pub asking if my dad was there. No son, he has gone on. And so on to the next. In the late summer of 1947, my father needed to return to Winchester on business, among other things, stocking up on painting materials. He brought me with him and took me back to my foster parents, bliss. When it came to return, I didn't want to go back. I did love him but it was the lifestyle that was the problem.

After some heart-breaking discussion and counsel with some Channel Island people he knew in Winchester and could trust, he accepted the situation and returned alone, leaving me at my foster home. There had been a time when my foster parents were willing to formally adopt me, but understandably he didn't want this. He had made a promise to my mother.

In November 1947 I was surprised to hear from my father that he had remarried and that I had acquired a stepmother. Again he collected me from Winchester to return to Alderney leaving my foster mother heartbroken once more. After a few months it became evident that mutually my stepmother and I were not compatible and I was sent to a boarding school on Guernsey. Came the summer holiday of 1948 and my father asked me if I would like to go to stay with my foster parents in Winchester. I was sent a single plane ticket to Southampton Airport and I never returned to Alderney.

My father became terminally ill and died in May 1951. My stepmother wanted me back in Alderney and work. I tacitly refused, whereupon she tried to send me to Australia under the post war immigration scheme. Advised by my foster father, Uncle Fred, I sought professional help from our local church who took up legal advice resulting in my being placed in the technical care of the NSPCC with my foster parents becoming my legal guardians. In hindsight, my father ensured I was returned to a place of safety and loving care, just as I had been in 1940.

My foster parents died, Uncle Fred on 11 August 1985 at the age of eighty-three, and Ma on 13 August 1995 aged ninety-three. They lie together in Magdelen Hill Cemetery in Winchester. It wasn't difficult to consider an epitaph for their headstone. It reads, 'Remembering all their loving kindness'. This says it all for me and the countless others who received their kindness and care in some form or another during their lifetime.[34]

The organisation of evacuee reunions has allowed evacuees to reconnect after years apart and to give thanks to the communities which cared for them during the war. Memorials have been installed in many of the places where evacuees were billeted. Lowestoft evacuees hold regular meetings where they share wartime memories and a plaque has been placed at Lowestoft railway station. Some of the evacuees make a yearly pilgrimage to Glossop where they were billeted. The wartime presence of Ben Howard's school at Sayers Camp has been preserved for ever:

Early in 1942, the art master had the idea of painting murals on the blank chimney breasts at each end of the dining hall. Two talented boys were appointed to produce a design, each was to be fifty-four inches square and to take the form of fifteen diamond shapes. Each diamond to depict one of the camp's activities. The murals were painted in oils and kept a number of artistic boys busy for some months. They depicted various winter and summer activities and are now registered as war memorials.

Stained glass 'evacuee windows' have been installed in a number of churches. In Sudbury's All Saints Church there is such a memorial which was presented to the community by former evacuees from Manchester. The three schools that were evacuated to Kettering installed stained glass windows in the new St Edward's church. Each school had their school badge and motto set into their window.

Channel Island evacuees will never forget the families who cared for them during the war. On 9 May 1946 a Liberation Day Parade in Guernsey gave thanks to communities on the British mainland. Between 1945 and 1953, Guernsey sent gifts to many of the towns and villages that had cared for evacuees.

Evacuees from Jersey have installed a plaque at Weymouth and communities in England, Scotland and Wales which received Channel Islanders have installed plaques and memorials. Every May, Disley church, in Cheshire, raises the Guernsey flag in memory of the evacuees who came to their village. In May 2010 Guernsey held an evacuee reunion and unveiled a plaque at the harbour. In June 2010, a blue plaque was installed at Stockport railway station[35] and the Bailiff of Guernsey gave an emotional speech regarding the kindness of the wartime community.

In 1995, The British Evacuees Association was formed to ensure that the true story of the great evacuation would become better known and preserved for future generations.[36] Founded by former evacuee James Roffey, it aims to place on record the impact that the evacuation had upon communities throughout the United Kingdom, not just those in the departure areas, but also those in the reception areas.

After all, the events surrounding the evacuees are as much a part of the UK's wartime experiences as for those who fought on land, at sea or in the air.

References and Notes

Chapter 1: 'The Bomber Will Always Get Through' – Plans for Evacuation

1. For a detailed account of Government evacuation planning see Titmuss, R.M., *Problems of Social Policy* (HMSO, London, 1950).
2. Brown, Mike, *Evacuees of the Second World War* (Shire Publications, Oxford, 2009), p.12.
3. Testimony of Ester Nickson; author's collection.
4. Testimony of Lorraine Chadwick; author's collection.
5. Letter from Southwold Council, January 1939; author's collection.
6. *Leek Post and Times*, 16 March 1940, p.5.
7. Testimony of George Osborn; author's collection.
8. Testimony of Jean Noble; author's collection.
9. 'Notice for Parents of Birmingham Evacuees'; author's collection.
10. See Brown, Mike, p.11.
11. Logbook of Meon School, Portsmouth, courtesy of George Osborn.
12. Titmuss, R.M., p.93.

Chapter 2: 'A Huge Decision to Make' – The Parents' Dilemma

1. Roffey, James, *A Schoolboy's War in Sussex* (History Press, Stroud, 2010), p.11.
2. Undated letter from West Bromwich Grammar School, Bedford Archive Service.
3. Testimony of John Hawkins; author's collection.
4. Diary of A.D. Wilshere, August 1939; courtesy of George Osborn.
5. Testimony of Jean Hoban; author's collection.
6. Testimony of Anthony Pakenhem; author's collection.
7. Testimony of Jean Noble; author's collection.
8. Testimony of John Payne; author's collection.
9. *Hansard* (Commons) vol.35, col.828.
10. *The Times*, 26 June 1940.
11. Folkestone evacuation notice, 27 May 1940; courtesy of Andy Parson.
12. Testimony of Peter Campbell; author's collection.
13. *History of Earls Hall School*, Whaley Bridge Local History Library.
14. Testimony of Derrick McGarry; author's collection.

15. Testimony of Philip Doran; courtesy of Catherine Sing and Mike Paice.
16. *Hansard* (Commons) vol.351, col.830.
17. Read, Brian Ahier, *No Cause for Panic* (Seaflower Books, Jersey, 1995), p.9.
18. Journal of Ursula Malet de Carteret, 1940-1945: courtesy of the Malet de Carteret family.
19. Testimony of Rev Mr Milnes, June-July 1940; author's collection.
20. Testimony of Rachel Rabey; author's collection.
21. Testimony of Therese Riochet; author's collection.
22. Testimony of Hazel Knowles, *née* Duquemin; author's collection.
23. Testimony of Rex Carre; author's collection.
24. Galliano, Lourdes, *A Rocky Passage to Exile* (Aquila Services, Gibraltar, 1997), p.21.
25. ibid, pp.29-30.
26. Testimony of Gerry Mullan; author's collection.
27. Testimony of Dan Muir; author's collection.
28. Testimony of John Partridge; author's collection.
29. Howard, Ben, *From Brown Hill to Pitch Hill: The Wartime History of Two Catford Schools* (Sayers Croft War Memorials Preservation Fund), p.21.
30. *Blyth News,* 16 September 1939.
31. 'Evacuation and Air Raids: Effects on Children', *British Medical Journal,* 8 November 1941, pp.661-2.
32. Hill, May, *An RAF Mother's WWII Diary Blog - January 1944-December 1944: 'Sorrows and Salvation'* (Ambridge, November 2014).

Chapter 3: "Evacuation Begins' – The Journey

1. Jessie Hetherington, quoted on Discover Your History, http://www.history-hub.com/dyh.
2. Testimony of Maureen Brass, courtesy of Parish of St Edward, Kettering, quoted on www.stedwardskettering.org.uk.
3. Wilshere, p.2.
4. Testimony of Harry Flack; author's collection.
5. Testimony of James Martin; author's collection.
6. Testimony of Doreen Gates, née Frisby; author's collection.
7. Museum of English Rural Life, University of Reading, DDX1883/1; personal papers of Mary and Elizabeth Hodges.
8. Testimony of John Hawkins; author's collection.
9. Testimony of Ronald Eric Gould; author's collection.
10. Testimony of Lily Dwyer; author's collection.
11. Testimony of Marion Wraight; author's collection.
12. Testimony of Doreen Acton, née Mason; author's collection.
13. Testimony of Jean Noble; author's collection.
14. Testimony of Alfred Goble courtesy of Nathan Goodwin.
15. Testimony of Peter Campbell; author's collection.
16. Testimony of Peter Hopper; author's collection.

17. Testimony of Audrey Patterson, née Woodhatch; author's collection.
18. Testimony of Alan Boast, courtesy of Lowestoft Evacuee Association.
19. Testimony of Francis Rutter, courtesy of Melissa J. Rutter.
20. *Hansard*, (Commons) vol. 351, col. 852.
21. Testimony of John Mallett; author's collection.
22. Testimony of Irene Wood Taylor; author's collection.
23. Testimony of George Osborn; author's collection.
24. Testimony of Derek Trayler; author's collection.
25. Testimony of Ronald Brash, courtesy of Kelvinside Academy.
26. Testimony of Ralph Risk; author's collection.
27. Mawson, G., *Guernsey Evacuees: The Forgotten Evacuees of the Second World War* (History Press, Stroud, 2012), p.21.
28. Testimony of Merle Roberts, Weston family papers.
29. Minutes of Guernsey Education Council meeting, 28 June 1940, Le Pelley family papers.
30. Journal of Cliff Witchell, June 1940, courtesy of Judith Wilbourn.
31. Testimony of John Petit; author's collection.
32. Testimony of Violet Hatton; author's collection.
33. Read, Brian Ahier, p.51.
34. Testimony of Graeme Cox; author's collection.
35. Testimony of Marjorie Lewis, courtesy of Eric Brett.
36. Testimony of Grace Fry, Guernsey Retired Teachers Association.
37. Testimony of Frederick Veale, courtesy of Mr John Veale and Elizabeth Cannon.
38. Testimony of Philip Godfray, courtesy of Anne Mauger.
39. Testimony of Lourdes Richardson (née Cavilla); author's collection.
40. Galliano, Lourdes, pp.40-5.

Chapter 4: 'We Will Find You a Nice One' – The Evacuees' New Homes

1. Wilshere, p.3.
2. Testimony of Mary Sinclair (née Richardson), courtesy of Margaret Brown.
3. *Hansard* (Commons) vol.351, col.862.
4. Testimony of Ruby Nicolle, courtesy of Valerie Winder.
5. *Evening Times*, Glasgow, 11 April 2014.
6. Glasgow, John, *A Rolling Pebble* (John Glasgow, 2014), pp.19-24.
7. A stained glass window from Stockport Sunday School is preserved in the Stockport Story Museum.
8. Testimony of Mavis Brown, née Duquemin; author's collection.
9. Testimony of Hazel Knowles, née Duquemin; author's collection.
10. Testimony of Alfred Goble, courtesy of Nathan Goodwin.
11. Testimony of Sarah Murray, courtesy of Dunning Parish Historical Society, and quoted on www.dunning.uk.net.
12. Testimony of Sheila Brown; author's collection.
13. Diary of Jean Le Prevost, Le Prevost family papers.
14. Testimony of Grace Fry; author's collection.

15. Testimony of John Tippett; author's collection.

16. Gillian Mawson, *Guernsey Evacuees*, p.53.

17. Testimony of Joan Simon; author's collection.

18. *Hansard* (Commons) vol.351, col.870.

19. Testimony of Mr J. Savident; author's collection.

20. Testimony of Margaret Jones; author's collection.

21. *Hansard* (Commons) vol. 55, col.1230W.

22. Testimony of Anne Mauger; author's collection.

23. Testimony of Marjorie Townsend; author's collection.

24. Woodhorn Archive Service, CC/CM/CC/50/p.267, 1939.

25. Testimony of John Payne; author's collection.

26. Testimony of Mary Sinclair (née Richardson) courtesy of Margaret Brown.

27. Testimony of Frances Gillies, courtesy of Kelvinside Academy.

28. *Hansard* (Commons) vol.351 col.854.

29. Bury Archive Service, Channel Islands Evacuees, 6/2/9; Telegram from Sergeant Aylward, 26 May 1942.

30. Testimony of Peter St John Dawe; author's collection.

31. Testimony of George Osborn; author's collection.

32. Frisby, Terence, *Kisses on a Postcard: A Tale of Wartime Childhood* (Bloomsbury, London, 2010), pp.25-8.

33. Testimony of Peter Hopper; author's collection. Mrs Elsa Barrett later became a leading light of Skegness Urban District Council, but to Peter, she was always 'The Evacuation Officer'.

34. Galliano, Lourdes, pp.49-54.

35. Testimony of Harry Flack; author's collection.

36. Testimony of Irene Wood Taylor; author's collection.

37. Testimony of Norton Myhill; author's collection.

38. Testimony of Doreen Sporle (née Moss); author's collection.

39. Testimony of Philip Doran, courtesy of Catherine Sing and Mike Paice.

40. Testimony of Alan Boast; author's collection.

41. Testimony of Joseph Parry, courtesy of Becky Williams.

42. Testimony of Ben Halligan courtesy of Martin Jones.

43. Testimony of Barry Fletcher; author's collection.

44. Testimony of Derek Trayler; author's collection.

45. Woodhorn Archive Service, T539; Testimony of Kenneth Grant.

46. Northumberland County Council Report, 2 November 1939, CC/CM/CC/50/pp.266-267.

Chapter 5: 'It Was Like Another World' – First Impressions

1. Testimony of Audrey Patterson; author's collection.

2. Glasgow, John, pp.24-5.

3. Testimony of Derek Trayler; author's collection.

4. Testimony of Rita Roberts; author's collection.

5. Testimony of Ronald Eric Gould; author's collection.

6. Roffey, James, *The Evacuation of British Children During the Second World War* (Evacuee Reunion Association, Retford, 2014), p.64.
7. Jessie Hetherington, quoted on Discover Your History, http://www.history-hub.com/dyh.
8. Testimony of Philip Doran courtesy of Catherine Sing and Mike Paice.
9. Testimony of Bob Cooper; author's collection.
10. Testimony of Mavis Robinson, courtesy of Caerleon History Group, and quoted on www.caerleon.net.
11. Testimony of Richard Singleton; author's collection.
12. Testimony of June Somekh; author's collection.
13. ibid.
14. Testimony of Brenda Harley; author's collection.
15. Testimony of John Martin, courtesy of Ursula Martin.
16. Testimony of Peter Staples; author's collection.
17. Testimony of John Honeybone; author's collection.
18. Testimony of Richard Singleton; author's collection.
19. Clifford Broughton's story is courtesy of Cwmamman History website, and quoted on www.cwmammanhistory.co.uk.
20. Testimony of Jean Hoban; author's collection.
21. Testimony of Ken Chamberlain; author's collection.
22. Testimony of Eric Scott; author's collection.
23. Testimony of Ruth Alexandre; author's collection.
24. Quin, Olive, *The Long Goodbye* (Guernsey Press, Guernsey, 1985), p.50.
25. Testimony of Agnes Camp; author's collection.
26. Testimony of Rex Carre; author's collection.
27. *Daily Mirror,* 17 June 1940.
28. Testimony of Margaret Duquemin; author's collection.
29. Testimony of Derek Dunn; author's collection.
30. Testimony of John Honeybone; author's collection.
31. Testimony of Marion Gilbert, née Wraight; author's collection.
32. Memories of David Forbes, courtesy of Dunning Parish Historical Society, quoted on www.dunning.uk.net.
33. Frisby, Terence, pp.32-4.
34. Testimony of Alan Boast; author's collection.
35. Diary of Muriel Parsons, p.24; author's collection.
36. Testimony of Bob Gill, Guernsey Retired Teachers Association.
37. Testimony of Lawson Allez; author's collection.
38. Testimony of Ronald Eric Gould; author's collection.
39. Hamel, E.J., *X Isles* (Paramount, Guernsey, 1975), p.26.
40. Testimony of Len Robilliard; author's collection.
41. Testimony of Joan Wilson; author's collection.
42. Testimony of Mrs Evelyn Brouard; author's collection.
43. Roffey, James, *A Schoolboy's War*, p.20.
44. Testimony of Philip Doran, courtesy of Catherine Sing and Mike Paice.

45. Jessie Hetherington, quoted on Discover Your History, http://www.history-hub.com/dyh.
46. Testimony of John Windett; author's collection.
47. Testimony of Jean Noble; author's collection.
48. Testimony of George Osborn; author's collection.
49. Testimony of Marjorie Chilvers, née Parker); author's collection.
50. Le Poidevin, N., *Torteval School in Exile* (Seaflower Books, Jersey, 2010), p.32.
51. Testimony of Doreen Acton, née Mason; author's collection.
52. Testimony of Doreen Sheffield; author's collection.
53. Testimony of Jim Marshall; author's collection.
54. Testimony of Michael Stedman; author's collection.
55. Lang, Suzanne, *Displaced Donkeys* (Pinknote Press, New Zealand, 2009), pp.103-10.
56. Testimony of Len Roberts; author's collection.
57. Axford, Jessica (née Young), *I lived in a Castle* (Antony Rowe, 1994), pp.43-5.
58. Testimony of Vera Liniham, Marple website, quoted on www.marple-uk.com/woodville-hall.htm.

Chapter 6: "I Hope You are Safe and Well' – Contact With Home

1. Testimony of George Osborn; author's collection.
2. Roffey, James, *A Schoolboy's War*, p.120.
3. Roffey, James, *Send them to Safety* (Evacuee Reunion Association, 2009), p.43.
4. James Roffey, *A Schoolboy's War*, p.120.
5. Postcard in the Daniel Kirmatzis and Emanuel School Archive.
6. Telegram dated 2 September 1939, Miller family papers.
7. Frisby, Terence, pp.19-20.
8. ibid, pp.35-9.
9. Buckingham County Council archive, MB3/10/5/125; letter dated 6 October 1940.
10. Testimony of Elaine Pritchard; author's collection.
11. *The Telegraph*, 2 September 2009.
12. Britton, Phyllis, Britton, Sally, and Boulton, Alison, *Phyllis's War: An Evacuee's Story in her Own Words* (Windmill Hill, Bristol, 2015), p.17.
13. Letter in the Daniel Kirmatzis and Emanuel School Archive.
14. Imperial War Museum, Department of Documents, reference 6803; undated letter from Dorothy King to Mrs King. Private papers of Miss D.E. King.
15. Testimony of Dorothy Miller, née King; author's collection.
16. Undated letter from Mrs King to Dorothy King, Miller family papers.
17. ibid.
18. Museum of English Rural Life, University of Reading, DDX1883/1; Personal papers of Mary and Elizabeth Hodges.
19. ibid, DDX1883/2.
20. ibid, DDX1883/11.
21. ibid, DDX1883/7.

22. ibid, DDX1883/6.
23. Frisby, Terence, pp.93-6, and pp.199-200.
24. Letter from Geoff Wright, 3 November 1943, courtesy of Kelvinside Academy.
25. *History of Earls Hall School*, Whaley Bridge Local Heritage Library.
26. Testimony of June Somekh; author's collection.
27. Testimony of Lily Dwyer; author's collection.
28. Testimony of Len Page courtesy of Andy Parsons.
29. Letter from Mr Campbell dated 9 June 1940, courtesy of the Campbell family and Les Haigh.
30. Testimony of Ronald Eric Gould; author's collection.
31. Testimony of William Crawford, courtesy of Bruce Crawford.
32. Testimony of George Osborn; author's collection.
33. Testimony of Marion Gilbert, née Wraight; author's collection.
34. Testimony of Roisin Toole, courtesy of Parish of St Edward, Kettering, and quoted on http://www.stedwardskettering.org.uk.
35. *Hansard* (Commons) vol.351, col.1466.
36. Letter from Frank Le Poidevin, 24 June 1940, Le Poidevin family papers.
37. Letter from Derby School, 4 June 1940, courtesy of Gordon Lancaster.
38. Testimony of Gordon Lancaster; author's collection.
39. Testimony of Ben Howard; author's collection.
40. Truro newspaper cutting, 8 August 1940.
41. Testimony of Dorothy Miller, née King; author's collection.
42. Testimony of Peter Staples; author's collection.
43. Testimony of Richard Singleton; author's collection.
44. Testimony of Barry Fletcher; author's collection.
45. Parents' Visiting Day notice, early 1940, Hanson family papers.
46. *Hansard* (Commons) vol.351, col.1341.
47. Testimony of Jim Davey; author's collection.
48. Testimony of Philip Doran, courtesy of Catherine Sing and Mike Paice.
49. Testimony of Jean Griffin, née Pare; author's collection.
50. Testimony of Marjorie Chilvers, née Parker; author's collection.
51. Memoirs of Mrs B. Paulding, *The Evacuee Magazine*, November/December 2015, p.5.
52. Frisby, Terence, pp.46-50.
53. Testimony of George Osborn; author's collection.
54. Testimony of Jean Bell; author's collection.
55. Testimony of Lily Dwyer; author's collection.
56. Glasgow, John, p.30.
57. Testimony of Jean Flannery; author's collection.
58. Testimony of John Payne; author's collection.
59. Jones, Audrey, *Farewell Manchester* (Didsbury Press, Manchester, 1989), p.105.
60. Testimony of John Hawkins; author's collection.
61. *Hansard* (Commons) vol.351, col.1341.
62. Testimony of Bob Cooper; author's collection.
63. Testimony of Hazel Gould (née Hall); author's collection.

64. Testimony of Joan Ozanne; author's collection.
65. Percy Martel Diary, March 1944, file 2, p.194; author's collection.
66. Testimony of Lorraine and Lloyd Savident; author's collection.

Chapter 7: 'God Keep You Safe From Harm' – The Kindness of Strangers
1. Testimony of Kathleen Potts, MBE; author's collection.
2. Testimony of Rev. Bernard Elson; author's collection.
3. Testimony of Marian Greenhalgh; author's collection.
4. *Manchester Guardian*, 12 July 1940.
5. Bury Archives, Channel Islands Evacuees, 6/2/9.
6. ibid, cinema letters.
7. Testimony of Peter Hopper; author's collection.
8. Galliano, Lourdes, p.54.
9. Strange, Joan, *Despatches from the Home Front, The War Diaries of Joan Strange 1939-1945* (Monarch Publications, 1989); see diary entry for 23 October 1940.
10. *Intermedian Magazine*, Guernsey States Intermediate School for Boys, 1939.
11. Bury Archives, ABU/6/2/, CIRC memo, 21 September 1940.
12. Testimony of Eva Le Page; author's collection.
13. Testimony of Len Robilliard; author's collection.
14. Testimony of Irene Moss (née Hawkins); author's collection.
15. Testimony of Agnes Scott; author's collection.
16. Russell, Yvonne, *A Guernsey Girl Evacuee joins the WAAF in Wartime England* (Toucan Press, Guernsey, 1988), p.7.
17. Yorkshire newspaper report, July 1940; Whittaker family papers.
18. Testimony of Marlene Whittaker; author's collection.
19. *Stockport Advertiser*, 12 July 1940.
20. Account courtesy of *Life and Work*, and quoted on www.lifeandwork.org.
21. *War News*, No.3 1941, Ramsbottom Heritage Society.
22. Testimony of Roisin Toole, courtesy of Parish of St Edward, Kettering, and quoted on www.stedwardskettering.org.uk.
23. Testimony of David Forbes, courtesy of Dunning Parish Historical Society and quoted on www.dunning.uk.net.
24. Testimony of Stella Marlow, courtesy of Jean Noble.
25. *Eastern Evening News*, 6 January 1940; author's collection.
26. *Leek Post & Times*, 6 January 1940, p.8.
27. Testimony of Pamela Le Poidevin; author's collection.
28. Testimony of Roisin Toole, courtesy of Parish of St Edward, Kettering, and quoted on www.stedwardskettering.org.uk.
29. Testimony of Dennis Camp; author's collection.
30. Testimony of Alice Thornton; author's collection.
31. *Worthing Herald*, December 1944.
32. Vancouver Channel Islanders Society Minutes, October 1941; Diary of Percy Martel.
33. Note from Mrs Collett, Canada, p.0277; Diary of Percy Martel.

34. For further reading on the FPP see Henry D. Molumphy, *For Common Decency: the History of Foster Parents Plan 1937-1983* (FPP, Rhode Island, 1984).

35. Testimony of Maureen Muggeridge; author's collection.

36. Testimony of Beryl Linehan, née Merrien; author's collection.

37. Testimony of Mrs Mavis Pike, née Fitzpatrick; in author's collection. Mavis still owns a doll and Easter card sent by her sponsor.

38. FPP Archives, FDR Presidential Library; Paulette Le Mescam biography sheet, dated February 1943.

39. Testimony of Paulette Le Mescam; author's collection.

40. FPP Archives, FDR Presidential Library; Letter written by Paulette Le Mescam, February 1943.

41. On 9 May 1945, British forces liberated Guernsey and the children and staff of La Chaumière began to plan their return to Guernsey. Father Bleach was not there to share their joy. He had left his pupils in 1943 to become Director of FPP operations in Malta and Italy. As a result of his work with the FPP, Father Bleach gained a private audience with The Pope.

42. FPP Archives, FDR Presidential Library; Letter from the FPP, 27 October 1943.

43. For Paulette, the return to Guernsey in July 1945 was tinged with sorrow as she discovered that her Grandmother had died during the war. Sent into the home of an Uncle whom she did not know. In December 2010 a BBC documentary described Paulette's wartime experiences in Cheshire and Paulette returned to Moseley Hall. She stated: 'It was wonderful to go back to look at all the rooms that I remembered so well. It also made me think about Mrs Roosevelt – it was so lovely to receive letter and parcels during the war from someone who cared about me.'

44. Churcher family papers; letter from New Barn nursery dated 23 December 1941.

45. ibid; letter from New Barn Nursery dated 25 May 1942.

46. ibid; letter from New Barn Nursery dated 25 June 1942.

47. ibid; letter from New Barn Nursery dated 22 May 1945.

Chapter 8: 'She Was Supposed to be Sent to Safety' – Out of the Frying Pan

1. *Hansard* (Commons), vol.362, cc699-760.

2. ibid.

3. Item 11222108, BBC News online; accessed 17 March 2016.

4. ibid.

5. Obituary for Bess Cummings, née Walder; *The Daily Telegraph*, 19 August 2010.

6. ibid.

7. ibid. During their rescue efforts the crew of HMS *Hurricane* miscounted the lifeboats from SS *City of Benares* that had been launched. As a result, Lifeboat 12 was missed. Its passengers had three weeks supply of food, but enough water for only one week. Amongst the forty odd people in the lifeboat were Father Rory O'Sullivan (a Roman Catholic priest who had volunteered to be an escort for the evacuee children) and six evacuee boys from the CORB program. They spent eight days afloat in the Atlantic before being sighted and rescued.

8. *Derby Daily Telegraph*, 26 June 1940.
9. Frisby, Terence, pp.142-4.
10. First Report of the Select Committee on Estimates, 1947: House of Commons Sessional Papers 1946-47 (96) VI.
11. Quoted in 'Don't Touch', *Britain at War* Magazine, Issue 32.
12. Army Notice Board Information Sheet No.87, April 1944.
13. *Gloucester Citizen*, 25 August 1942.
14. *Western Daily Press*, 24 April 1943.
15. *Western Daily Press*, 12 July 1941.

Chapter 9: 'The Most Wicked Woman we had Ever Met' – Mishaps, Misdeeds and Murder

1. Testimony of Pauline Burford; author's collection..
2. Testimony of Beryl Blake-Lawson; author's collection.
3. Testimony of Brian Russell; author's collection.
4. Testimony of Jenny Horne; author's collection.
5. *Western Gazette*, 5 April 1940.
6. *Edinburgh Evening News*, 6 September 1939.
7. ibid, 13 September 1939.
8. *Dundee Evening Telegraph*, 14 October 1939.
9. *Hansard* (Commons), vol.351, col.884.
10. *Gloucester Citizen*, 8 January 1941.
11. *Western Times*, 13 September 1940.
12. *Northampton Mercury*, 8 September 1939.
13. Testimony of Sheila Whipp; author's collection.
14. Testimony of Faith Catchpole; author's collection.
15. Testimony of Philip Doran courtesy of Catherine Sing and Mike Paice.
16. Testimony of Jean Noble; author's collection.
17. Testimony of Peggy White; author's collection.
18. Testimony of Mrs Jennifer Wallen, née Williams, quoted in *The Evacuee Magazine*, Nov/Dec 2015, p.4.
19. Testimony of Rosemary Hall; author's collection.
20. Testimony of Eileen Parker; author's collection.
21. Testimony of Rose Gillett; author's collection.
22. Testimony of George Osborn; author's collection.
23. ibid.
24. Testimony of Edna Dart; author's collection.
25. Testimony of Jean Gibbs; author's collection.
26. Memories of Francis Rutter, courtesy of Melissa J. Rutter.
27. Testimony of Jean Bell; author's collection.
28. John Welshman, *Churchill's Children: The Evacuation Experience in Wartime Britain* (OUP, Oxford, 2010), p.80.
29. Testimony of Jean Gibbs; author's collection.
30. Testimony of Ann Smith; author's collection

Chapter 10: 'We Will Take Care of Them' – The Wartime Foster Families
1. Testimony of Frances Gillies; courtesy of Kelvinside Academy.
2. Testimony of Val Morrish; author's collection.
3. Testimony of Margaret Nolan, courtesy of Ramsbottom Heritage Society.
4. Testimony of Linda Mitchelmore; author's collection.
5. Testimony of Judy Jones; author's collection.
6. Testimony of Ruth Harrison; author's collection.
7. Testimony of Jean Flannery; author's collection.
8. Testimony of Fred Jones; author's collection.
9. Testimony of Sheila Da Costa; author's collection.
10. Phyllis Britton, p.30.
11. Letter to Mrs Hanson from Birch Grove House, 15 January 1941, Hanson family papers.
12. Letter from Ada Tullett to Mrs Hanson, 1944, Hanson family papers.
13. *Derby Evening Telegraph*, 9 June 2008, p.22.
14. Testimony of Ben Howard; author's collection.
15. Percy Martel Diary, 19 July 1941, p.127; author's collection.
16. *Hansard* (Commons) vol.351, col.831.
17. *Hansard* (Commons) vol.351, col.840.
18. The testimony of Faith Shoesmith can be found in Chapter 9.
19. Testimony of Geraldine Barker; author's collection.
20. Percy Martel Diary, August 1940, p.97. As it turned out, the child was not removed from this billet and relations within the family improved. The family remained in touch with the child for many years after the war.
21. *Stockport Advertiser*, 12 October 1939.
22. The defence was the wife's bad health – the couple would have liked children but could not manage them.
23. *Leek Post and Times*, 11 August 1944, p.1.

Chapter 11: 'I Had Mixed Feelings' – Saying Goodbye
1. M.B. Martel and E.M. Gill, *Wartime Memories of Two Sisters*, 2007, Martel family papers.
2. Interview with Winifred Le Page (née West) 2006, courtesy of Second World War Experience Centre.
3. Testimony of Lloyd Savident; author's collection.
4. E. Hamel, *X Isles*, p.35.
5. Testimony of Alan Pike, in author's collection, and *Burnley Express*, 12 May 1945.
6. *The Bury Times*, 30 June 1945.
7. *Eastern Daily Press*, 13 June 1945.
8. *Picture Post*, 23 June, 1945, pp.11-3.
9. *Channel Islands Review,* August 1945, p.1.
10. N. Le Poidevin. p.62.
11. *News Chronicle*, 21 July 1945.
12. *Bury Times,* 21 July 1945.

13. Testimony of Lily Dwyer; author's collection.
14. Testimony of Keith Llewellyn; author's collection.
15. Testimony of Adelaide Harris; author's collection.
16. Testimony of Richard Singleton; author's collection.
17. This interviewee wished to remain anonymous.
18. Oldham Local Studies, Guernsey Boys' file, caption provided by un-named billeter underneath photograph of Guernsey evacuee, George, for an exhibition and reunion held in June 1990.
19. Frisby, Terence, pp.207-8.
20. Roffey, James, *A Schoolboy's War*, pp.125-6.
21. Testimony of Mavis Robinson, courtesy of Caerleon History Group.
22. Testimony of Douglas Wood; author's collection.
23. Testimony of William Crawford, courtesy of Bruce Crawford.
24. Glasgow, John, pp.30-2.
25. Journal of Ursula Malet de Carteret, 1940-1945, courtesy of the Malet de Carteret family.
26. Testimony of Dorothy Miller, née King; author's collection.
27. Testimony of Janet Day; author's collection.
28. Testimony of Irene Moss (née Hawkins); author's collection.
29. Testimony of Peter Aves; author's collection.
30. Testimony of Ruby Nicolle, courtesy of Valerie Winder.
31. Testimony of Bob Cooper; author's collection.
32. Testimony of John Noble; author's collection.
33. Testimony of Jim Marshall; author's collection.
34. Galliano, Lourdes, pp.123-7.
35. Testimony of Brian Russell; author's collection.
36. Testimony of George Osborn; author's collection.
37. Testimony of John Martin; author's collection.
38. Testimony of John Mallett; author's collection.
39. Bury Local Archives, ABU6/2/16; MOH memo NW199/45, 18 July 1945, p.2.
40. Testimony of Peter Hopper; author's collection.
41. *Daily Mail*, 13 October 2015.
42. Testimony of Len Rumens; author's collection.
43. Testimony of Marion Gilbert, née Wraight; author's collection.
44. Testimony of John Payne; author's collection.
45. Testimony of Richard Smith; author's collection.
46. Testimony of Derek Pilling; author's collection.

Chapter 12: 'It Shaped My Life' – The Aftermath of Evacuation

1. Welshman, J., pp.314-5.
2. Testimony of Grace Fry, courtesy of Guernsey Retired Teachers Association.
3. Testimony of John Tippett; author's collection.
4. Testimony of June Somekh; author's collection.
5. Testimony of John Helyer; author's collection.

6. Testimony of Rex Carre; author's collection.

7. Testimony of Sheila Gibson; author's collection.

8. Testimony of Douglas Wood; author's collection.

9. Testimony of Philip Doran, courtesy of Catherine Sing and Mike Paice.

10. Testimony of Ronald Eric Gould; author's collection.

11. Testimony of Richard Singleton; author's collection.

12. Testimony of Win de la Mare; author's collection.

13. Testimony of Dorothy Miller, née King; author's collection.

14. Testimony of Len Page courtesy of Andy Parsons.

15. Frisby, Terence, pp.208-9, and testimony of Terence Frisby in author's collection.

16. Testimony of Derek Trayler; author's collection.

17. Titmuss, R., p.181.

18. Testimony of Alice Greenston; author's collection.

19. This is a pseudonym as this evacuee did not wish to be named.

20. Testimony of Lily Dwyer; author's collection.

21. Testimony of Val Sarre; author's collection.

22. Testimony of Geoff Durrant; author's collection.

23. *Daily Mail*, 13 October 2015.

24. Testimony of Bill Smith, courtesy of Dunning Parish Historical Society and quoted on www.dunning.uk.

25. Testimony of Peter Hopper; author's collection.

26. Testimony of Edna Dart; author's collection.

27. Testimony of Jean Bell; author's collection.

28. Testimony of Sheila Whipp; author's collection.

29. See, for example, S. Isaacs, *The Cambridge Evacuation Survey, A Wartime Study in Social Welfare and Education* (London, Methuen, 1941).

30. *The Evacuation from Guernsey – The Experience of School Children and its Effects: a Biographical Study by Guernsey MIND, 1986*, pp.6-8.

31. Testimony of Marion Gilbert, née Wraight; author's collection.

32. Testimony of Lloyd and Lorraine Savident; author's collection.

33. Galliano, Lourdes, p.128.

34. Testimony of Ben Howard; author's collection.

35. Stockport provided homes for the largest number of Channel Islanders during the war.

36. The association was formerly known as the Evacuee Reunion Association. The association publishes books about the evacuation, organises reunion meetings and publishes a monthly newsletter, entitled *The Evacuee*, which is sent free to members, not all of whom are evacuees. The 'Lost Touch' section has helped many people to trace old friends. The association is currently raising funds to place a memorial in the National Memorial Arboretum near Lichfield. It will pay tribute, not just to the evacuees, but to everyone involved in the evacuation – including foster parents, teachers, volunteers, nurses, train drivers and billeting officers.

Bibliography

Ainger Lois, M., *My Case Unpacked* (Lois M. Ainger, 1995).

Axford, Jessica, (née Young), *I Lived in a Castle* (Antony Rowe, 1994).

Britton, Phyllis, Britton, Sally, and Boulton, Alison, *Phyllis's War: An Evacuee's Story in Her Own Words* (Windmill Hill, Bristol, 2015).

Brooks, Christopher J., *When Will I See You Again? The Story of East Coast Evacuees* (Rushmere, 1991).

Frisby, Terence, *Kisses on a Postcard: A Tale of Wartime Childhood* (Bloomsbury, London, 2010).

Glasgow, J.D., *A Rolling Pebble: Reminiscences of an Alderney Boy* (Self-published, copies available from John Glasgow, 27 Fox Lane, Winchester SO22 4DY).

Galliano, Lourdes, *A Rocky Passage to Exile: The War Memoirs of a Gibraltarian Child Evacuee 1940-1945* (Self-published, copies available from maggie_galliano@hotmail.com).

Goodwin, Nathan, *Hastings Wartime Memories and Photographs* (Phillimore & Co Ltd, 2011).

Hamon, Simon, *Channel Islands Invaded: The German Attack on the British Isles in 1940* (Frontline, Barnsley, 2015).

Hill, May, *An RAF Mother's WWII Diary Blog – January 1944-December 194e: 'Sorrows and Salvation'* (Ambridge Books, November 2014).

Hobbs, Pam, *Don't Forget to Write: The True Story of an Evacuee and Her Family* (Ebury Press, London, 2009).

Hollingsworth, Hilda, *They Tied a Label on my Coat* (Virago, 1991).

Holmes, Neil, *Liverpool Blitzed: Seventy Years On* (Halsgrove, 2011).

Howard, Ben, *From Brown Hill to Pitch Hill: The Wartime History of Two Catford Schools* (Sayers Croft War Memorials Preservation Fund).

Johnson, B.S. (Ed.), *The Evacuees* (Victor Gollancz, 1968).

Jones, Audrey, *Farewell Manchester: The Story of the 1939 Evacuation* (Didsbury Press, 1989).

Kirmatzis, Daniel, *The Biggest Scrum That Ever Was: A History of Emanuel School at War* (Troubador/Matador Press, 2014).

Le Poidevin, Nick, *Torteval School in Exile* (ELSP, 2010).

Mawson, Gillian, *Evacuees: Children's Lives on the WW2 Home Front* (Pen & Sword, Barnsley, 2014).

_____, *Guernsey Evacuees: The Forgotten Evacuees of the Second World War* (History Press, Stroud, 2012).

_____, 'Guernsey Mothers and Their Children: Forgotten Evacuees', in Professor Maggie Andrews and Dr Janis Lomas (Eds.) *The Home Front in Britain: Images, Myths and Forgotten Experiences 1914-2014* (Palgrave Macmillan, London, 2014).

Noble, Jean C., *Golden Girls and Downham Days* (J.C. Noble, 1999).

Roberts, Rita, *Toffee Apples and Togas* (Rita Roberts, 2011).

Roffey, James, *A Schoolboy's War in Sussex* (History Press, Stroud, 2010).

Russell, Yvonne, *A Guernsey Girl Evacuee Joins the WAAF in Wartime England* (Toucan Press, Guernsey, 1988).

Titmuss, R.M., *Problems of Social Policy* (HMSO, London, 1950).

Wallace, Lorne A., *Here Come the Glasgow Keelies: Vivid Recollections of World War II Evacuees and a Wee Scottish Village* (Dunning Parish Historical Society, 1999).

WEBSITES AND BLOGS

British Evacuees Association: www.evacuees.org.uk

Gillian Mawson's evacuation research blog: https://evacueesofworldwartwo. wordpress.com

Index